Arkham House Books

Arkham House Books

A Collector's Guide

LEON NIELSEN

FOREWORD BY BARRY ABRAHAMS

McFarland & Company, Inc., Publishers

Jefferson, North Carolina, and London

All cover illustrations, photographs and colophons are
copyrighted by Arkham House Publishers, Inc., Sauk City,
Wisconsin, and reproduced here with permission.

LIBRARY OF CONGRESS CATALOGUING-IN-PUBLICATION DATA

Nielsen, Leon.
    Arkham House books : a collector's guide / Leon Nielsen;
foreword by Barry Abrahams.
        p.   cm.
    Includes bibliographical references and index.

    ISBN 0-7864-1785-4 (softcover : 50# alkaline paper) ∞

    1. Arkham House—Bibliography.   2. Fantasy fiction—
Bibliography—Catalogs.   3. Horror tales—Bibliography—
Catalogs.   4. Sauk City (Wis.)—Imprints—Catalogs.
5. Book collecting—United States.   6. Rare books—Collectors
and collecting—United States.   7. Rare books—Prices—United
States.   8. Arkham House—History.   9. Publishers and publishing—Wisconsin—Sauk City—History.   I. Title.
Z473.A68N54   2004
813'.08766'075—dc22   2004014709

British Library cataloguing data are available

Cover image: Howard Phillips Lovecraft as a young boy

Manufactured in the United States of America

McFarland & Company, Inc., Publishers
  Box 611, Jefferson, North Carolina 28640
  www.mcfarlandpub.com

In truth he was a strange and wayward wight,
Fond of each gentle, and each dreadful scene,
In darkness, and in storm he found delight;
Nor less than when on ocean-wave serene,
The southern sun diffus'd his dazzling sheen.
Even sad vicissitude amus'd his soul;
And if a sigh would sometimes intervene,
And down his cheek a tear of pity roll,
A sigh, a tear, so sweet, he wish'd not to control.
Ann Radcliffe
The Mysteries of Udolpho

In Memoriam:
August William Derleth
(1909–1971)

Acknowledgments

I first became acquainted with Arkham House Publishers, Inc., in the late 1970s, when searching for samples of Howard Phillips Lovecraft's literary work. I had recently read a magazine article on the life of this remarkable author of supernatural fiction, but I was largely unfamiliar with his writings. From a local bookseller, I acquired first editions of *The Dunwich Horror and Others* and *Dagon and Other Macabre Tales* for $15.00 each. The rest, as the saying goes, is history. Over the past 25 years, I have collected, bought and sold Arkham House books, and have seen a remarkable increase in their value, especially in the last 15–20 years. At the present the two titles mentioned above list at about $200 each, depending on condition. On the basis of scarcity, author and literary merit, some Arkham House titles have appreciated considerably since publication, while others have ascended the price scale more slowly.

But this book is not so much a price guide—for price guides often become outdated shortly after publication—as it is a tribute to Arkham House; to August Derleth, its founder and for 32 years its editor; and to the more than 230 titles produced by Arkham House Publishers, Inc., since 1939.

In the preparation of the book I want to acknowledge my debt and express my appreciation to the authors of three books that no Arkham House collector or bookseller should be without. They are *Thirty Years of Arkham House: 1939–1969,* by August Derleth (Arkham House Publishers, Inc., 1970); *The Arkham House Companion,* by Sheldon Jaffery (Starmont House, Inc., 1989); and *Sixty Years of Arkham House,* compiled by S.T. Joshi (Arkham House Publishers, Inc., 1999). While the first two titles are difficult to find and demand premium prices, Mr. Joshi's work, which contains a wealth of bibliographical information, is still available from the publisher.

Acknowledgments

I also want to convey my gratitude to Allen and Patricia Ahearn, whose guides to values, book collecting books and author price guides have given me much information and insight.

A special acknowledgment of gratitude goes to Ms. April Derleth, president of Arkham House Publishers, Inc., for her support and encouragement. Ms. Derleth freely gave permission to reprint the dust jacket art shown throughout the text and graciously provided photographs of her father, August Derleth, and of H.P. Lovecraft. She also took time to review the manuscript and make helpful suggestions to insure its accuracy.

My appreciation and thanks to Barry Abrahams, a friend, teacher and fellow Arkham House aficionado, a collector and bookseller, who wrote the foreword, read the manuscript and offered numerous suggestions for improvements. With his profound interest in Arkham House and its publishing history, Barry was the first person who came to mind for this task.

While this book would not have been possible without the resources, references, assistance and encouragement provided by the aforementioned, any errors or omissions found in the text are my responsibility alone.

Contents

Foreword

One of the greatest rewards of being a book collector is to meet other people who understand and share a passion for collecting, buying and selling books. Crossing paths with individuals who genuinely appreciate books in the way that collectors and booksellers do can provide an interesting exchange at the very least, and on occasion, the foundation for a friendship.

Over the years, I have corresponded with many collectors and booksellers. Our mutual interest in science fiction, fantasy, horror and mystery first editions has enabled me to make friends with people across the country. This has occurred often enough to prompt me to travel throughout the United States to meet these friends, first found because of our penchant for collecting these particular types of books.

My friendship with Leon Nielsen, the author of this work, began some years ago in just such a way. Over the years, Leon and I have had many lively discussions by telephone, letter or email, and it has been a pleasure to exchange information and opinions on the finer points of collecting, buying and selling books. More often than not, our conversations have been focused on Arkham House Publishers, the books and the charismatic people associated with this enterprise.

It was early in my days as a collector of genre first editions that I came to value the books published by Arkham House. I was particularly impressed by August Derleth and Donald Wandrei's recognition of the talent of H. P. Lovecraft and their persistence in keeping his writings in print, which led to the founding of Arkham House Publishers in Sauk City, Wisconsin. I was also taken by the quality of the book bindings and the dust jacket art, which always seemed to catch the mood of the writing in the book. Another thing that struck me was Derleth's tenacity, which not only kept Arkham House going under difficult circumstances, but also managed to garner the writings of such prominent authors as H.P. Lovecraft, Clark Ashton Smith, William H. Hodgson, Robert E. Howard and Donald Wandrei, not to mention Derleth's own work. In a larger perspective August Derleth's enduring perseverance in perpetuating his small publishing company has enabled us to enjoy and appreciate the works of many unique writers who might otherwise have faded into obscurity.

With the added advantage of living only two hours away from Sauk City in Wisconsin, a circumstance which has deepened his interest in Arkham House and August Derleth, Leon Nielsen has authored a book which will be an invaluable resource for Arkham House devotees, collectors and booksellers alike. An avid book collector himself, partial to Arkham House, Edgar Rice Burroughs and Robert E. Howard, Leon is an experienced and meticulous researcher with an ability to obtain, compile and present information in a concise and organized format that is easy for anyone to understand and use.

His in-depth knowledge of the material presented herein and a strong sense of responsibility to fellow collectors and Arkham House devotees, combined with a profound respect and admiration for August Derleth and his legacy, is evident throughout the book. I have no doubt that any book collector, but particularly collectors or booksellers who have an interest in Arkham House, H.P. Lovecraft or science fiction, fantasy or horror literature in general, will benefit from the comprehensive and up-to-date information in the text that follows.

Barry Abrahams
Lincoln, Nebraska
June 2004

Preface

This book was written as a reference source for collectors, booksellers, libraries, universities and other institutions or individuals who have an interest in the macabre, supernatural and science fiction found in the books published by Arkham House Publishers, Inc., from 1939 to date.

In the opening pages the reader will find brief discussion of the more salient points of book collecting, such as edition identification, grading, major defects, restoration, book care and associated topics. Although more comprehensive volumes have been written on these matters, I hope that the comments herein may provide a measure of guidance for both new and seasoned collectors. For general information on book collecting, refer to the bibliography at the end of the text.

The main body of the text consists of a description of the titles released by Arkham House and its two imprints: Mycroft & Moran and Stanton & Lee. Emphasis is on the first printing of the first edition. Except for Lovecraft's works, Arkham House did not reprint many of its early titles. Reprints have become more common in later years but are still relatively scarce. Where deemed appropriate and where reprints may be confused with first editions, they have been included in the title descriptions.

I have chosen to list individual titles chronologically, rather than alphabetically. An alphabetical index of titles has also been included to provide quick access to information on a particular book. All titles are numbered in order of publication, and these numbers are used throughout the book as references to guide the reader to a certain title or the work of a particular author. For the purpose of locating all the writings of an author published by Arkham House, an alphabetical index of authors is also included.

Because this book was not intended to be a biography or a work of literary review, I have refrained from the inclusion of author profiles or comments on the literary merits of their work. Supplementary notes in the title descriptions are brief. Much more extensive detail on authors, contents and literary criticism can be found in the relevant books listed in the reference bibliography at the end of the text. For the reader who wants to learn more about the men and women who wrote or still write for Arkham House, these resources are comprehensive and invaluable. No Arkham House collector or aficionado should be without a minimum knowledge of the writers who created and populated the strange and wondrous worlds that have become the hallmark of Arkham House's books and the wellspring of its continuing success.

Arkham House books are published in small printings, from as few as 500 (even fewer in some cases) to 7000 copies; the average printing is approximately 2000 to 3000 copies. This relative scarcity has made Arkham House titles a particularly attractive and challenging subject for book collectors. Furthermore, Arkham House books are not distributed through the usual conduit of retail bookstores, but sold directly from the publisher through mailed catalogs, announcements of new titles and the publisher's Internet website. Arkham House books in print may also be ordered through a bookstore. A few titles have been remaindered in the past, but they are the exception.

I have included ranking lists for both value and scarcity, which are not necessarily synonymous, to provide the reader with a quick reference to the most desirable and usually most elusive titles. A list of stock lists and catalogs issued by Arkham House, my personal suggestions for the quintessential Arkham House book collection, and the bibliography of reference literature complete the book.

Ideally, a work of this nature would include a picture of each title listed. Since that would have added far too many pages, I have instead chosen to include only particular jackets, focusing on 1) specific key issues; 2) author's first book; 3) first edition covers, which are different from reprints; and 4) samples of the art of prominent Arkham House cover artists. All cover art illustrations shown are reproduced (with permission of Arkham House) from first edition/first printing copies.

Titles listed as still in print may be obtained directly from Arkham House Publishers, P.O. Box 546, Sauk City, WI 53583, USA. Phone: 608-643-4500. Fax: 608-643-5043. Internet: sales@arkhamhouse.com and www.arkhamhouse.com.

Preface

The foundation of information on which the book was prepared and written derives from a number of sources, foremost from my personal collection and experience, but also from the sources mentioned in the acknowledgments. It is my hope that the book may become a worthy successor to those references that came before and a beneficial addition to the literature on that most remarkable and enduring publishing enterprise known as Arkham House.

1

Howard Phillips Lovecraft, August Derleth and Arkham House

On August 20, 1890, in Providence, Rhode Island, a son was born to Winfield Scott Lovecraft and Sarah Susan (Phillips) Lovecraft, both of English descent. The boy was christened Howard Phillips Lovecraft and raised primarily by a doting but possessive and neurotic mother, who saw it as her motherly duty to shelter her young son from the difficulties and travails of life. Winfield Lovecraft, a traveling salesman who suffered from paralysis, did not participate significantly in his son's upbringing and died from severe paralytic complications eight years after Howard's birth.

The young Lovecraft was a gifted but sickly child who spent much of his time in the voluminous library of his maternal grandfather. He taught himself to read at the age of four and was fascinated by fairy tales and adventure stories. In spite of a measure of public schooling, compromised by frequent absences because of ill health, Howard was largely self-educated. As he grew older, but not healthier, he developed a strong interest in subjects such as chemistry, geography and astronomy. At the age of seven he began writing essays on these subjects and had several published in the local papers. Some years later, enthralled by the stories by Edgar Allan Poe and other writers of the supernatural and macabre, and profoundly influenced by the quaint, eighteenth century character of his native town, Lovecraft began writing weird stories. He wrote his first, "The Beast in the Cave," at the age of fifteen.

Lovecraft joined the United Amateur Press Association in 1914 and found not only an outlet for his literary aspirations, but also the company of fellow writers and thinkers. The magazine *Home Brew* published Lovecraft's first professional work, "Herbert West: Reanimator," in 1922, an event followed by the publication of "Dagon," in *Weird Tales* in 1923.

Following his maternal grandfather's death in 1904, the family fortune had dwindled steadily. Being physically unfit to hold regular employment, Lovecraft found himself living on an average of fifteen dollars per week. The death of his grandfather also brought him under increasing dominance by his mother and her two sisters, Mrs. Frank C. Clark and Mrs. Edward F. Gamwell, until 1919 when the mentally and physically exhausted Mrs. Lovecraft was hospitalized. She died two years later.

After his mother's death, Lovecraft, who had pulled further away from human society to the point of being nearly reclusive, continued to write weird fiction prolifically. He summarized his reasons in a single assertion: "There is no field other than the weird in which I have any aptitude for fictional composition. Life has never interested me so much as the escape from life."

Out of financial necessity and because he did not believe he could make a living from his own writing, be began to earn a meager income by revising or ghostwriting the works of aspiring writers. This undertaking generated many friendships, and his stories were now being published in *Weird Tales* with greater regularity. Through his revision work, he met Mrs. Sonia Greene of New York, a tall, well-educated and gracious woman, ten years older than Lovecraft and a successful Fifth Avenue fashion executive. After a two-year courtship, mainly by correspondence, they were married in New York in 1924. They had no children and the marriage did not last. They separated after two years and were eventually divorced in 1929.

In the summer of 1926, Lovecraft received a letter from a young Wisconsin writer, August Derleth, an admirer of Lovecraft's *Weird Tales* stories. Only seventeen years of age, Derleth had recently had his first story, "Bat's Belfry," published in *Weird Tales*, following numerous rejections of other stories. Derleth's letter to Lovecraft, whose address he had obtained through the editor of *Weird Tales*, Farnsworth Wright, was about the Welsh writer Arthur Machen's fantasy novel *Hills of Dreams*, a work much admired by both men. The letter started an exchange of correspondence that would continue to Lovecraft's untimely death in 1937.

Lovecraft was impressed by Derleth from the start. In a letter to the distinguished fantasy writer Clark Ashton Smith, he wrote: "I have just discovered a boy of seventeen who promises to develop into something of a fantaisiste.... August William Derleth, whose name you may have seen as author of some rather immature stories in *Weird Tales*... turns out to be a veritable prodigy." In another letter to J. Vernon Shea, he wrote: "When I say Derleth will soon lead all the rest of the gang, I speak seriously and advisedly. He has a profundity, seriousness, simplicity and human insight that none of the rest of us can even begin to duplicate."

Over the years Lovecraft and Derleth discussed freely a multitude of subjects, thoughts, ideas, the work of other writers, and a host of social issues in their letters. Oddly enough, the two men, who came to develop the greatest respect for each other and each other's work and were so close in their correspondence friendship, never met. Lovecraft was loath to leave his native Providence, and Derleth was equally dismayed to depart his beloved Sauk City; hence a realistic opportunity for a meeting between the two men never occurred.

Derleth was only one of many aspiring young writers with whom

Top: Howard Phillips Lovecraft as a young boy. *Bottom:* Howard Phillips Lovecraft, 1930s.

9

Lovecraft maintained a steady and prodigious correspondence. Among the notables were Robert Bloch, Alfred Galpin, Robert E. Howard, Maurice W. Moe, J. Vernon Shea, Clark Ashton Smith, Donald Wandrei, and others, whom Lovecraft in general discourse would refer to affectionately as his "grandchildren."

August William Derleth was born on February 24, 1909, in Sauk City, Wisconsin, to William Julius Derleth and Rosella Louise Volk Derleth. His family ancestry was predominantly Bavarian and French. The name Derleth was derived from the name of an ancestor, a French count d'Erlette, who escaped from France to Bavaria during the revolution. The young August Derleth was an inquisitive and intelligent child who took pleasure in many things, including canoeing, hiking, fishing, and collecting comic books, cartoon strips, stamps, books and other things. He was a prolific reader and particularly captivated by adventure, action and supernatural stories. Derleth's formal education began at St. Aloysius Parochial School, continued at Sauk City High School and culminated in a B.A. from the University of Wisconsin, Madison, in 1930. He began writing at thirteen years of age and sold his first story at seventeen. In addition to his many sales of stories to *Weird Tales* from 1926, he began writing more serious works and had several other stories, novels and regional writings, including a volume of poetry and the first novel in his ambitious Sac Prairie Saga, *Still Is the Summer Night,* published between 1932 to 1937.

Following a year-long period of debility, Howard Phillips Lovecraft died on March 15, 1937, of intestinal cancer and Bright's disease (an affliction of the kidneys). He was not yet 47 years old. When the news of Lovecraft's passing reached Derleth, it affected him greatly. Far too distraught to attend to his usual schedule, he sought consolation by walking in the marshes near his home. After three months of mourning, August Derleth and a colleague, Donald Wandrei (one of Lovecraft's "grandchildren"), made plans to collect and attempt the publication of a memorial volume of Lovecraft's best weird fiction. The idea was encouraged by J. Vernon Shea (another "Lovecraft grandchild"). While many of Lovecraft's stories had been published in pulp magazines, such as *Weird Tales,* only two books and a few pamphlets had been published prior to his death. Lovecraft's will, however, named a Robert H. Barlow as the executor of the estate, and Barlow had his own plans to publish Lovecraft's stories. This idea did not sit well with Derleth, and with his considerable faculty of persuasion, he managed to talk Barlow into turning the project over to him. This was confirmed by Robert Barlow in a letter to Mrs. Edward F. Gamwell, Lovecraft's only surviving aunt. After carefully selecting the stories for the Lovecraft memorial volume, Derleth and Wandrei submitted a manuscript titled *The Outsider and Others* to two of the larger publishers in New York. Rejections were not long in coming from both of them.

This discouraging turn of events was only a temporary setback to Derleth. With the support of Barlow and Mrs. Gamwell, and backed by a bank loan originally secured for building a house, Derleth and Wandrei decided to publish the book themselves. The name of the new publishing venture was derived from the fictitious community of Arkham, which was Lovecraft's place name for Salem, Massachusetts, a setting that figured prominently in many of his stories. In late 1939, more than two years after

August Derleth at home in Sauk City, 1940s.

Lovecraft's death, 1,268 copies of *The Outsider and Others* with cover art by Virgil Finlay (another Lovecraft devotee) were delivered to Derleth by the printer, the George Banta Company of Menasha, Wisconsin. The cover price of the book was $5.00, a fair amount of money at the time, and it took four years to sell the only printing.

11

In spite of the disheartening slowness of their first sales, Derleth and Wandrei felt encouraged to continue the Arkham House imprint and followed in 1941 with a collection of Derleth's own weird tales, titled *Someone in the Dark*. The third volume in the Arkham House saga was Clark Ashton Smith's *Out of Space and Time*, published in 1942. At this time Donald Wandrei had entered the army, and he stayed in the service until the end of World War II.

In the years that followed, Arkham House published the works of many of the foremost American and British writers of weird fiction, including Cynthia Asquith, Basil Copper, Lord Dunsany, Robert E. Howard, Frank Belknap Long, Brian Lumley, Seabury Quinn, and Lucius Shepard. In addition, Arkham House also published the first book of several notable writers, including Robert Bloch, Ray Bradbury, Joseph Payne Brennan, J. Ramsey Campbell, Frederick S. Durbin, and A. E. van Vogt.

In addition to managing the publishing house with a minimum of help, August Derleth continued his writing, correspondence, editorial duties and a multitude of other projects. He received a Guggenheim Fellowship in 1938; became a lecturer in American Regional Literature, University of Wisconsin, 1939-1943, and the Writer's Institute, University of Wisconsin, 1958-1959; director of the Board of Education, Sauk City, Wisconsin, 1937-1943; contributing editor to *Outdoors Magazine*, 1934-1943; literary editor for *The Capital Times*, Madison, Wisconsin, 1941 *et seq.*; and columnist for *The Capital Times* from 1960. Derleth was also a prodigious reader who could take in several books in a day, and he owned a library of several thousand volumes. Few collectors could match his enormous collection of comic books, pulp magazines and recorded jazz music.

On April 6, 1953, Derleth married Sandra Evelyn Winters (the daughter of Millard and Roberta Alexander Winters). Two children were born into the marriage. April Rose on August 9, 1954, and William Walden on August 22, 1956. Unfortunately, the personalities of August and Sandra (Sandy) were not compatible and the marriage was short-lived. A divorce was granted on March 23, 1959. The custody of the children was awarded to Derleth.

In the meantime, Arkham House continued to publish on a more or less regular basis. Some years were sterling, with several releases, while others were meager with only a few or a single title published.

The economy of the enterprise at the time was precarious, and the sale of books relied almost entirely on subscribers and collectors of the genre literature published by Arkham House. Somehow, though, the printing bills got paid and the company moved along, to a great extent supported by Derleth's earnings from his many novels and regional writings printed by other publishers.

August Derleth at his desk, 1960s.

In spite of his robust physique and rugged appearance, August Derleth's health was in decline. In August of 1969, at the age of sixty, he entered St. Mary's Hospital in Madison, Wisconsin, for a gall bladder operation. His hospital visit became an extended stay, during which he learned that he suffered from a collapsed lung, pleuritis, hepatitis, peritonitis, moniliasis, and proteins in the urine. He was discharged on October 19, 1969, and returned home to attend to a large accumulation of work, including reviews, correspondence and new writing projects. For almost two years, he managed to keep up his hectic work schedule and take pleasure in the steady progress of Arkham House.

Nevertheless, his health was not improving. In the morning of Sunday, July 4, 1971, Derleth went outside to rest on a bench under a favorite tree on his property. It was here that death stilled the heart of one of the most prominent and prolific American writers of his time. The death certificate noted the cause of death as a sudden heart attack, but other conditions may have played a role.

August Derleth left a literary legacy of more than 150 published books and countless stories, articles, essays and other writings. Few writers have achieved such distinction.

Following Derleth's death, Donald Wandrei briefly assisted with the management of Arkham House. He was succeeded by Roderic Meng, who had worked for Arkham House for years and now was saddled with handling the backlog of managerial duties left by Derleth's passing. In 1974, James Turner, a talented, dynamic, and controversial individual became managing editor. During his tenure, more science fiction was incorporated into the traditional Arkham House genre literature. This move, though criticized by some Arkham House devotees, garnered such eminent writers as Greg Bear, Michael Bishop, Lucius Shepard and James Tiptree, Jr. In 1980, S.T. Joshi joined the editorial staff and participated in several important collaborations with Turner.

Sixty-five years after its humble beginnings, Arkham House is still going strong, managed by April Derleth, August's daughter, with Peter Ruber of Candlelight Press as the consulting editor. For further information on Arkham House Publishers, Inc., please visit www.arkham-house.com.

2

Collecting Arkham House Books

BOOK TERMINOLOGY

To understand the description of books listed for sale in catalogs, in advertisements or on Internet web sites, and for general information and discourse, it is important that the collector know the proper terms for the parts of a book. The terminology may be applied or expressed differently by collectors and booksellers alike; however, the following are the most commonly used descriptive terms.

A book consists of two major parts: the *text block*, which is made up of a number of *signatures* (groups of pages) sewn or glued together, and the *case* or *binding* that encloses the text block. The top of the text block is the *head* of the book, the bottom is the *tail*, and the right side, where the pages open, is the *fore edge*. The case consists of the *front board* and *back board*, connected by the *spine*. The outside groove where the boards swing on the spine is the *outer joint*, which may either be a *flush joint* or a *french groove*. Inside the front board is a double page, half of which is pasted to the inside of the board, with the other half being the first page of the book. This is the *front end paper*, divided in the *pasted down front end paper* or *board paper*, and the *free front end paper*.

The following leaf, if blank, is the *front flyleaf*, after which there is a right hand page with the title in lesser type. This is the *half title*, followed by another blank page and a right hand page with the title, the author's name, illustrator, publisher, colophon and other capital information. This is the *full title* and the reverse is the *copyright* page, which lists copyright data, publisher, printing history, credits, ISBN number, edition, printing and other material information. The opposite page is the *dedication page*. Inside the book, the inner margin where the pages are joined, is the *gutter* and at the very back of the book, if blank, is the *rear flyleaf*, followed by the *rear end paper*, half of which is pasted to the inside of the back board—the *pasted down rear end paper*—with the other half, the *free rear end paper*, being the last page of the book.

The inside groove where the boards swing from the spine is the *front/rear hinge* or *front/rear inner joint*. Where additional strength of the spine is required, some books have multicolored bands at the head and tail of the text block at the spine. These are called *headbands* and *tailbands* respectively.

The term *case-bound* indicates a *hardcover* or *hardbound* book as opposed to a *paperback* or *soft-cover* book. The description of a dust jacket includes the *front panel* with a *front flap*, the *spine* and the *rear panel* with a *rear flap*. *Wrapper* or *wraps* are terms used for the covers of a paperback or soft-cover book. A *chapbook* is a small unbound pamphlet, usually center stapled and with heavy paper covers.

The system of designating book sizes is based on the size of the sheet used and the size into which it is folded to make each signature. The five most common sizes are *folio* (fo): greater than 12" in height; *quarto* (4to): 10" to 12" in height; *octavo* (8vo): 8" to 10" in height; *duodecimo* (12mo): 7" to 8" in height; and *sextodecimo* (16mo): 6" to 7" in height.

PAPER

Until fairly recently the paper used in the production of books contained varying degrees of acid, which accelerated the aging and associated deterioration process. This is evident in the gradual browning and brittleness of pages in many older books. Newspaper print and comic books are particularly susceptible to this process because of the paper's high acid content. During the war years, 1941 through 1945, special government restrictions were imposed on the publishing industry to save resources, and books from this period were often printed on cheaper, thinner and more acidic paper. The war-years books are usually more affected by browning and brittleness of the pages than are books from before or after the war. Today more acid-free paper is being manufactured and used in publishing, yet not all modern books are printed on acid-free paper.

DUST JACKETS

Dust jackets or dust wrappers are folded paper covers used to protect the binding of hardcover books. They are a product of the early 20th century. Previously books were bound in cardboard, cloth or leather or in combinations thereof.

The dust jacket is an essential part of a book, without which it is incomplete and of less value. On the average, the dust jacket may constitute as much as 75 percent or more of a book's value. An example is the first edition of Ray Bradbury's first book *Dark Carnival* (Sauk City: Arkham House, 1947), which sells for about $300 without its dust jacket, while a copy with jacket demands a price of $1,000 to $1,500 depending on the book's condition.

Most publishers print overruns of dust jackets for replacements, but Arkham House did not do so for its early titles. Later on Arkham began printing extra dust jackets for each new title. Thus the Arkham House books most often seen without dust jackets are the early titles, while the majority of later books still have the original dust jacket. One reason for this discrepancy could be an emerging awareness in the 1940s and 1950s that without its dust jacket a collectible book would be less valuable. This was not the case in the 1910s and 1920s. When dust jackets first appeared, they were considered of little worth and frequently discarded. It was not uncommon that dust jackets were thrown away deliberately to facilitate a desired decorative effect on bookshelves with the jacketless bindings. Pre–1930s books without dust jackets are therefore much more common than copies with jacket.

It is well worth the cost to preserve the original dust jacket of any collectible book with a clear Mylar cover. This will protect the book from shelf wear, handling and spills and make the dust jacket look more attractive. A prominent source for dust jacket covers and other book preservation products is the Brodart Co., 100 North Road, P.O. Box 300, McElhattan, PA 17748. (www.brodart.com).

CONDITION

While demand and scarcity of a book cannot be discounted, condition is the foremost factor by which its market value is determined. No matter how rare a book may be, if in poor condition it is not considered collectible and is therefore of little value. In order to standardize how the condition of a book is described, the following general terms have been agreed upon by the rare book trade.

Mint (MT) or **As New** describes a book that is immaculate and complete in every aspect, including its original dust jacket, and appears as if it just came off the press, with no visible signs of wear, defects or imperfections. In short, a perfect copy. Books in this condition are rare.

Fine (FN) describes a book that is close to mint and complete, but without the crispness and with slight signs of wear. Minor defects, repairs or restorations must be noted.

Very Good (VG) describes a book that is visibly used with signs of wear, but complete and with no major defects. Any defects, repairs or restorations must be noted.

Good (GD) describes the average used book that is noticeably worn, but still complete. Spine roll, tears and other defects, and repairs or restorations must be noted.

Fair (FR) describes a book that is worn and incomplete, but with the text pages and inside illustrations (plates) intact. All defects and repairs must be noted. Unless extremely rare, a fair book is seldom considered a collectible.

Poor (PR) describes a book that is so worn and defective that it is only a reading copy and not a collectible. Major defects, such as torn, loose or missing pages, are common and must be noted.

Ex–public library copies, private lending library copies and **book club editions**, regardless of their condition must always be described as such with all defects, including ex-library labels, lending card pockets, location and date stamps.

Books that fall between the above listed categories may be graded "**very fine**" (VF) or "**near mint**" (NM). The condition of a book can be further defined by adding a plus (+) or minus(-) to a grade to indicate a better or lesser copy: for example, VG+ and FN-. Some sellers and collectors may also use terms such as "near very good" or "near fine" in describing a book's condition.

Dust jackets are graded separately. The condition of the book is listed first, followed by a slash and the condition of the dust jacket: for example, "FN/VG." The majority of collectible books are in the grades "fine," "very good" or "good."

GRADING BOOKS

The grading of collectible books is a skill that takes patience and experience to learn and must be executed with a high degree of objectivity. This is particularly important to keep in mind when the grader has a commercial interest in a book and knows that a step up or down in grade can mean a difference of hundreds of dollars earned or lost. Human wants have a way of affecting human objectivity. At one book fair, I noticed a decent copy of an Arkham House title on a seller's table graded "very good." It sold for $75 shortly after the fair opened. Later in the afternoon, I saw the same book, now graded "fine," on another seller's table and offered for sale at $200. It sold at that price.

Grading is done as a preliminary step for selling or buying a book or to establish the book's value for insurance or inventory purposes. Whenever possible and financially feasible, it is preferable to have an experienced, impartial appraiser grade the books. Where this is not possible or practicable, the grading must be done with detachment and honesty.

One thing to keep in mind is that there are few true "mint" copies in existence. As soon as a book comes off the press, it is handled, packed, unpacked, shelved, and browsed, leaving early signs of wear, however imperceptible they may be. There may be fingerprints, nail marks, soiling and bumped corners from being dropped, or printers' and binders' imperfections. For that reason, the term "mint" is seldom used. The next highest sub-grade, "near mint" is used more often, but most high grade, collectible books are "fine," and many booksellers do not grade their books higher than that.

The dust jacket is graded separately from the book and by the same grading scale. Unless protected with a Mylar cover from the time of printing, the dust jacket will usually show more wear than the book. This is a natural result of handling, reading and shelving. Consequently it is not uncommon that the dust jacket grades lower than the book, a condition reflected in a description such as "FN/VG" which indicates a fine book in a slightly worn but still very good dust jacket.

The technique of grading varies from one individual to another. Every collector and bookseller has his or her own way of determining a book's condition. A newer book will often grade fine, but as it ages and is subjected to more wear, fading, humidity and other damages, the book will slip in grades to very good and eventually good and fair unless its decline is arrested by the appropriate protective measures.

My personal technique for grading the condition of books may be comparable to the judging of horses (which I did many years ago) and consists of starting every book, regardless of condition, with 100 points. From there I deduct points for every fault, flaw or defect that I can find. Major defects detract more points than lesser flaws and wear, and at the end I have a number of points which I correlate to a grading scale. In the case of borderline grades, the lower grade is used.

Poor	Fair	Good	Very Good	Fine	Very Fine	Near Mint	Mint
0—10	11—20	21—40	41—60	61—80	81—90	91—99	100

MAJOR DEFECTS

Books are made from paper, cloth, cardboard or leather—fragile materials—and are subject to wear and aging. High acid content in the paper, fading, mildew, insect damage, water damage, fire, rough handling and incorrect storage are some of the agents that bring about the deterioration or destruction of thousands of valuable books every year. The term major defects, as used here, does not refer to normal wear, but to specific, identifiable things to look for which will lower the grade of a book—sometimes by several steps, depending on the severity of the defect. The order of significance is subjective. The following list is a personal ranking of the most common, major defects.

Missing pages or plates. Any page or plate missing from a book, including end papers (which may be removed to obliterate an inscription, name, notes or library markings) will instantly drop a book to a "fair" copy only. Such a book is not considered a collectible.

Missing dust jacket. Without its original dust jacket, a book is incomplete. The lack of a dust jacket may drop a book's value by 75 to 80 percent or more, even when the book itself is graded "fine." This is not likely, though, for without its dust jacket the book is unprotected, and a grade of "good" or at best "very good" is more likely for a jacketless book.

Water damage. This is a matter of degree, but the general rule is that any water damage such as stains, warping, wrinkling or color change (bleed) will drop the book to "good" or below. A barely perceptible ring from a water glass on the rear panel of a dust jacket, for example, will not detract as much as more serious damage. In general, collectors should avoid books that show signs of water damage, since there may be associated hidden problems such as decay in the spine, mildew, rotting stitching or disintegration of glue.

Cracked hinge or hinges. If the hinge or hinges, also known as inner joints, are broken or nearly broken—which will show as a splitting or separation of the front or rear end paper—the book is nearly worthless. A result of heavy use and rough handling, this is a major defect that cannot be remedied without extensive restoration. Books with broken hinges are graded no higher than "good." Collectors should avoid books with cracked or starting to crack hinges. Minor splits may be repaired, but this repair should be noted.

Spine roll. This is also known as slanting or sloping of the spine. When viewed from the head or tail of the book, the spine is not at a right angle to the front and back boards, but slants more or less and usually towards the front board. Spine roll is caused by wrongly breaking in a new book, by repeated careless readings or by storing the book at a slant on a bookshelf. It is a common defect and very undesirable, for it is almost impossible to correct. Regardless of the condition of the book, it looks bad. Even moderate spine roll will drop the condition of a book one full grade.

Foxing. This defect results in spotting of pages and page edges by light, reddish-brown spots, predominantly caused by mildew. As always the result is a matter of degree. If the condition is arrested, a few spots may not lower the grade of the book very much, but a more severe affliction can drop an otherwise decent book to as low as "fair" or "poor," effectively removing it from the realm of collectible books.

Damage to the binding. Defects in the case or binding of a book include damaged or creased boards, bumped corners due to the book having been dropped, bumped and frayed head and tail of the spine, cracked spine, spine wrinkles, rubbing, edge wear and torn cloth. Depending on the seriousness of the damages, the book may drop several grades to as low as "good" or "fair."

Damage to the text block. Damage to the text block includes separation of pages at the gutter, tearing of pages, missing corners or parts of pages, creases and stains, browning or discoloration. Because of the acid contents in the paper used in older books, natural aging of a book may cause browning of pages or page edges. Unless excessive or accompanied with brittleness, which can make the pages fall apart when touched, a moderate, naturally occurring browning (or tanning) due to age does not downgrade a book. Separations, tears, creases, stains and other page defects, however, will downgrade a book in accordance with the extent of the damage.

Loose binding. As a book ages and is read and handled more often, the binding may become loose through normal wear. For books graded "good" or lower a certain amount of looseness may be expected. If the binding is excessively loose, which usually means that the hinges and spine are weakened and may be about to crack or break, the book should be downgraded accordingly.

Inscriptions and bookplates. It is not uncommon that a previous owner of a book may write an inscription, a name or a date, usually on the front end papers or half title. Such writing may be small and neat, in which case it does not detract much from the book. In other cases, the writing may be large and sprawling or consist of extensive notations on everything from the occasion of receipt to a pagelong critique of the book. In that case, the book should be downgraded accordingly. Bookplates are another common way of showing ownership of a book and while some are small, neat and tasteful, others are garish and obtrusive. Unless inscriptions are by the author or associated with the author or publisher in some way, such as "association" and "dedication" copies (in which case the value of the book usually increases), bookplates and writing will downgrade a book in accordance with the degree that they affect the appearance of the book. There are many collectors who will not purchase a book with either bookplates or writing.

Remainder marks. These are special stamps, marker dots, slashes or colored sprays on the head or tail of the text block, indicating that the publisher has relinquished a number of copies for resale in book-stores at a reduced price. In most cases, the books are publisher's overstock sold directly to retail outlets. The presence of a remainder mark is undesirable from a collector's point of view and will drop the book one grade. Some collectors will not buy books with remainder marks.

Unpleasant smells. A musty, moldy, mildewy smell or a strong smell of tobacco smoke emanating from the pages of a book when opened will detract from the value of the book. These smells may be caused by storage of the book in a high humidity location or by smoking while reading. Books with this flaw should not be graded above "very good" regardless of condition.

GRADING DUST JACKETS

Dust jackets are relatively fragile paper wraps whose main purpose is to protect the binding of a book. The average dust jacket is subjected to a fair amount of handling, wear and abuse. While some overall wear of an older dust jacket should be expected, tears, flaking or chipping of edges and corners will downgrade a jacket. Missing pieces will further downgrade the jacket in accordance with how large a piece of the jacket is gone and how the loss may affect the jacket's illustration or text. Price clipping (the removal of a triangular piece of the jacket's front flap on which the original price was printed) is another defect that may or may not downgrade a jacket. On a common dust jacket the drop in value would be slight, but when the price is the only indicator of a first-state jacket, the value of a price-clipped dust jacket will drop and the jacket should be listed as possibly a later issue.

I have seen several examples of dust jackets cut in pieces and pasted into the book. It may be a front panel illustration tipped into the book at the relevant text, or it may be a resume or review of the book glued onto the pasted down-end paper. While the original intention may have been to enhance the book, this practice will decrease the value of the book by as much as one full grade.

23

REPAIRS

Book repairs may range from the finest, most professional work to the do-it-yourself tape mechanic's effort. Minor professional repairs, such as closed tears, will usually not have any effect on the grade, but tape or tape remnants will lower the book's grade. Commercial tape is generally considered a scourge in the book trade and when used to hold a dust jacket to the binding of a book, fasten loose pages, and repair major page tears, cracked hinges, and so forth, it will downgrade the book or dust jacket one or more grades.

The extent of repairs on a book and the quality of the work will determine the effect on the grading. Professionally executed repair may enhance the value of a book, while amateurish or poor quality attempts to fix a problem can send an otherwise acceptable copy plummeting to the bottom of the grading scale. Such books are usually best left alone.

RESTORATIONS

To restore or not ... that is the question. If and to what extent a worn or damaged book should be restored depends largely on the status of the book. If it is an heirloom (rather than a historical or collectible book), such as a family bible, a special gift, an inscribed book, a favorite novel or a beloved children's book, professional restoration may be well worth while; it can bring new life and longevity to old paper. If the subject is a rare, valuable and collectible book, however, the merits of restoration becomes debatable. While many collectible books might benefit from restoration, the more extensively a book is restored or reconstructed, the less of the original work remains, which in turn makes the book less valuable and less desirable.

When deemed appropriate or necessary, restoration should be done sparingly, carefully and professionally. As much as possible of the original book should be preserved. When done right, restoration can fix minor problems while having little effect on the value of the book; in the best of cases, restoration can enhance a book's worth. Dust jackets, boards and pages can be cleaned. Slight tears can be closed nearly invisibly and weak hinges can be reinforced. Loose pages and plates can be tipped in, and small rips and splits in the binding can be glued in place. Since these types of restorations do not replace any original part of the book and are in most cases unobtrusive, they do not have any great impact on the value of the book. More extensive restoration, which may require replacement of original parts of the book (for example, the end papers), will drop its value proportionally to the amount of restoration done.

Restoration should not be used as a means of pushing an inferior copy up to a higher grade for commercial gains; the primary purpose of restoration is preserving that which might otherwise be lost. As an alternative to restoration and for storage of rare and valuable books, custom-made clamshell book boxes or slip cases are recommended.

Any repair or restoration should be listed if the book is offered for sale or catalogued for other purposes. Professional restoration is expensive and the value of the book to be restored needs to be taken into consideration.

REPLACEMENT AND FACSIMILE DUST JACKETS

A first edition, first printing in the original dust jacket is the most desirable book from a collecting point of view and demands the highest price. Publishers often print overruns of dust jackets, and a book that has lost its original jacket may be refurbished with a replacement jacket. Although the replacement may be a genuine first edition overrun jacket, it is not the original jacket issued with the book, and the "mating" of an old book with a new replacement jacket may have a negative impact on its value. How much depends on the usual factors of condition, scarcity and demand.

With today's computer and color reproduction technology, faux dust jackets have proliferated at an astounding rate in the last ten years. Early color copies and photographic reproductions have been replaced by laser printed facsimiles, dye-ink replications and reconstruction jackets. Most are copies of the original first edition jacket, and the better ones are so close to the original that it can be difficult to tell the difference. Some show the word "facsimile" or other indicators that the jacket is a copy or reproduction, but others do not.

As a book ages, so does its dust jacket, with the inevitable signs of wear, rubbing, fading, stress lines, small tears, and so forth, and if the dust jacket on an older book is new and fresh with a near mint look and feel, it is most likely a new overrun or facsimile jacket. The paper the jacket is printed on may also provide a clue to its origin. The early Arkham House dust jackets were printed on heavy, non-glossy paper (there are exceptions). It is these early titles that are most often found with facsimile dust jackets.

Does a quality facsimile or reproduction dust jacket enhance the value of a book? It will certainly enhance the appearance of the book and furnish information printed on the original dust jacket, such as contents, author profile, reviews, other titles, etc., but it does not affect the value of the book as a collectible. It is fair that a bookseller add the retail cost of a facsimile jacket (usually around $20 to $30 for a high quality jacket) to the price of the book, but otherwise, the value of a book in a facsimile jacket is the same as the value of the book without a dust jacket.

FIRST EDITIONS

To the discriminating collector the only collectible books are the first printings of the first edition (including advance reading copies, issued before the first trade edition). For that reason, it is important that the collector know how to identify first editions and understand the difference between editions and printings. A first edition may have numerous printings, all of which are first editions, but only the first printing is considered a true "first" and collectible book. When corrections are made in the text or the format, jacket illustration or some other aspect is changed, the book becomes a second or subsequent edition.

Publishers designate their editions and printings in any number of ways, and it is not always easy to determine with certainty if a book is a first edition or printing. The classification of older books especially can be confusing and difficult. For more specific information on first edition identification, refer to the sources listed in the bibliography at the end of this book.

To aid in the identification of Arkham House first editions, the publishers made following statement in 1976: "All Arkham House books are limited (first editions) with the exceptions of the collected works of H.P. Lovecraft, the subsequent reprintings of which are acknowledged in the end colophon to each volume." This is not correct, since there are reprints of Arkham House books where the reprinting was not acknowledged in the colophon. (The present work discusses these cases in the description of individual titles.)

In 1981, Arkham House issued the following statement: "Initial pressruns of Arkham House books (from 1980 to the present) are identified by the term 'First Edition' on the copyright page. If the title subsequently is reprinted, the 'First Edition' designation is either removed from the copyright page or is replaced by an appropriate acknowledgment such as 'Second Printing,' 'Third Printing,' et cetera." In 1988 and again in 1993, Arkham House issued the following statement: " All Arkham House first editions are designated by the term 'First Edition' which invariably occupies the final line on our copyright pages (p. iv). Should a book enter subsequent printings, this line will be replaced by 'Second Printing,' 'Third Printing," or whatever notification is appropriate. With the exception of our collected critical Lovecraft editions, Arkham House seldom reprints its titles." In later years, however, Arkham House has reprinted titles other than the Lovecraftian collections, which are correctly identified in this book. For more information on the identification and printing history of individual titles, the reader should consult the relevant chapter.

ARKHAM HOUSE BINDINGS, HEADBANDS AND COLOPHONS

Most Arkham House books are bound in black Holliston Novelex cloth with gold lettering on the spine, but there are exceptions as noted in this work's individual title descriptions. Later editions are bound in a similarly textured black cloth, designated as Holliston Roxite B grade, also with gold lettering on the spine. With the exception of a smaller number of volumes published in wraps without dust jackets and some specially bound volumes without dust jackets, Arkham House titles are hardcover books with dust jackets. In general, up to 1965, the books were not bound with the additional spine support of head- and tailbands. The bands were introduced that year as a standard binding feature and are present on all titles thereafter (there are exceptions).

From the early books, all Arkham House books had a brief colophon on the last printed page, which listed the approximate print number, printer and binder, the type in which the book was composed, typesetting, paper and binding material. The colophon was discontinued in 1980, but a few titles thereafter carried a brief notation on the types used in the book in place of the colophon. The colophon was reinstated in its original format in 1998 and has been continued in all new titles thereafter.

The familiar "Haunted House" Arkham House colophon or trademark was designed by the Wisconsin artist Frank Utpatel and appeared first in the 1944 title *The Eye and the Finger* by Donald Wandrei. With few exceptions, the "Haunted House" has appeared unchanged on the title page of all titles to the present.

AUTHOR SIGNED, ASSOCIATION AND DEDICATION COPIES

A book signed by its author is more valuable than an unsigned copy because of the closer association with the author. The signature of some authors remains constant in form and legibility, while the signature of others may change over time with the name becoming more and more indistinct, until it is little more than a scribble. This is a modern phenomenon caused by the demand on authors to sign increasingly larger number of books at fairs, on book signing tours and at other promotions. An early, complete and legible signature will increase the value of the same title and edition to a greater level than a recent, less complete or legible signature. How much a signed copy will increase in value over an unsigned copy is a matter of author, title, edition, demand, scarcity and condition of the book.

There are several ways that an author may sign a book, and some are more favored than others. The most desirable is the distinct, full name signature, usually written on the free front end paper, half title or title page. This is know as a **flatsigned** signature. If the book is signed and inscribed to a person or persons, the signature is an **inscription** signature, which is slightly less desirable. An author's signature may be written on a bookplate pasted into the front of the book. For promotional purposes, an author may sign hundreds of bookplates which are then affixed to the book before or after sale. The **bookplate** signature is only indirectly associated with the book and consequently less desirable. A special plate or signature card bearing the author's signature may be **tipped in** at the front of the book, usually after the free front end paper. The author has signed the plates or cards in advance, and they are bound into the book. Finally the author's signature may be cut from a letter, a cancelled check or other writing and pasted into the book. The **cut and paste** method is the least desirable signature form.

Association copies are copies which have a particular association to the author or publisher, expressed by an inscription, bookplate, marking or signature connecting the book with a person, a special date, event or circumstance. **Dedication copies** are copies especially dedicated and signed by the author to relatives, friends, associates or acquaintances. If the copy is dedicated to a family member of the author, publisher, fellow writer or other prominent person, its value will increase accordingly. As a general rule, true association and dedication copies are more valuable than plain, signed copies of the same title and edition.

BRIEF NOTES ON BOOK CARE

Books are comparatively fragile objects made from paper, cardboard, fabric or leather. Every year, thousands of books are lost in floods, fires, earthquakes, mud slides, hurricanes and tornados—not to mention ordinary hazards. To ensure the preservation of collectible books, steps must be taken to protect them.

Sunlight. Exposure to sunlight (ultraviolet light) will quickly fade the colors of a book or dust jacket, especially the exposed spine when the book is placed in a bookcase. Sunlight will cause browning of pages and make them brittle. It will also dry leather-bound volumes and make them crack or chip. Do not leave books where sunlight might reach them at any hour, and remember that windows in a room with books should be shaded during the day, except if facing north.

Water. Water or moisture can destroy a book beyond restoration. Books that have been submerged in water, even briefly, will swell or disintegrate and cannot be salvaged. A more insidious, but equally detrimental factor is humidity. If there is a high atmospheric moisture content where books are kept or stored (as in a basement, garage, attic or in tropical climates), they will deteriorate proportionally with the degree of humidity. The case may unglue and deteriorate, signature stitching may rot and cause the pages to fall apart, seeping glue may discolor end papers and inside pages may warp and discolor. High humidity commonly causes mildew, which shows as brown spots known as "foxing." Hardcover and leather-bound books are prone to warping and molding due to moisture.

Keep books away from areas that may be flooded, leaking or subject to potential plumbing problems (e.g. frozen pipes), such as basements, garages and attics. Faulty plumbing and unexpected sewer backup during heavy rains have destroyed many rare books. In the winter, prevent gutter ice dams, resulting in water from melting snow running inside ceilings and walls, by keeping the first three to four feet of the roof from the gutter clear of snow. Boxes of books stored in basements should be at least 12 inches off the floor, and boxes stored in attics should be covered with plastic to protect against water damage from potential roof leaks.

Maintain a constant temperature of 60 to 70° F and a relative humidity of 40 to 50 percent where books are kept. Most central heating and air conditioning systems can be equipped with a humidity control, and where high humidity is a problem, a dehumidifier can bring atmospheric moisture down to an acceptable level. In tropical climates, valuable books should be kept in a climate-controlled environment.

Fire. There is little to be said about fire. It burns and destroys books either directly or by smoke damage. Do not keep or store books in or near a potentially flammable environment. Make sure that fire and smoke detectors are installed and working. Change batteries twice yearly and follow the local fire department's recommendations for fireproofing. Keep fire extinguishers accessible, but avoid installation of automatic sprinklers in rooms where books are kept; in case of activation the water may do as much damage as the fire. Especially valuable books may be kept in fireproof safes or file cabinets, vaults or bank boxes.

Insects and rodents. Insects and rodents can do a tremendous amount of damage to books that are boxed and stored undisturbed for long periods of time. Insects and rodents eat the glue that holds the binding together, the glue in the pages, the paper and the leather binding. They may also shred pages for nesting material and leave a mess with their droppings. The result is books that are seriously and irreparably damaged. Keep books in an environment that is free of these pests. Do not store books in basements, garages or attics undisturbed for long periods of time. If this becomes necessary, seal boxes completely with heavy packing tape and place insect and rodent poison or repellent around and under the boxes. Periodically check and rearrange the boxes to detect any damage as early as possible.

Rough handling. One of the most common and most easily prevented causes of harm to books is rough or thoughtless handling. Books are broken open to lie flat, which will crack the spine; they may be dropped, spilled on, used as drink coasters or note pads, have page corners bent as book marks, left in sunlight, tossed around and generally handled with little regard for their worth or care. Handle books carefully and ask others to do the same. Do not break them open to lie flat, but support them in half-open position for reading. Do not permit food, drinks or smoking near or around collectible books. Tobacco smoke may cause discoloration and leaves an offensive, lingering smell in a book. Rare books should be handled with cloth gloves to avoid the transfer of fingerprints, oil, dirt or sweat from the hands to the book. The cardinal rule of caring for collectible books is not to lend them out to anyone for any reason.

Shelving. Although most books are kept standing upright on shelves where they are the most accessible, larger and heavier volumes are best preserved lying flat on the side, which is how books originally were kept. When standing upright, weighty volumes will drop the text block to rest on the shelf, which will pull the pages off the binding at the top and deform the top of the spine into a concave shape. Thick books with glossy pages are particularly prone to this. Much depends on the thickness and weight of the pages and the method of binding, but as a rule any rare or valuable book over two inches in thickness should be shelved horizontally.

Books are best kept in bookcases behind glass. This will protect them from dust and changes in the environment. Shelves with books in upright position should be filled, but not so tightly packed that the books are difficult to pull out, since this may damage the top of the jacket, spine or headband. Books placed upright on half-empty shelves lean against other books, which gradually warps the case and spine. Place heavy books horizontally against vertical copies. Valuable copies may be protected in slip cases or clamshell book cases made to order by a bookbinder.

Bookmarks. Bookmarks are any flat object used to indicate a specific place in the text block of a book. They come in many shapes, sizes and materials, and most of them should not be used as markers in collectible books. Bookmarks made from acidic papers (newsprint, for example) will leave a shadow on the page if left for a time, and magazine paper may leave a text or color imprint. Paper clips leave indentations and at times rust marks on pages. Many bookmarks sold in bookstores are patently harmful. Some that I have seen for sale include small cloth animals (which will force the pages apart and distort the binding), metal book marks (which may cut, tear or dent the pages), leather bookmarks (which may exude oil and stain the pages), and laminated old paperback covers (which will leave impressions in the pages). The only bookmark that should be used is a strip of plain, white acid free paper without printing or writing.

INSURANCE

Regardless of how well protected a collection is, accidents, thefts or natural disasters which cannot be foreseen or prevented may happen. Collections of rare books should be insured. This may require a professional appraisal, but it is money well spent. Talk to your agent.

Most insurance companies will add a special rider for a collection to a home insurance policy, but there are also companies that specializes in insuring collectibles. One such company is the Collectible Insurance Agency (CIA), P.O. Box 1200, Westminster, MD 21158-0299, www.collectinsure.com.

3

Buying and Selling Arkham House Books

BUYING BOOKS

Every collector and bookseller dreams of going to a rummage sale, finding a box of books with a $10 price tag and discovering a dozen early Arkham House first editions in impeccable condition. While this may have been possible a quarter of a century ago, it is unlikely to happen today. I have visited hundreds of rummage sales, flea markets and junk fairs over the years, with fewer than 20 collectible books to show for it. I am not saying that the dream scenario cannot happen, but the most likely place to find a bargain would be moving or estate sales where the seller might not be cognizant of the value of individual titles. Sometimes, the executors of an estate may let a book collection go for a reduced price in order to liquidate the assets of the estate quickly.

Such finds are exceptions, and few collectors are lucky enough to stumble onto such deals. Today collections of rare books are often sent to auction houses, where specialists are keenly aware of their values. In most cases, collectors are left with the options of purchasing books from booksellers, on the Internet or from other collectors specializing in Arkham House books. While there may be room for some negotiation, prices are usually firm and largely based on the condition and current catalog value of a book. When buying from a bookseller, be prepared to pay the asking price. It may seem difficult to get a good deal that way, but Arkham House books will most likely appreciate in value as demand and scarcity increases and a book purchased from a bookseller 10–15 years ago may well be worth double or triple its price today. Keep checking rummage sales, estate and moving sales, auctions, and used book stores, but for acquiring high grade copies, find and develop a good relationship with several reputable booksellers. Let them know what you are looking for and what you are prepared to pay. Some of the ways of finding booksellers who are selling Arkham House books are through recommendations from other collectors, relevant Internet sites and visits to rare book stores.

Buying on the Internet. The evolution of the worldwide web or Internet has revolutionized the book trade and provided collectors with instant and almost unlimited access to the world's rare book market. Book searches that would have required days, weeks or months to carry out by traditional means a few years ago can now be done within minutes with a few key strokes or mouse clicks. A book that has eluded the intrepid collector for years may now be found in less than ten minutes; not only one copy, but several of varying conditions and prices. For the bookseller, the Internet has opened a whole new world of marketing possibilities: For a small fee, books that have lingered on the shelf waiting for a walk-in customer can now be spotlighted electronically to millions of potential buyers.

The first thing that one notices is the sheer number of Arkham House titles available on the Internet. The largest book search service, www.abebooks.com (the Advanced Book Exchange), for example, has 1268 Arkham titles listed at the time of writing, with new items being added or sold daily. When the abebooks.com search is limited to first editions in dust jackets, the count is 787 titles, still an impressive number. Another website well worth looking at is www.abaa.com, the Antiquarian Bookseller's Association of America (ABAA), which lists about 1000 Arkham House titles with 667 being first editions in dust jackets. Other sites such as Alibris, Barnes & Noble.com and Amazon.com show the occasional Arkham title, but mostly the newer reprints. In addition, many booksellers maintain their own website, but can be difficult to locate unless one knows the name of the business or the address of the website.

This leaves the Arkham House collector with primarily www.abebooks.com and www.abaa.com as the two largest book search services for buying books. Looking at the titles offered on these two sites, there is some repetition since many booksellers list their books on both sites. As for quality, the books offered by the ABAA are usually a better grade and more accurately described than on other sites. Higher prices reflect the greater level of quality. The sellers know their books and their values. The books offered by abebooks.com are usually well described and fairly correctly represented, but there are occasional inaccuracies and inconsistencies in edition identification and description. Regardless of site reputation, description and price, buying books unseen on the Internet can be a gamble, so following are a few suggestions which can make the experience less chancy.

Compare price and condition. Very recently, I found 37 copies of *Someone in the Dark* by August Derleth (Arkham House, 1941) on abebooks.com and abaa.com, all first editions in the original dust jacket. The books were listed in various condition from "very good" to "fine" and priced accordingly, but not consistently. One copy described as "fine/near fine" (meaning the book was "fine," the dust jacket "near fine") listed at $1000 while another book described as "very good/very good" was priced at $950. Another "fine/very good" copy listed at $650. A different "near fine/near fine" book was priced at $400. Obviously there are substantial differences in the asking prices for books within a comparable grade range. It is possible to pick up good, high grade copies for a reasonable price, if one takes the time to look instead of jumping on the first book that is available. Patience is the password. The inconsistencies in sellers' prices have made the job of compiling a realistic guide to values a challenging task.

Contact the seller. Ask questions. Most web sites have a service that facilitates direct communication between a potential buyer and the seller through email. Do not buy a high-priced book without first contacting the seller and asking specific questions: Is this a true first edition/first printing? Is the binding tight and square, with no spine roll and good hinges? To what degree are the boards and spine faded or discolored and is the text on the spine still readable? Are any plates or pages missing? Does the book have writing, bookplates, stamps, tears, tape repairs, stains or remainder marks? Is the dust jacket the original, issued with the book, or is it a later state dust jacket? Is the jacket faded, chipped, or repaired, or are pieces missing? Is the jacket price clipped? Most importantly: May I return the book for a refund if I am not satisfied?

This may seems like a lot of trouble, but it only takes a few minutes to email the questions, and when several hundred dollars are at stake, it is well worth the effort. If some of the answers are provided in the description of the book, there is no need to ask those questions. If the seller does not answer positively within a reasonable time (usually one to three business days), do not buy the book. If the seller answers your questions honestly and courteously, you are less likely to end up with a book that you would not have bought if you had seen it beforehand. If asked, some sellers will email electronic scans or photographs of high-priced items.

Buying on Internet auctions. Buying books on auctions such as www.ebay.com, yahoo.com, uBid.com, amazon.com, bidville, and buynsellit.com, to mention a few, is entirely different from buying from a bookseller and can be a chancy proposition. While the sellers on abebooks.com or abaa.com know their books and price accordingly, this is not necessarily so with auction sites. In many cases the seller does not know the difference between a first edition and a reprint or a variant; the condition and consequent value of a book may be misrepresented or the book may be inadequately described, giving the bidder little information on which to base a decision. On the other hand, it is possible to make some good deals on auctions, if one knows what to look for and how to develop a winning bidding strategy.

As a rule of thumb, the winning bid paid for Arkham House books on www.ebay.com is about 50 to 70 percent of the price charged by sellers for the same title in comparable condition through book search services such as abebooks.com and abaa.com. Before bidding on a book, know its current catalog value and determine the top price that you are prepared to pay.

The most important thing when buying at an Internet auction is to make sure that the seller has a return guarantee so a book purchased may be returned for a refund if it is not satisfactory.

SELLING BOOKS

For the book collector who wants to dispose of duplicate copies, single titles or an entire collection of Arkham House books, there are five basic options available.

Sale to collectors. This is the option that brings the best price. The seller can set the price in accordance with current price guides, but may give a discount to make the sale. The greatest challenge is to find collectors who are interested in buying the book(s) and can pay the price. Mailing lists from collectors' organizations, advertisements in specialty publications and listings on the Internet are commonly used to reach interested buyers.

Sale by auction. Larger collections may be offered for sale through auction houses. Auctions attract both booksellers and collectors and will often bring the best price for the least amount of hassle. The seller can set a minimum (reserve) price or leave the conditions of sale to the auctioneer. The percentage commission charged by the auction house per book is paid by the buyer.

Sale at book fairs and exhibitions. Nearly all larger cities have one or more used and rare book fairs or exhibitions per year. Many have several and a few areas have monthly shows. Some of these events are reserved for bona fide booksellers, but in many cases it is possible for anyone to rent space, a booth or a table with chairs and offer books for sale. The seller should be prepared to negotiate within a set margin. Potential buyers expect to find bargains at these events, but may also be nitpicking at insignificant flaws and unfairly criticize a book or its condition to bring the price down. This tactic cheapens the buyer and demeans the seller. Don't fall for it. Determine a fair price and stick to it.

Sale to booksellers. When selling to booksellers, remember that this is how they make a living. They cannot buy at catalog prices if they want to stay in business. If a seller has a ready buyer or knows that there is a high demand for a certain book, he or she may be prepared to pay up to 70 percent of guide value. If a seller believes that the book is scarce enough to sell within a reasonable time, he or she may offer 30 to 40 percent of guide value. If a book is common and most likely will linger on the shelf (or website) for more than a year, don't expect more than 10 to 20 percent of guide value—that is, if the seller wants the book at all.

Instead of selling a book or a collection outright to a bookseller, one might consider trading for credit towards the purchase of other books. This may give more buying power than a cash deal, since most sellers would be willing to give more store credit than cash. That said, don't expect a bookseller to accept a boxful of common titles for a high priced item. Much depends on the prospective demands for the books in trade.

Selling on the Internet. The internet presently offers three choices for selling books.

PERSONAL WEBSITE. Many booksellers post their own websites with customer access to their inventory through a user-friendly search engine, together with listings of services, news items, links and other matters of interest. Depending on one's assets, these sites can be elaborate and very artistically designed. Individual titles can be better represented and are easier to find on a personal website than in the thousands of titles listed by the book search services. The seller determines the price for the books offered for sale. A personal website might be listed in various Internet directories, or a potential buyer may need to know the name of the seller or the website address to find and access it.

BOOK SEARCH SERVICES. Like *www.abebooks.com*, *www.abaa.com* and others, these services are massive databases containing millions of books and representing thousands of booksellers worldwide. For a nominal fee, abebooks.com, for example, will list books for sale, collect credit card payments, provide a small personalized website and a free download book database program to keep track of inventory, sales, etc. The seller sets the price for which the book will be offered. The downside is that with more than 1000 Arkham House titles online, the few books listed by a private seller may easily disappear into the vastness of such inventory, unless they are exceptional books of exceptional value and at exceptional prices. The average book might wait online for a long time before anyone buys it.

While abebooks.com will list books from anyone who registers successfully, abaa.com will accept book listings only from members of the ABAA.

ONLINE AUCTIONS. If you are more interested in a quick sale than a higher profit, the online auction is the way to go. There are several possibilities, but *www.ebay.com* is probably the best known and has a large following in the United States. Auctions usually run for 7 days, but can be more or less if required. There is a small listing fee and a percentage is deducted from the winning bid price. Ebay.com also provides online payment services and has an accessible feedback system for buyers and sellers—a good thing to check when in doubt. The seller determines the auction starting price, but can set a reserve line, which means a price below which the book cannot be sold. Most early Arkham House first edition titles sold on ebay.com have reserve lines. As mentioned before, one can expect about half the price for a book sold on an ebay.com auction that it would sell for on a book search service.

In summary, regardless of which of the above listed options the seller may choose, know the books offered for sale. Consider titles, authors and editions and keep in mind that condition, supply and demand will influence values. Grade the books accurately and conservatively. A "very good" book should be graded as such, not as a "fine" copy. The informed buyer will know the difference. Study catalogs and price guides to get a realistic fix on the asking price. Be prepared to negotiate, but decide on the lowest acceptable price and stick to it.

VALUE GUIDE CRITERIA

The values listed in this work are based on the conditions described in the previous chapter. They are not definitive, but provide a guide for pricing a particular book based on current information. The prices suggested are retail prices that a collector can expect to pay when purchasing a book from a bookseller. They are not the prices that a bookseller may pay for a book. Demand, scarcity and condition constitute the foundation of pricing; the greater the demand for a book, the scarcer it is, and the better its condition, the higher the price. Like any collectible, a book is worth no more and no less than someone is willing to pay for it. Use the information in this book as a guide, but the final word on pricing is the compromise between what a seller is asking and what a buyer is prepared to pay.

For the purposes of this guide, the values listed for books published from 1939 through 1974 are for titles in "fine" condition in an original issue "fine" dust jacket. Books in better condition will demand higher prices than those listed and books in lesser condition will cost less. Prices listed for books published from 1975 through 2003 are for books in "very fine" to "near mint" condition for book and dust jacket. Books in lower grades will sell for less. While the values of some reprints have been listed where appropriate for completeness, the listing is primarily for first edition, first printing copies.

The following table may be used to determine the value of lower or higher grade copies for books published from 1939 through 1974, using the grade "fine" as the baseline. The percentages listed indicate the increase or decrease in value for lower or higher grade copies. A "good" book, for example, would be 50 percent of the value of a "fine" book, while the value of a "near mint" would be 115 percent of a "fine." The same table may be used to determine the value of a dust jacket, which is then included in the price of the book. For example, the value of a FN/VG book would be 87.5 percent of a FN/FN copy, while the value of a VF/FN book would be 105 percent of a FN/FN copy.

Poor	Fair	Good	Very Good	Fine	Very Fine	Near Mint	Mint
10%	20%	50%	75%	100%	110%	115%	120%

FUTURE TRENDS

As with many other collectible books, Arkham House books saw a significant upswing in values between 1980 and 1997. Since then there have been fluctuations in prices as authors and titles move in and out of vogue; however, the appreciation of Arkham House books has remained fairly predictable. A rough overall average shows that Arkham House titles published from 1939 to 1989 have doubled in value since 1990. This is a median figure, and not all titles have achieved such a rise. Some titles have appreciated as much as 300 percent in the same time period, but the doubling of values over the past 13 years seems to be a relative constant.

As with other future trends, the potential appreciation of Arkham House books is difficult to predict. Research for this book suggests that the early Arkham House titles (1939 to 1965), and particularly books by Robert Bloch, Ray Bradbury, Joseph Payne Brennan, August Derleth, William Hope Hodgson, Robert E. Howard, Howard Phillips Lovecraft, Stanley McNail, Clark Ashton Smith, Donald Wandrei, and Henry S. Whitehead, will continue to appreciate in value, not only because of their age and increasing scarcity, but also because of their literary merits. Of the newer titles (1966 to 2002), books by Greg Bear, Michael Bishop, J. Ramsey Campbell, Basil Copper, Tanith Lee, Brian Lumley, Barry N. Malzberg, Lucius Shepard, and James Tiptree, Jr., appear to be among the most likely to experience noticeable appreciation in years to come.

Some price guides increase the value of books (and other collectibles) by customarily adding an annual percentage, with little consideration to actual market prices. The problem with this approach is evident, since book values may rise or fall above or below any arbitrarily set percentage in accordance with scarcity and demand. The greatest pitfall of the 'annual percentage increase' method is that given enough time, the suggested value of a book may become so overinflated that it is utterly out of balance with the market. This happened some years ago in the comic book industry, where the guide prices had become so inflated that a drastic 'price regulation' from one year's guide to the next became necessary and sent the value for the majority of later comic books plummeting by as much as 60 to 80 percent in order to get catalog values back in line with market values. In addition to devaluating thousands of private collections, the sudden price regulation contributed to the closing of several hundred comic book stores nationwide.

Price guides should be based primarily on the prices paid currently on the market with consideration given to a book's scarcity, demand and condition—not what a seller is asking for a book, but what a buyer has actually paid or is prepared to pay. While this approach requires more research, it is the only way to establish a realistic, up-to-date price guide. The values listed herein are based on current market research and personal experience buying and selling Arkham House books.

In closing, collectors and would-be collectors would do well to seek out and acquire the early Arkham House books (1939 to 1965) first, although they are more costly than later and more accessible editions. The early titles, in collectible condition, are becoming proportionally scarcer with age and seem to continue to appreciate in value. When possible, buy now; these books will not become any less expensive with the passing of time. The value of an early Arkham House book bought today may well double or triple within the next decade. For the books published from 1965 to 1990, there are more copies in "fine" condition available at a lower cost and with consequently lesser appreciation. Books published after 1990 (with few exceptions) have not yet appreciated beyond the cover price, since many are still in print. Start at the beginning and work forward in time.

ARKHAM HOUSE BOOKS
AS INVESTMENTS

When the value of collectible books began a near meteoric rise in the early 1980s, it seemed that rare books might be a good financial investment. In order to make the right choices of any investment instruments, however, one must anticipate future demands for the prospective product or service. As has been shown repeatedly by the volatility of the stock market and other economic indicators, this is far from an easy undertaking. In the above, I have briefly outlined some thoughts on the prospective appreciation of Arkham House books. There is little doubt that the high-end authors and early titles will continue to increase in value, perhaps at a slower pace than in the past 20 years, but I do not believe that starting a collection at this time for the single purpose of investment and in hope of a hefty return in the future is a viable option. As far as the lesser or low-end titles, with the exception of the premier works of yet undiscovered authors, I do not expect these books will appreciate at nearly the same rate as the high-end items. Nevertheless, I believe that most collectible titles will increase in value, but in slower increments. Books are fragile objects and every year thousands are lost or discarded, making those remaining that much more scarce and valuable.

One argument against collectible books as an investment is that unlike stocks, bonds and precious metal, books are not easily turned into money. A buyer who is willing and able to pay the asking price must be found, a process which might require weeks, months or years if the collection is large or particularly valuable. If the right buyer cannot be found or a collection must be sold quickly because of financial needs, the seller may take a loss and in some case recover little more than the original price paid for the books. An enjoyable hobby, perhaps, but a poor investment. It also seems that the younger generations, nurtured by television, video, computers and other electronic marvels, have little interest in books and book collecting. There will always be people who appreciate and collect rare books, but they will be progressively fewer in number, making book collecting solely for investment purposes a precarious proposition.

All things considered, I cannot advocate book collecting as a feasible instrument of investment. Books should be enjoyed for their own sake, for a favorite author or literary merit, a beautiful binding or an artistically rendered dust jacket. In short, collecting should be for the appreciation of books and not for prospective monetary gain.

4

Arkham House Bibliography (1939–2003)

All titles are listed and numbered in chronological order as published. The majority of Arkham House titles are out of print. Titles still in print are noted accordingly.

During its history, Arkham House has published a multitude of booklets, pamphlets, chapbooks, leaflets and announcements with information on upcoming titles or other timely topics. They are usually not numbered in the Arkham House list; however, special printings of particular interest or importance have been included and numbered in this bibliography. Because of these inclusions, the numbering of titles herein varies slightly from the official Arkham House publishing list.

The term "No reprints" indicates that the title has not been reprinted by any publisher. The term "No AH reprints" indicates that the title has not been reprinted by Arkham House, but may have been reprinted by other publishers.

Arkham House stock lists and book catalogs are not included in this bibliography, but they are listed in Chapter 9. Additional information on Arkham House special printings and ephemera may be found in the books listed in the reference bibliography.

The suggested values listed here for books published from 1939 through 1974 are for titles in "fine/fine" condition. Books in better condition will demand higher prices, and books in lower grade will cost less. Values listed for books published from 1975 through 2003 are for books in "very fine" to "near mint" condition. Books in lower grade will sell for less. While the values of some reprints have been included where appropriate or necessary for completeness, the listing is primarily for first edition/first printing copies. The first noted value is for books in the original

45

dust jacket; the second is for books without dust jackets or with facsimile jackets.

BIBLIOGRAPHY

1. **The Outsider and Others,** by Howard Phillips Lovecraft. Compiled by August Derleth and Donald Wandrei, the first book published by Arkham House contains many of H.P. Lovecraft's best supernatural stories. (1939.) 533 pp. 1268 copies printed. Cover price $5.00. Jacket art by Virgil Finlay.

Contents: *Howard Phillips Lovecraft: Outsider* by August Derleth and Donald Wandrei; *Dagon; Polaris; Celephais; Hypnos; The Cats of Ulthar; The Strange High House in the Mist; The Statement of Randolph Carter; The Silver Key; Through the Gates of the Silver Key; The Outsider; The Music of Eric Zann; The Rats in the Wall; Cool Air; He; The Horror at Red Hook; The Temple; Arthur Jermyn; The Picture in the House; The Festival; The Terrible Old Man; The Tomb; The Shunned House; In the Vault; Pickman's Model; The Haunter of the Dark; The Dreams in the Witch-House; The Thing on the Doorstep; The Nameless City; The Lurking Fear; The Call of Cthulhu; The Color out of Space; The Dunwich Horror; The Whisperer in Darkness; The Shadow over Innsmouth; The Shadow out of Time; At the Mountains of Madness;* Supernatural Horror in Literature.

The Outsider and Others, by H.P. Lovecraft (1939). Cover art by Virgil Finlay. No. 1.

The title for the book was chosen from one of its stories and with reference to Lovecraft, who regarded himself an outsider from ordinary human society. At the time of issue $5.00 was a hefty price to pay for a book. A pre-publication price of $3.50 brought only 150 responses, and it took better than four years to sell the book's only printing. The dust jacket art is a montage of

46

drawings done for *Weird Tales* by Virgil Finlay. Jacket proofs were printed in black, green and blue, with the final choice being blue. It appears that no extra dust jackets were printed at the time and this is one of the Arkham House titles that is most often seen without the original dust jacket. A reprint (facsimile) dust jacket was produced later, but is considered to be of esthetic value only. High grade copies in the original dust jacket are relatively scarce and caution is advised when purchasing this title in dust jacket. Counterfeits are not uncommon and with today's technology relatively easy to produce. Three of the stories, *The Dunwich Horror, At the Mountains of Madness,* and *Dagon*, were published later by Arkham House as separate collections in 1963, 1964 and 1965 respectively. *The Outsider and Others* is the definitive key title. No other AH reprints, but some of the stories have been reprinted by other publishers. $3,000/400

2. **Someone in the Dark**, by August Derleth. Collection of stories previously published in *Weird Tales*. (1941.) 335 pp. 1115 copies printed. Cover price $2.00. Jacket art by Frank Utpatel.

Contents: *When the Night and the House Are Still; Glory Hand; Compliments of Spectro; A Gift for Uncle Herman; McGovern's Obsession; Three Gentlemen in Black; Muggridge's Aunt; Bramwell's Guardian; Joliper's Gift; Altimer's Amulet; The Shuttered House; The Sheraton Mirror; The Wind from the River; The Telephone in the Library; The Panelled Room; The Return of Hastur; The Sandwin Compact.*

Someone in the Dark, by August Derleth (1941). Cover art by Frank Utpatel. No. 2.

Because of Derleth's contractual obligations, the manuscript was first submitted to Charles Scribner's Sons. It contained what Derleth believed to be the best short stories he had written. It was felt, however, that Scribner's would not be able to do as well commercially as a smaller press, and it was suggested that Derleth might consider publishing the collection under the Arkham House imprint. This was a departure from the original concept of Arkham House, which was founded for the purpose of publishing Lovecraft's work exclusively. After some consideration, Derleth did have the book published by Arkham House and it outsold the first title. The first edition of *Someone in the Dark* is 17.60 cm tall and has no headband. An offset edition was reprinted in 300 copies by Hunter Publishing Company for Arkham House in 1965. This book is 18.35 cm tall with headband. 335 pp. Cover price $5.00. A key title. No other reprints. First printing $1,250/300; 1965 reprinting $300/75

3. **Out of Space and Time,** by Clark Ashton Smith. The author's first collection of supernatural stories. (1942.) 370 pp. 1054 copies printed. Cover price $3.00. Jacket art by Hannes Bok.
Contents: *Clark Ashton Smith: Master of Fantasy,* by August Derleth & Donald Wandrei; *The End of the Story; A Rendezvous in Averoigne; A Night in Malnéant; The City of the Singing Flame; The Uncharted Isle; The Second Interment; The Double Shadow; The Chain of Aforgomon; The Dark Eidolon; The Last Hieroglyph; Sadastor; The Death of Ilalotha; The Return of the Sorcerer; The Testament of Athammaus; The Weird of Avoosl Wuthoqquan; Ubbo-Sathla; The Monster of the Prophesy; The Vaults of Yoh-Vombis; From the Crypts of Memory; The Shadows.*

Out of Space and Time, by Clark Ashton Smith (1942). Cover art by Hannes Bok. No. 3.

The third Arkham House title, is the first collection of weird fiction by the uniquely talented Clark Ashton Smith. Most of the stories were written between 1930 and 1935 and thought by the author to be among his best works up to 1942, when this volume was published. The collection covers a range of Smith's writings and includes stories from all of his major series, such as *Zothique, Hyperborea, Averoigne* and *Poseidonis*. As the first collection of stories by a popular, fantasy writer and of considerable literary merits, the book is a key title and consequently difficult to find. No AH reprints, but many of the stories have been reprinted by other publishers. $1,000/250

4. **Beyond the Wall of Sleep,** by Howard Phillips Lovecraft. The second Lovecraft collection of supernatural stories. (1943.) 458 pp. 1217 copies printed. Cover price $5.00. Jacket art by Burt Trimpey.

Contents: *By Way of introduction,* by August Derleth & Donald Wandrei; *Autobiography: Some Notes on a Nonentity; The Commonplace Book; History and Chronology of the Necronomicon; Memory; What the Moon Brings; Nyarlathotep; Ex Oblivione; The Tree; The Other Gods; The Quest of Iranon; The Doom That Came to Sarnath; The White Ship; From Beyond; Beyond the Wall of Sleep; The Unnameable; The Hound; The Moon-Bog; The Evil Clergyman; Herbert West-Reanimator; The Dream Quest of Unknown Kadath; The Case of Charles Dexter Ward; The Crawling Chaos* (w/ Elizabeth Berkeley); *The Green Meadow* (w/ Elizabeth Berkeley); *The Curse of Yig* (w/ Zealia Brown-Reed); *The Horror in the Museum* (w/ Hazel Heald); *Out of the Eons* (w/ Hazel Held); *The Mound* (w/ Zealia Brown-Reed); *The Diary of Alonzo* Typer (w/ William Lumley); *The Challenge from Beyond* (w/ C.L. Moore, A.

Beyond the Wall of Sleep, by H.P. Lovecraft (1943). Cover art by Burt Trimpey. No. 4.

Merritt, R. E. Howard and F. B. Long); *In the Walls of Eryx* (w/ Kenneth Sterling); *Ibid; Sweet Ermengarde; Providence; On a Grecian Colonnade in a Park; Old Christmas; New England Fallen; On a New England Village Seen by Moonlight; Astrophobos; Sunset; A Year off; A Summer Sunset and Evening; To Mistress Sophia Simple, Queen of the Cinema; The Ancient Track; The Eidolon; The Nightmare Lake; The Outpost; The Rutted Road; The Wood; Hallowe'en in a Suburb; Primavera; October; To a Dreamer; Despair; Nemesis; Psychopompos; The Book; Pursuit; The Key; Recognition; Homecoming; The Lamp; Zaman's Hill; The Port; The Courtyard; The Pigeon-Flyers; The Well; The Howler; Hesperia; Star-Winds; Antarktos; The Window; A Memory; The Gardens of Yin; The Bells; Night-Gaunts; Nyarlethotep; Azathoth; Mirage; The Canal; St. Toad's; The Familiars; The Elder Pharos; Expectancy; Nostalgia; Background; The Dweller; Alienation; Harbour Whistles; Recapture; Evening Star; Continuity; Yule Horror; To Mr. Finlay; To Clark Ashton Smith; Where Once Poe Walked; Christmas Greetings to Mrs. Phillips Gamwell; Brick Row; The Messenger; The Cthulhu Mythology: A Glossary*, by Francis T. Laney; *An Appreciation of H.P. Lovecraft*, by W. Paul Cook.

Burt Trimpey's unique jacket art is a collage of photographs of sculptures by Clark Ashton Smith. The collection consists of a wider array of Lovecraft's work than *The Outsider and Others*, although considered to be of slightly lesser quality. Nevertheless, it contains two previously unpublished short novels, *The Dream-Quest of Unknown Kadath* and *The Case of Charles Dexter Ward*, both excellent works. Several of the stories are collaborations or revisions of other author's work. Two of these, *The Curse of Yig*, by Zealia B. (Reed) Bishop and *The Horror in the Museum*, by H.P. Lovecraft and Others, were published by Arkham House as separate collections in 1953 and 1970 respectively. *Beyond the Wall of Sleep* was well received, but because of wartime paper shortage and consequent restrictions, only 1217 copies were printed and sold out quickly. Because of its popularity, the book is difficult to find and demands a hefty price on the rare book market. No reprints other than those separate editions by AH mentioned in the above. $2,250/400

5. **The Eye and the Finger,** by Donald Wandrei. Collection of weird and supernatural stories. (1944.) 344 pp. 1617 copies printed. Cover price $3.00. Jacket art by the author's brother, Howard Wandrei. Contents: *Introduction; The Lady in Gray; The Eye and the Finger;*

The Painted Mirror; It Will Grow on You; The Tree-Men of M'Bwa; The Lives of Alfred Kramer; The Monster From Nowhere; The Witch-Makers; The Nerveless Man; Black Fog; The Blinding Shadows; A Scientist Divides; Earth Minus,; Finality Unlimited; The Crystal Bullet; A Fragment of a Dream; The Woman at the Window; The Messengers; The Pursuers; The Red Brain; On the Threshold of Eternity.

Donald Wandrei was co-founder of Arkham House, but entered the Army in 1942 and remained in service to the end of the hostilities. The material in *The Eye and the Finger* was consider by Wandrei to be some of his best work. The stories had

The Eye and the Finger, by Donald Wandrei (1944). Cover art by Howard Wandrei. No. 5.

previously been published in magazines such as *Weird Tales, Esquire, Argosy, Astounding Stories* and others. Following the war, Donald Wandrei continued his editorial duties at Arkham House, but did not pursue an active literary career. The three books by Wandrei published later by Arkham House, *The Web of Easter Island* (1948), *Poems for Midnight* (1964), and *Strange Harvest* (1965) all contain pre-war material. This was the first Arkham House title to display Frank Utpatel's 'Haunted House' colophon on the title page. No reprints. $400/100

6. **Jumbee and Other Uncanny Tales,** by Henry S. Whitehead. Collection of supernatural and macabre stories. (1944.) 394 pp. 1559 copies printed. Cover price $3.00. Jacket art by Frank Wakefield.

Contents: *Henry S. Whitehead*, by R.H. Barlow; *Jumbee; Cassius; Black Tancrède; The Shadows; Sweet Grass; The Black Beast; Seven Turns in a Hangman's Rope; The Tree-Man; Passing of a God; Mrs. Lorriquer; Hill Drums; The Projection of Armand Dubois; The Lips; The Fireplace.*

A great introductory collection of the works of one of the finest weird fiction writers of the day. The majority of stories were originally published in magazines such as *Weird Tales* and *Adventure*. Most of the tales in this collection are set in the West Indies. No AH reprints. $375/100

7. **Lost Worlds,** by Clark Ashton Smith. The author's second volume of weird fiction. (1944.) 419 pp. 2043 copies printed. Cover price $3.00. Jacket art by Burt Trimpey.

Contents: *The Tale of Satampra Zeiros; The Door to Saturn; The Seven Geases; The Coming of the White Worm; The Last Incantation; A Voyage of Sfanomoë; The Death of Malygris; The Holiness of Azèdarac; The Beast of Averoigne; The Empire of the Necromancers; The Isle of the Torturers; Necromancy in Naat; Xeethra; The Maze of Maal Dweb; The Flower-Women; The Demon of the Flower; The Plutonian Drug; The Planet of the Dead; The Gorgon; The Letter from Mohaun Los; The Light from Beyond; The Hunters from Beyond; The Treader of the Dust.*

Jumbee and Other Uncanny Tales, by Henry S. Whitehead (1944). Cover art by Frank Wakefield. No. 6.

Burt Trimpey's jacket art is another collage of photographs of sculptures by the author. Many of the stories in this collection are reprinted from *Weird Tales* and most are from Smith's series *Atlantis, Averoigne, Hyperboria, Zothique and Xiccarph.* Although considered by some to be of slightly lesser literary merit than *Out of Space and Time,* it is a key title which is well worth reading and collecting. In the majority of cases one cannot go wrong with the works of Clark Ashton Smith. No AH reprints. $450/100

8. **Marginalia,** by Howard Phillips Lovecraft. Collection of stories, essays and memoirs by

H.P. Lovecraft and other writers. (1944.) 377 pp. 2035 copies printed. Cover price $3.00. Jacket art by Virgil Finlay. Illustrated.

MARGINALIA
By H. P. LOVECRAFT

Marginalia, by H.P. Lovecraft (1944). Cover art by Virgil Finlay. No. 8.

Contents: Foreword, by August Derleth & Donald Wandrei; *Imprisoned With the Pharaohs*, by Houdini; *Medusa's Coil*, by Zealia Brown (Reed) Bishop; *Winged Death*, by Hazel Heald; *The Man of Stone*, by Hazel Heald; *Notes on the Writing of Weird Fiction; Some Notes on Interplanetary Fiction; Lord Dunsany and His Work; Heritage or Modernism: Common Sense in Art Forms; Some Backgrounds of Fairyland; Some Causes of Self-Immolation; A Guide to Charleston, South Carolina; Observations on Several Parts of North America; The Beast in the Cave; The Transition of Juan Romero; Azathoth; The Book; The Descendant; The Very Old Folk; The Thing in the Moonlight*, by J. Chapman Miske; *Two Comments; His own Most Fantastic Creation*, by Winfield Townley Scott; *Some Random Memories of H.P. Lovecraft*, by Frank Belknap Long; *H.P. Lovecraft: An Appreciation*, by T.O Mabbott; *The Wind That Is in the Grass: A Memoir of H.P. Lovecraft in Florida*, by R.H. Barlow; *Lovecraft and Science*, by Kenneth Sterling; *Lovecraft as a Formative Influence*, by August Derleth; *The Dweller in Darkness*, by Donald Wandrei; *To Howard Phillips Lovecraft*, by Clark Ashton Smith; *H.P.L.*, by Henry Kuttner; *Lost Dreams*, by Emil Petaja; *To Howard Phillips Lovecraft*, by Francis Flagg; *H.P. Lovecraft*, by Frank Belknap Long; *Elegy: In Providence the Spring...*, by August Derleth.; *For the Outsider: H.P. Lovecraft*, by Charles E. White; *In Memoriam: H.P. Lovecraft*, by Richard Ely Morse.

The first of several volumes of Lovecraft marginalia and miscellany. The jacket art by Virgil Finlay is a reproduction of his exquisite illustration for H.P. Lovecraft's *The Shunned House*, which first appeared in *Weird*

Tales in October 1937, seven months after the author's death. The book includes several biographical sketches, essays, tributes, critical comments, illustrations, photographs and Lovecraft drawings, together with a reproduction of Alfred Galpin's *Lament for H.P.L.* No reprints. $450/100

9. **Something Near,** by August Derleth. The author's second collection of weird fiction. (1945.) 274 pp. 2054 copies printed. Cover price $3.00. Jacket art by Ronald Clyne.
   Contents: *A Thin Gentleman with Gloves; Mr. Ames' Devil; A Wig for Miss Devore; Mrs. Corter makes Up Her Mind; Pacific 421; Headlines for Tod Shayne; No Light for Uncle Henry; Lansing's Luxury; Carousel; Lady Macbeth of Pimley Square; Here, Daemos!; McElwin's Glass; An Elegy For Mr. Danielson; The Satin Mask; Motive; The Metronome; The Inverness Cape; The Thing That Walked on the Wind; Ithaqua; Beyond the Threshold; The Dweller in Darkness.*
   The stories in this collection are primarily derived from Derleth's earlier work for *Weird Tales.* The cover artist, Ronald Clyne, was a young

New Yorker without any formal art training. Recognizing Clyne's talent, August Derleth commissioned him to do several other jacket designs, which shows an impressive progression in artistic accomplishment. No reprints. $225/50

10. **The Opener of the Way,** by Robert Bloch. Collection of *Weird Tales* stories. (1945.) 309 pp. 2065 copies printed. Cover price $3.00. Jacket art by Ronald Clyne.
   Contents: *By Way of Introduction; The Cloak; Beetles; The Fiddler's Fee; The Mannikin; The Strange Flight of Richard Clayton; Yours Truly, Jack the Ripper; The Seal of the Satyr; The Dark*

The Opener of the Way, by Robert Bloch (1945). Cover art by Ronald Clyne. No. 10.

54

Demon; The Faceless God; The House of the Hatchet; The Opener of the Way; Return to the Sabbath; The Mandarin's Canaries; Waxworks; The Feast in the Abbey; Slave of the Flames; The Shambler from the Stars; Mother of Serpents; The Secret of Sebek; The Eyes of the Mummy; One Way to Mars.

The author's first book. A collection of supernatural stories, which in most cases were published in *Weird Tales* in the 1930s and 1940s. This was the book that launched Robert Bloch on a writing career that would make him one of the foremost supernatural fiction writers of the century and produce novels such as *Psycho* and other masterpieces. A key title. No AH reprints. $400/75

11. **Witch House**, by Evangeline Walton. The first full-length novel published by Arkham House. (1945.) 200 pp. 2949 copies printed. Cover price $2.50. Jacket art by Ronald Clyne. It was also the first fantasy novel to be published by Arkham House. In spite of its exquisitely crafted, atmospheric story about witchcraft, the book was not well received and it took several years to sell out the only printing. No reprints. $125/30

12. **Green Tea and Other Ghost Stories**, by J. Sheridan Le

Top: Witch House, by Evangeline Walton (1945). Cover art by Ronald Clyne. No. 11. *Bottom: Green Tea and Other Ghost Stories,* by J. Sheridan Le Fanu (1945). Cover art by Ronald Clyne. No. 12.

Fanu. First American collection of the author's best short stories. (1945.) 357 pp. 2026 copies printed. Cover price $3.00. Jacket art by Ronald Clyne.

Contents: *Foreword*, by August Derleth; *Schalken the Painter; Squire Toby's Will; Green Tea; Wicked Captain Walshawe, of Wauling; Carmilla; The Sexton's Adventure; Madam Crowl's Ghost; Sir Dominick's Bargain; The Vision of Tom Chuff; Ultor De Lacy; Dickon the Devil; The House in Aungier Street; Mr. Justice Harbottle; The Familiar.*

A capital collection of the best weird fiction and ghost tales by the Irish writer, including the classic vampire story *Carmilla*. A key title. No reprints. $350/80

13. **The Lurker at the Threshold**, by H.P. Lovecraft, and August Derleth. A novel in the Cthulhu Mythos. (1945.) 196 pp. 3041 copies printed. Cover price $2.50. Jacket art by Ronald Clyne.

Contents: *Billington's Wood; Manuscript of Stephen Bates; Narrative of Winfield Phillips.*

An addition to the Ctulhu Mythos, this novel in three parts about an accursed stone tower in Billington's Wood and the fate of its inheritor, was composed by August Derleth from two unrelated story fragments found among H.P. Lovecraft's papers following the death of his first executor, Robert H. Barlow. Derleth conceived the notion of forging the two fragments into one story and wrote the novel almost entirely in his own words. No AH reprints. $175/35

14. **The Hounds of Tindalos**, by Frank Belknap Long. Collection of weird fiction. (1946.) 316 pp. 2602 copies printed. Cover price $3.00. Jacket art by Hannes Bok.

Contents: *A Visitor from Egypt; The Refugees; Fisherman's Luck; Death-Waters; Grab Bags are Dangerous; The Elemental; The Peeper; Bridgehead; Second Night Out; The Dark Beasts; Census Taker; The Ocean Leech; The Space-Eaters; It will Come to You; A Stitch in Time; Step into My Garden; The Hounds of Tindalos; Dark Vision; The Flame Midget; Golden Child; The Black Druid.*

The first Arkham House collection of the author's best weird fiction, originally published in *Weird Tales* in the 1920s and 1930s. Frank Belknap Long was a longtime friend of both H.P. Lovecraft and August Derleth. A key title. No AH reprints. $250/45

15. **The Doll and One Other,** by Algernon Blackwood. A collection of two novelettes. (1946.) 138 pp. 3490 copies printed. Cover price $1.50. Jacket art by Ronald Clyne. Contents: *The Doll; The Trod* The last book by the famous British horror writer, who was known as one of the outstanding early contributors to the gothic and weird fiction genre. This was the first publication of both novelettes. Regrettably, the book did not sell well and remained in print for some time. No AH reprints. $100/25

16. **The House on the Borderland and Other Novels,** by William Hope Hodgson. Collection of four short novels. (1946.) 639 pp. 3014 copies printed. Cover price $5.00. Jacket art by Hannes Bok.

The House on the Borderland and Other Novels, by William Hope Hodgson (1946). Cover art by Hannes Bok. No. 16.

Contents: *William Hope Hodgson, Master of the Weird and Fantastic,* by H.C. Koenig.; *The Boats of the "Glen Carrig"; The House on the Borderland; The Ghost Pirates; The Night Land; Bibliography,* by A Langley Searles.

The first Arkham House book with a four-color dust jacket. A voluminous book that introduces the British writer William Hope Hodgson. The novels and stories by Hodgson, who was killed in 1918, while serving in the British Army in World War I, was little known in the United States before this publication. The appearance or rediscovery of Hodgson's works and the dust jacket makes this book a key title. No AH reprints. $600/100

17. **Skull-Face and Others,** by Robert Ervin Howard. Collection of fantasy stories. (1946.) 475 pp. 3004 copies printed. Cover price $5.00. Jacket art by Hannes Bok.

Contents: *Foreword,* by August Derleth; *Which Will Scarcely Be Understood; Robert Ervin Howard: A Memoriam,* by H.P. Lovecraft; *A Memory of R.E. Howard,* by E. Hoffman Price; *Wolfshead; The Black Stone; The Horror from the Mound; The Cairn on the Headland; Black Canaan; The Fire of Asshurbanipal; A Man-Eating Jeopard; Skull-Face; The Hyborian Age; Worms of the Earth; The Valley of the Worm; Skulls in the Stars; Rattle of Bones; The Hills of the Dead; Wings in the Night; The Shadow Kingdom; The Mirrors of Tuzun Thune; Kings of the Night; The Phoenix on the Sword; The Scarlet Citadel; The Tower of the Elephant; Rogues in the House; Shadows in Zamboula; Lines Written in the Realization that I Must Die.*

The first Arkham House collection of fantasy stories by Robert E. Howard, the creator of *Conan, Solomon Kane* and other memorable characters. It was the second Arkham House book with a four-color dust jacket, also by Hannes Bok. The collection includes many of Howard's best fantasy and 'sword and sorcery' stories. Because of similarities in size and dust jacket design it is often thought of as a companion volume to *The House on the Borderland and Other Novels.* A key title. No AH reprints. $800/125

Skull-Face and Others, by Robert E. Howard (1946). Cover art by Hannes Bok. No. 17.

18. West India Lights, by Henry S. Whitehead. The second collection of the author's weird stories. (1946.) 367 pp. 3037 copies printed. Cover price $3.00. Jacket art by Ronald Clyne.

Contents: *Black Terror; West India Lights; "Williamson"; The Shut Room; The Left Eye; Tea Leaves; The Trap; The Napier Limousine; The Ravel Pavane; Sea Change; The People of Pan; The Chadbourne Episode; Scar Tissue; "–In Case of Disaster Only"; Bothon; The Great Circle; Obi in Caribbean.*

The second and last collection of the author's supernatural tales, mostly reprinted from *Weird Tales, Strange Tales and Amazing Stories.* No reprints. $150/30

19. **August Derleth: Twenty Years of Writing 1926–1946,** by August Derleth. A small, promotional pamphlet, bound in printed wrappers and prepared by Arkham House to commemorate Derleth's twenty year writing career. (1946.) 22 pp. No print numbers given. No cover price. Provides some brief biographical and bibliographical information on Derleth and was given away free to subscribers. It is one of the rarest Arkham House collectibles, and the first of three booklets on Derleth's writing career. $500

20. **Fearful Pleasures,** by Alfred E. Coppard. Collection of weird stories. (1946.) 301 pp. 4033 copies printed. Cover price $3.00. Jacket art by Ronald Clyne.
   Contents: *Foreword; Adam and Eve and Pinch Me; Clorinda Walks in Heaven; The Elixir of Youth; Simple Simon; Old Martin; The Bogie Man; Polly Morgan; The Gollan; The Post Office and the Serpent; Crotty Shinkwin; Ahoy, Sailor Boy!; Gone Away; Rocky and the Bailiff; Ale Celestial?; The Fair Young Willowy Tree; Father Raven; The Drum; Cheese; The Homeless One; The Kisstruck Bogie; The Tiger; The Gruesome Fit.*
   The only Arkham House collection of supernatural stories by this British writer and poet. Coppard, a fine author of horror and ghost stories was not widely read, but this collection which contains nearly all of his weird tales, is well worth its price. No reprints. $125/20

21. **The Clock Strikes Twelve,** by Russell H. Wakefield. Collection of ghost stories. (1946.) 248 pp. 4040 copies printed. Cover price $3.00. Jacket art by Ronald Clyne.
   Contents: *Why I write Ghost Stories; Into Outer Darkness; The Alley; Jay Walkers; Ingredient X; "I Recognized the Voice"; Farewell Performance; Not Quite Cricket; In Collaboration; A Stitch in Time; Lucky's Grove; Red Feathers; Happy Ending?; The First Sheaf; Masrur; A Fishing Story; Used Car; Death of a Poacher; Knock! Knock! Who's There?*
   The first Arkham House collection of mostly ghost stories by this author was an expanded reprint of a 1940 British edition. Thus, the book is not a true first edition, but a first American edition. A second

Top: Slan, Albert E. Van Vogt (1946). Cover art by Robert E. Hubbell. No. 22. *Bottom: This Mortal Coil*, by Cynthia Asquith (1947). Cover art by Ronald Clyne. No. 23.

Arkham House collection of Wakefield's stories was published in 1961 (No. 63.) No AH reprints. $150/30

22. Slan, by Alfred E. Van Vogt. Futuristic novel. (1946.) 216 pp. 4051 copies printed, Cover price $2.50. Jacket art by Robert E. Hubbell. This novel, about a benevolent superman, could probably be considered Arkham House's first venture into science fiction. The novel was originally serialized in *Astounding Science Fiction* in 1940, and in book form it became the author's first book. A key title. No AH reprints. $350/80

23. This Mortal Coil, by Cynthia Asquith. Collection of weird stories. (1947.) 245 pp. 2609 copies printed. Cover price $3.00. Jacket art by Ronald Clyne.
 Contents: *In a Nutshell; The White Moth; The Corner Shop; "God Grante That She Lye Stille"; The Playfellow; The Nurse Never Told; The Lovely Voice; The First Night; The Follower.*
 The only Arkham House collection of supernatural stories by this prominent British editor and author. The dust jacket attained the distinction of being ranked among the 50 best book dust jackets of the year. No reprints. $150/25

24. Dark of the Moon, by August Derleth (ed.). Classic collection of fantasy, ghostly and macabre poems. (1947) 418 pp. 2634 copies printed. Cover Price $3.00. Photography jacket art by Smith-Wollin Studios, lettering by Frank Utpatel and re-designed by Gary Gore.

Contents: *Introduction,* by August Derleth; *The Twa Corbies; A Lyke-Wake Dirge; William and Marjorie; The Wee Wee Man; The Wife of Usher's Well; Fair Eleanor,* by William Blake; *Address to the Deil; Tam o' Shanter; Death and Doctor Hornbook,* by Robert Burns; *Kilmeny,* by James Hogg; *The Eve of St. John,* by Sir Walter Scott; *Kubla Khan; Phantom,* by Samuel Taylor Coleridge; *The Lake of the Dismal Swamp,* by Thomas Moore; *The Hand of Glory,* by Richard Harris Barham; *The Erl King,* by Wolfgang von Goethe; *La Belle Dame Sans Merci,* by John Keats; *The Haunted House; The Dream of Eugene Aram; Pompey's Ghost; The Ghost,* by Thomas Hood; *The Phantom-Wooer; The Ghosts' Moonshine,* by Thomas Lovell Beddoes; *The Phantom Ship; The Legend of Rabbi Ben Levi; The Ghosts,* by Henry Wadsworth Longfellow; *The Raven; Dream-Land; Ulalume,* by Edgar Allan Poe; *Rizpah,* by Alfred Lord Tennyson; *A Lowland Witch Ballad,* by William Bell Scott; *The Legend of the Glaive,* by J. Sheridan Le Fanu; *The Weird Lady; The Sands of Dee,* by Charles Kingsley; *Keith of Ravelston,* by Sidney Thompson Dobell; *The Witch Bride; The Fairies,* by William Allingham; *The Flying Dutchman,* by Charles Godfrey Leland; *The Lost Steamship; The Three Gannets; The Demon of the Gibbet,* by Fitz-James O'Brien; *Sister Helen,* by Dante Gabriel Rossetti; *Goblin Market; The Ghost's Petition,* by Christina Rossetti; *The City of Dreadful Night,* by James Thomson; *The Wind,* by William Morris; *The Highwayman's Ghost,* by Richard Garnett; *The Ballad of Judas Iscariot,* by Robert Buchanan; *The Song of the Ghost,* by A.P. Graves; *A Glimpse of Pan; The Witch of Erkmurden,* by James Whitcomb Riley; *A Windy Night; Roads; An April Ghost; Bitters,* by Lizette Woodworth Reese; *The True Lover,* by A.E. Housman; *Lazarus,* by José Asunción Silva; *All Soul's Night; The Fair Little Maiden; The Fetch; The Fairy Thorn-Tree,* by Dora Sigerson Shorter; *Luke Havergal,* by Edwin Arlington Robinson; *The Superstitious Ghost,* by Arthur Guiterman; *The Listeners; The Little Green Orchard; The Ghost,* by Walter de la Mare; *A Dracula of the Hills; The Paper in the Gate-Legged Table; Haunted,* by Amy Lowell; *The Witch of Coös,* by Robert Frost; *The Little Dead Child,* by Josephine Daskam Bacon; *Dave Lilly,* by Joyce Kilmer; *The Sorceress of the Moon,* by William Rose Benet; *221B; Changeling; Vis-*

itation; Legend; Gooseflesh; Extraordinary Visit; Sea Story, by Vincent Starrett; *Lonesome Water; Old Christmas,* by Roy Helton; *Psychopompos; Fungi from Yuggoth (The Book; The Pursuit; The Key; Recognition; Homecoming; The Lamp; Zaman's Hill; The Port; The Courtyard; The Pigeon-Flyers; The Well; The Howler; Hesperia; Star-Winds; Antarktos; The Window; A Memory; The Gardens of Yin; The Bells; Night Gaunts; Nyarlathotep; Azathoth; Mirage; The Canal; St. Toad's; The Familiar; The Elder Pharos; Expectancy; Nostalgia; Background; The Dweller; Alienation; Harbour Whistles; Evening Star; Continuity); The Messenger; The Ancient Track,* by Howard Phillips Lovecraft; *The Warning,* by Robert P. Tristam Coffin; *The Eldritch Dark; Warning; The Hashish-Eater; Nightmare; Outlanders; Nyctalops; Shadows; The Envoys; Fantaisie d'Antan; In Thessaly; Resurrection,* by Clark Ashton Smith; *The Owls,* by Timeus Gaylord; *The Orchard Ghost,* by Mark Van Doren; *Werewolf,* by Arthur Inman; *Metropolitan Nightmare; Nightmare Number Three,* by Stephen Vincent Benét; *The Goblin Tower; In Mayan Splendor; Sonnet; A Knight of La Mancha; On Reading Arthur Machen; The Abominable Snow Men; The Horror on Dagoth Wold,* by Frank Belknap Long; *Just Then the Door,* by Merrill Moore; *Forgetful Hour; The Specter's Tale; The Haunted Stairs,* by Yetza Gillespie; *The Snake; The Dreamer in the Desert,* by Francis Flagg; *Strange; Forest God; Tree Woman; The Wolves of Egremont,* by Dorothy Quick; *The Harp of Alfred; Futility; The Singer in the Mist; Solomon Kane's Homecoming; Moon Mockery; The King and the Oak; Recompense; Always Comes Evening; The Ghost King; The Last Hour; Which Will Scarcely Be Understood; Lines Written in the Realization That I must Die,* by Robert Ervin Howard; *Sonnets of the Midnight Hours (After Sleep; Purple; The Hungry Flowers; The Eye; The Torturers; The Statues; The Old Companions; The Head; In the Attic; The Cocoon; The Metal God; The Little Creature; The Pool; The Prey; The Rack; Escape; Capture; In the Pit; The Bell; The Ultimate Vision),* by Donald Wandrei; *Weldon House; Lois Malone; Ted Birkett; Bart Hinch; The Shores of Night; Man at the Window; Stranger in the Night; Mark of Man-Mark of Beast,* by August Derleth; *Sonnet of the Unsleeping Dead,* by Anthony Boucher; *Fox Hunters of Hell,* by Byron Herbert Reece; *Dreams of Yith,* by Duane W. Rimel; *Nostalgia; Echidna,* by Mary Elizabeth Counselman; *Changeling; Wood Wife; In the Shadows; The Path Through the Marsh; The Tenants; All-Saints' Eve; The Ballad of Jabberwock; Heard on the Roof at Midnight,* by Leah Bodine Drake; *Wayfarers; Two Hunters,* by Harvey Wagner Flink; *Star Gazer; Death at Sea; The Goats of Juan Fernandez,* by Coleman Rosenberger.

A sterling collection of weird and macabre poems, chronologically arranged from the Middle Ages to the present. Includes a large selection of poems by H.P. Lovecraft, Clark Ashton Smith, Frank Belknap Long, Robert E. Howard, August Derleth, and Leah Bodine Drake. A superb volume and a key title. No AH reprints. $250/50

25. **Dark Carnival**, by Ray Bradbury. The author's first book. (1947.) A collection of weird and fantastic stories. 313 pp. 3112 copies printed. Cover price $3.00. Jacket art by George Burrows.

Contents: *The Homecoming; Skeleton; The Jar; The Lake; The Maiden; The Tombstone; The*

Dark Carnival, by Ray Bradbury (1947). Cover art by George Burrows. No. 25.

Smiling People; The Emissary; The Traveler; The Small Assassin; The Crowd; Reunion; The Handler; The Coffin; Interim; Jack-in-the-Box; The Scythe; Let's Play "Poison"; Uncle Einar; The Wind; The Night; There Was an Old Woman; The Dead Man; The Man Upstairs; The Night Sets; Cistern; The Next in Line.

This collection of fantasy/horror stories, many reprinted from *Weird Tales,* constitutes the first book of one of the finest science fiction writers of the century. Ray Bradbury would go on to write such masterpieces as *The Martian Chronicles, The Illustrated Man, Fahrenheit 451, Something Wicked This Way Comes* and many other bestsellers. The dust jacket is the first Arkham House photo montage cover. A key title. No AH reprints. $1,250/250

26. **Revelations in Black**, by Carl Jacobi. Collection of weird stories. (1947.) 272 pp. 3082 copies printed. Cover price $3.00. Jacket art by Ronald Clyne.

Contents: *Revelations in Black; Phantom Brass; The Cane; The Coach on the Ring; The Kite; Canal; The Satanic Piano; The Last Drive; The Spectral Pistol; Sagasta's Last; The Tomb from Beyond; The Digging at Pistol Key; Moss Island; Carnaby's Fish; The King and the Knave; Cosmic Teletype; A Pair of Swords; A Study in Darkness; Mive; Writing on the Wall; The Face in the Wind.*

The author's first Arkham House collection of stories, mostly reprinted from *Weird Tales* and other pulp magazines from the 1930s and 1940s. No AH reprints. $135/25

27. **Night's Black Agents,** by Fritz Leiber, Jr. Collection of fantasy and weird stories. (1947.) Collection of fantasy stories. 237 pp. 3084 copies printed. Cover price $3.00. Jacket art by Ronald Clyne.

Contents: *Foreword; Smoke Ghost; The Automatic Pistol; The Inheritance; The Hill and the Hole; The Dreams of Albert Moreland; The Hound; Diary in the Snow; The Man Who Never Grew Young; The Sunken Land; Adept's Gambit.*

The author's first book. With this work a promising career began and Fritz Leiber, Jr. would become a principal and outstanding writer of fantasy and science fiction for the next half century. A key title. No AH reprints. $300/75

28. **The Arkham Sampler,** by August Derleth (ed.). Volume I, Number One: Winter. Collection of stories and essays by various writers. (1948.) 100 pp. 1200 copies printed. Cover price $1.00. Cover design by Ronald Clyne.

Contents: *Messrs. Turkes and Talbot,* by H. Russell Wakefield; *History and Chronology of the Necronomicon,* by H.P. Lovecraft,

Night's Black Agents, by Fritz Leiber, Jr. (1948). Cover art by Ronald Clyne. No. 27.

together with some pertinent paragraphs by August Derleth; *Lamia; The Nameless Wraith; The City of Destruction,* by Clark Ashton Smith; *A Little Anthology,* edited by Malcolm Ferguson; *Mara,* by Stephen Grendon; *A Hornbook for Witches,* by Leah Bodine Drake; *Checklist: The Carvings of Clark Ashton Smith; The Dream-Quest of Unknown Kadath, Part I,* by H.P. Lovecraft; *Two Novels and an Anthology; From the Fan Press; The Shasta Checklist,* by August Derleth; *Through a Glass Darkly; A Thorne Off the Old Smith,* by Robert Bloch; *Three Anthologies,* by John Haley; *Short Notices; Editorial Commentary.*

All editions of *The Arkham Sampler* were identical in size, side stapled and bound in heavy paper wraps. The cover design by Ronald Clyne was the same on all issues, but printed in alternating colors. The *Sampler* was a quarterly publication that contained stories, poems, essays and prose by Arkham House writers and other contributors. The purpose of the magazine was to provide the readers with a taste of Arkham House writings and create a general interest in the publisher's books at an affordable price. The magazine lasted for eight issues over a two-year period (1948–1949.) No reprints. $75

29. The Arkham Sampler, by August Derleth (ed.). Volume I, Number Two: Spring. Collection of stories and essays by various writers. (1948.) 100 pp. 1200 copies printed. Cover price $1.00. Cover design by Ronald Clyne.

Contents: *A Damsel with a Dulcimer,* by Malcolm Ferguson; *Hellenic Sequel,* by Clark Ashton Smith; *A Group of Letters,* by H.P. Lovecraft; *The Blindness of Orion,* by Clark Ashton Smith; *West Country Legends,* collected by Robert Hunt; *The Wind in the Lilacs,* by Stephen Grendon;

The Arkham Sampler, by August Derleth (ed.) (1948–1949). Cover design by Ronald Clyne. Nos. 28–31, 38–41.

65

Unhappy Ending, by Leah Bodine Drake; *Fantasy on the March*, by Fritz Leiber, Jr.; *On the Cthulhu Mythos*, by George T. Wetzel; *On "The Lurker at the Threshold"*, by August Derleth; *From a Letter*, by Clark Ashton Smith; *A Memoir of Lovecraft*, by Rheinhart Kleiner; *The Dream-Quest of Unknown Kadath, Part 2*, by H.P. Lovecraft; *Ghosts in Great Britain; The Macabre in Pictures*, by August Derleth; *Top-Notch Science Fiction*, by John Haley; *"Deliver Us from Evil,"* by Robert Bloch; *Short Notices; Editorial Commentary.*
See comments for No. 28. No reprints. $65

30. **The Arkham Sampler,** by August Derleth (ed.). Volume I, Number Three: Summer. Collection of stories and essays by various writers. (1948.) 100 pp. 1200 copies printed. Cover price $1.00. Cover design by Ronald Clyne.
Contents: *A Kink in Space-Time*, by H. Russell Wakefield; *Night in the City*, by Geraldine Wolf; *The Novels of M.P. Shiel*, by A Reynolds Morse; *No Stranger Dream; On the Mount of Stone*, by Clark Ashton Smith; *The Loved Dead*, by C.M. Eddy, Jr.; *Howard Phillips Lovecraft*, by Samuel Loveman; *A Letter to E. Hoffmann Price*, by H.P. Lovecraft; *Old Wives' Tale*, by Leah Bodine Drake; *Strangers from Hesperus*, by Norman Markman; *Further West Country Legends*, collected by Robert Hunt; *The Dream-Quest of Unknown Kadath, Part 3*, by H.P. Lovecraft; *Dr. Keller's Stories*, by John Haley; *Wit and Satire; Studies in Murder*, by August Derleth; *Gremlins*, by Leah Bodine Drake; *Short Notices; Editorial Commentary.*
See comments for No. 28. No reprints. $60

31. **The Arkham Sampler,** by August Derleth (ed.). Volume I, Number Four: Autumn. Collection of stories and essays by various writers. (1948.) 100 pp. 1200 copies printed. Cover price $1.00. Cover design by Ronald Clyne.
Contents: *The Sign*, by Lord Dunsany; *Providence: Two Gentlemen Meet at Midnight*, by August Derleth; *A Note on Aubrey Beardsley*, by Malcolm Ferguson; *Only to One Returned*, by Clark Ashton Smith; *A Spell Useful Near Water*, by Peter Viereck; *Nut Bush Farm*, by Mrs. J.H. Riddell; *The Unknown Land*, by Leah Bodine Drake; *The Dream-Quest of Unknown Kadath, Conclusion*, by H.P. Lovecraft; *Change of Heart*, by Robert Bloch; *Anterior Life*, by Charles Baudelaire, translated by Clark

Ashton Smith; *The Machen Collection; Books of Magical Lore*, by August Derleth; *John Campbell's Stories*, by John Haley; *"The World is My Idea"*, by Robert Bloch; *A Cosmic Novel*, by Clark Ashton Smith; *Short Notices; Editorial Commentary.*
See comments for No. 28. No reprints. $60

32. The Travelling Grave and Other Stories, by Leslie P. Hartley. Collection of weird tales. (1948.) 235 pp. 2047 copies printed. Cover price $3.00. Jacket art by Frank Utpatel.

Contents: *A Visitor from Down Under; Podolo; Three, or Four, for Dinner; The Travelling Grave; Feet Foremost; The Cotillon; A Change of Ownership; The Thought; Conrad and the Dragon; The Island; Night Fears; The Killing Bottle.*

The only Arkham House collection of stories by the British writer Leslie Poles Hartley, primarily derived from two earlier collections (1924 and 1932.) No AH reprints. $135/30

33. The Web of Easter Island, by Donald Wandrei. Novel in the Cthulhu mythos. (1948.) 191 pp. 3068 copies printed. Cover price $3.00. Jacket art by Audrey Johnson. First written in 1932 with the title *Dead Titans, Waken!*, the manuscript was rejected by Harper & Brothers, completely revised and subsequently published by Arkham House. No AH reprints. $200/50

34. The Fourth Book of Jorkens, by Lord Dunsany. Collection of fantasy stories. (1948.) 194 pp. 3118 copies printed. Cover price $3.00. Jacket art by Ronald Clyne.

Contents: *Making Fine Weather; Mgamu; The Haunting of Hala-hanstown; The Pale-Green Image; Jorkens Leaves Prison; The Warning; The Sacred City of Krakovlitz; Jorkens Practises Medicine and Magic; Jarton's Disease; On the Other Side of the Sun; The Rebuff; Jorkens' Ride; The Secret of the Sphinx; The Khamseen; The Expulsion; The Welcome; By Command of Pharaoh; A Cricket Problem; A Life's Work; The Integrating Smile; The Last Bull; The Strange Drug of Dr. Caber; A Deal with the Devil; Strategy at the Billiards Club; Jorkens in Witch Wood; Lost; The English Magnifico; The Cleverness of Dr. Caber; Fairy Gold; A Royal Dinner; A Fight with Knives; Out West; In a Dim Room.*

The only Arkham House collection of stories by the Irish writer

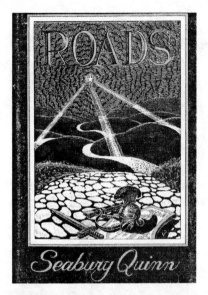

Lord Dunsany, who was considered one of the founding fathers and leading practitioners of early fantasy fiction. No reprints. $150/35

35. Roads, by Seabury Quinn. Short novel, originally from *Weird Tales.* (1948.) 110 pp. 2137 copies printed. Cover price $2.00. Jacket art and illustrations by Virgil Finlay. A delightful story about the origin of Santa Claus. The printing of the book was subsidized by Quinn. It was the first book with interior illustrations published by Arkham House. A key title. No reprints. $300/60

36. Genius Loci and Other Tales, by Clark Ashton Smith. Third collection of weird stories by the author. (1948.) 228 pp. 3047 copies printed. Cover price $3.00. Jacket art by Frank Wakefield.

Contents: *Genius Loci; The Willow Landscape; The Ninth Skeleton; The Phantoms of the Fire; The Eternal World; Vulthoom; A Star-Change; The Primal City; The Disinterment of Venus; The Colossus of Ylourgne; The Satyr; The Garden of Adompha; The Charnel God; The Black Abbott of Puthuum; The Weaver in the Vault.*

Top: Roads, by Seabury Quinn (1948). Cover art by Virgil Finlay. No. 35. *Bottom: Genius Loci and Other Tales,* by Clark Ashton Smith (1948). Cover art by Frank Wakefield. No. 36.

The author's third collection of weird and fantastic tales, primarily written between 1930 and 1935. No AH reprints. $250/60

37. Not Long for This World, by August Derleth. Collection of weird stories. (1948.) 221 pp. 2067 copies printed. Cover price $3.00. Jacket art by Ronald Clyne.

Contents: *Foreword; The Shadow on the Sky; Birkett's Twelfth Corpse; The White Moth; Nellie Foster; Wild Grapes; Feigman's Beard; The Drifting Snow; The Return of Sarah Purcell; Lagoda's Heads; The Second Print; Mrs Elting Does Her Part; A Little Knowledge; Mrs. Bentley's Daughter; Those Who Seek; Mr. Berbeck Had a Dream; The Tenant; The Lilac Bush; "Just a Song at Twilight"; A Matter of Sight; Prince Borgia's Mass; A Dinner at Imola; Lesandro's Familiar; The Bridge of Sighs; A Cloak from Messer Lando; He Shall Come; Mrs. Lannisfree; After You, Mr. Henderson; Baynter's Imp; The Lost Day; A Collector of Stones; The God-Box; Saunder's Little Friend.*

Many of the stories in this, the third volume of Derleth's weird tales by Arkham House, were originally published in *Weird Tales* and other pulp magazines in the 1930s and 1940s. No AH reprints. $175/40

38. The Arkham Sampler, by August Derleth (ed.). Volume II, Number One: Winter. Collection of science fiction stories and essays by various writers. (1949.) 100 pp. 2000 copies printed. Cover price $1.00. Cover design by Ronald Clyne.

Contents: *A Basic Science-Fiction Library,* by Forrest J. Ackerman, Everett Bleiler, David H. Keller, Sam Merwin, Jr., P. Schuyler Miller, Sam Moskowitz, Lewis Padgett, Paul L. Payne, A. Langley Searles, Theodore Sturgeon, A.E. Van Vogt, Donald Wandrei; *Avowal,* by Clark Ashton Smith; *The Spring Night,* by Ray Bradbury; *The Case for Science Fiction,* by Sam Moskowitz; *Dear Pen Pal,* by A.E. Van Vogt; *The Pool in the Wood,* by August Derleth; *Solution of Mind Problems by the Imagination,* by Jules Verne; *The Swallowers of Universes,* by Peter Viereck; *David Henry Keller and the Scientific Novel in the United States,* by Regis Messac; *Time to Rest,* by John Beynon Harris; *Open Sesame!,* by Stephen Grendon; *Travel Talk,* by Vincent Starrett; *The Moon as Goal,* by Everett Bleiler; *Charles William's Novel,* by Edward Wagenknecht; *From the Fan Presses,* by Fritz Leiber, Jr.,; *Frank Merriwell on Venus,* by Robert Bloch; *Factual Fantasies,* by Carl Jacobi; *Dr. Keller Again,* by Weaver Wright; *Whimsy and Whamsy,* by Leah Bodine Drake; *Short Notices; Editorial Commentary.*

See comments for No. 28. No reprints. $50

39. **The Arkham Sampler,** by August Derleth (ed.). Volume II, Number Two: Spring. Collection of stories and essays by various writers. (1949.) 100 pp. 1200 copies printed. Cover price $1.00. Cover design by Ronald Clyne.

Contents: *The Root of Ampoi,* by Clark Ashton Smith; *Fragment,* by Vincent Starrett; *The Mummy,* by Everett Bleiler; *Sed Non Satiata,* a poem from Baudelaire, by Clark Ashton Smith; *A Feather from Lucifer's Wing,* by Foreman Faulconer; *Lovecraft and the Stars,* by E. Hoffmann Price; *The Saints of Four-Mile Water,* by Leah Bodine Drake; *Technical Slip,* by John Beynon Harris; *The Last American,* by J.A. Mitchell; *Full Circle,* by Vincent Starrett; *The Realm of Redonda,* by August Derleth; *"Gougou",* by P. Schuyler Miller; *Characterization in Imaginative Literature,* by Jack C. Miske; *Jamesian Spectres,* by August Derleth; *Two Bibliographies,* by Everett Bleiler; *The Devil and Miss Barker,* by Leah Bodine Drake; *Christina,* by Joseph L. McNamara; *An Arkham Quartet,* by Edward Wagenknecht; *Messrs. Sturgeon, Williamson & DeCamp,* by August Derleth; *Short Notices; Editorial Commentary.*

See comments for No. 28. No reprints. $50

40. **The Arkham Sampler,** by August Derleth (ed.). Volume II, Number Three: Summer. Collection of stories and essays by various writers. (1949.) 100 pp. 1200 copies printed. Cover price $1.00. Cover design by Ronald Clyne.

Contents: *The One Who Waits,* by Ray Bradbury; *In the Year 2889,* by Jules Verne; *Hieroglyphics; Two Horsemen,* by Vincent Starrett; *Journey to the World Underground, Part I,* by Lewis Holberg; *Oblivion,* by Jose-Maria de Heredia, translated by Clark Ashton Smith; *Two Poems After Baudelaire (The Giantess, Lethe),* by Clark Ashton Smith; *The Door,* by David H. Keller; *The Derleth Science Fiction Collection,* by Everett F. Bleiler; *Ode to a Skylark,* by Robert Bloch; *More Caldecott,* by Edward Wagenknecht; *Poetry of Immortality,* by John Haley; *"American Dreams" and Utopias,* by Everett F. Bleiler; *Salem Again,* by Robert Bloch; *A Mixed Bag,* by August Derleth; *Editorial Commentary.*

See comments for No. 28. No reprints. $50

41. **The Arkham Sampler,** by August Derleth (ed.). Volume II, Number Four: Autumn. Collection of stories and essays by various writ-

ers. (1949.) 100 pp. 1200 copies printed. Cover price $1.00. Cover
design by Ronald Clyne.

Contents: *The Triumph of Death,* by H. Russell Wakefield; *Calenture; Pour Chercher Du Nouveau,* by Clark Ashton Smith; *Footnote to
Dunne,* by Anthony Boucher; *Journey to the World Underground, Part II,*
by Lewis Holberg; *The Death of Lovers,* by Charles Baudelaire, translated by Clark Ashton Smith; *Escape,* by Thomas H. Carter; *Sidney Sime
of Worplesdon,* by Martin Gardner; *Nightmare,* by Erasmus Darwin; *The
Song of the Pewee,* by Stephen Grendon; *A Little Anthology,* edited by
Malcolm Ferguson; *Abracadabra,* by Leah Bodine Drake; *The Rape of
Things to Come,* by Robert Bloch; *Perhaps the Future,* by John Haley;
Nelson Bond's New Stories, by August Derleth; *Anthropology and Fiction,*
by Everett F. Bleiler; *A Contrasting Duo,* by Fritz Leiber, Jr.; *A Selected
Shelf of Fantasy,* by August Derleth; — *Two Views of the Future,* by Frank
Belknap Long; *Short Notices; Editorial Commentary; Index.*

See comments for No. 28. $50

With the *issue of The Arkham Sampler,* II/4, the series was discontinued. Thirty-four years later, from 1983 to 1986, a printer under the
name "The Strange Company" in Madison, Wisconsin, published three,
four-issue volumes with the title *"The Arkham Sampler"* (Vol. I, II, and
III), each issue being 28 to 39 pages in length. It is unclear if or how
the printer obtained the right to use and copyright the title. The poor
quality of this publication is only surpassed by the lack of literary dis-
tinctions of its contents. It has no connection to Arkham House and is
of no value to Arkham House collectors.

42. **Something About Cats and Other Pieces,** by H.P. Lovecraft. Collection of stories, essays, poetry and revisions by Lovecraft and
other writers. (1949.) 306 pp. 2995 copies printed. Cover price
$3.00. Jacket art by Ronald Clyne.

Contents: *A Prefatory Note,* by August Derleth; *Something About
Cats; The Invisible Monster; Four O'Clock,* by Sonia H. Greene; *The Hor-
ror in the Burial Ground,* by Hazel Heald; *The Last Test; The Electric
Executioner,* by Adolphe de Castro; *Satan's Servants,* by Robert Bloch;
*The Despised Pastoral; Time and Space; Merlinus Redivivus; At the Root;
The Materialist Today; Vermont: A First Impression; The Battle That Ended
the Century; Notes for "The Shadow Over Innsmouth"; Discarded Draught
of "The Shadow Over Innmouth"; Notes for "At the Mountain of Madness";*

71

Notes for "The Shadow Out of Time"; Phaeton; August; Death; To the American Flag; To a Youth; My Favorite Character; To Templeton and Mount Monadnock; The House; The City; The Poe-et's Nightmare; Sir Thomas Tryout; Lament for the Vanished Spider; Regnar Lodburg's Epicedium; A Memoir of Lovecraft, by Rheinhart Kleiner; *Howard Phillips Lovecraft,* by Samuel Loveman; *Lovecraft as I Knew Him,* by Sonia H. Davis; *Lovecraft's Sensitivity; Lovecraft's "Conservative",* by August Derleth; *The Man Who Was Lovecraft,* by E. Hoffmann Price; *A Literary Copernicus,* by Fritz Leiber, Jr.; *Providence: Two Gentlemen Meet at Midnight,* by August Derleth; *H.P.L.,* by Vincent Starrett.

The second collection of marginalia, stories, essays, poems, revisions, memoirs and other items by H.P. Lovecraft and various writers. The book is illustrated with several photographs, including a photo of Lovecraft as a child, a photo of Mrs. Sonia H. Davis, Lovecraft's wife from 1924 to 1929, and a Lovecraft satirical design for his own gravestone sketched on an envelope. No AH reprints. $250/50

43. The Throne of Saturn, by S. Fowler Wright. Collection of science fiction stories. (1949.) 186 pp. 3062 copies printed. Cover price $3.00. Jacket art by Ronald Clyne.

Contents: *Justice; This Night; Brain; Appeal; Proof; P.N. 40; Automata; The Rat; Rule; Choice; The Temperature of Gehenna Sue; Original Sin.*

A collection of related science fiction stories about a bleak and science controlled future world by the British writer Sydney Fowler Wright. An early Arkham House science fiction title and the only Arkham House book by this author. No AH reprints. $135/30

A Hornbook for Witches, by Leah Bodine Drake (1950). Cover art by Frank Utpatel. No. 44.

44. A Hornbook for Witches, by Leah Bodine Drake. Collection of fantasy and weird poems. (1950.)

70 pp. 553 copies printed. Cover price $2.10. Jacket art by Frank Utpatel.

Contents: *A Hornbook for Witches; Unhappy Ending; Witches on the Heath; The Tenants; The Ballad of Jabberwock; Bad Company; Mouse Heaven; Rabbit-Dance; Wood-Wife; A Likely Story!; The Man Who Married a Swan-Maiden; All-Saint's Eve; The Last Faun; Changeling; In the Shadows; Figures in a Nightmare; The Witch Walks in Her Garden; The Seal-Woman's Daughter; They Run Again; The Path Through the Marsh; Old Wive's Tale; A Vase from Araby; The Fur Coat; House Accurst; The Vision; Sea-Shell; Willow-Woman; The Girl in the Glass; Heard on the Roof at Midnight; Terror by Night; Legend; The Heads on Easter Island; Haunted Hour; Goat-Song; The Nixie's Pool; The Stranger; Encounter in Broceliande; The Window on the Stair; The Old World of Green; Curious Story; The Steps in the Field; Midsummer Night; Old Daphne; Mad Woman's Song; Griffon's Gold; Black Peacock; The Centaurs.*

The cost of printing this slim volume of poetry was subsidized by the author, who, in turn, received 300 copies of the 553 copies printed. Thus, Arkham House had only 253 copies for sale, making this title one of the scarcest books published by Arkham House. One may speculate what happened to the 300 copies given to the author, who died in 1964, but with the passing of time, some may find their way back into the rare book market. No reprints. $1,750/400

45. August Derleth: Twenty-Five Years of Writing 1926–1951, by August Derleth. A small, promotional pamphlet, bound in wrappers, updating *Twenty Years of Writing 1926–1946.* (1951.) No page or print numbers given. No cover price. Provides some brief biographical and bibliographical information on Derleth and was given free to subscribers. A scarce Arkham House item, it is the second of three booklets on Derleth's writing career. $500

46. The Dark Chateau, by Clark Ashton Smith. Collection of fantasy and weird poetry. (1951.) 63 pp. 563 copies printed. Cover price $2.50. Jacket art by Frank Utpatel.

Contents: *Amithaine; Seeker; The Dark Chateau; Lamia; Pour Chercher du Nouveau; "O Golden-Tongued Romance"; Averoigne; Zothique; The Stylite; Dominium in Excelsis; Moly; Two Myths and a Fable; Eros of*

Ebony; Shapes in the Sunset; Not Theirs the Cypress-Arch; Don Quixote on Market Street; Malediction; Hellenic Sequel; The Cypress; The Old Water-Wheel; Calenture; Soliloquy in an Ebon Tower; Sinbad, It Was Not Well to Brag; Sonnet for the Psychoanalysts; Surréaliste Sonnet; The Twilight of the Gods; The Poet Talks with the Biographers; Desert Dwellers; Hesperian Fall; "Not Altogether Sleep"; Some Blind Eidolon; The Isle of Saturn; Oblivion; Revenant; In Slumber; Cambion; The Witch with Eyes of Amber; The Outer Land; Luna Aeternalis; Ye Shall Return.

A slim and limited printing of poetry which was intended to be a temporary work, while the much more voluminous collection *Selected Poems* by Clark Ashton Smith was in preparation. Nevertheless, because of the small print number, this title has attained a greater value on the rare book market than its considerably larger successor (No. 117). No reprints. $1,000/250

47. **Tales from Underwood,** by David H. Keller. Collection of weird tales and science fiction stories. (1952.)322 pp. 3500 copies printed. Cover price $3.95. Jacket art by Ronald Clyne.

Contents: *Introduction; The Worm; The Revolt of the Pedestrians; The Yeast Men; The Ivy War; The Doorbell; The Flying Fool; The Psychophonic Nurse; A Biological Experiment; Free as the Air; The Bridle; Tiger Cat; The God Wheel; The Golden Bough; The Jelly Fish; The Opium Eater; The Thing in the Cellar; The Moon Artist; Creation Unforgivable; The Dead Woman; The Door; The Perfumed Garden; The Literary Corkscrew; A Piece of Linoleum.*

The first Arkham House collection of stories, primarily reprinted from *Weird Tales* and other pulp magazines, by the American physician and writer, David H. Keller. This was the first book to be published by Pellegrini & Cudahy, New York, for Arkham House. The binding of this title is therefore not the customary Arkham House Holliston Black Novelex, but a reddish-brown cloth binding with black lettering on the spine. The usual Arkham House end colophon with printing information is also missing. $150/35

48. **Night's Yawning Peal: A Ghostly Company,** by August Derleth (ed.). An anthology of supernatural tales. (1952.) 280 pp. 4500 copies printed. Cover price $3.00. Jacket art by Robert Crane.

Contents: *Foreword*, by August Derleth; *Mr. George*, by Stephen

Grendon; *The Loved Dead,* by C.M. Eddy, Jr.; *The Sign,* by Lord Dunsany; *The La Prello Paper,* by Carl Jacobi; *The Gorge of the Churels,* by H. Russell Wakefield; *Dhoh,* by Manly Wade Wellman; *The Churchyard Yew,* by J. Sheridan Le Fanu; *Technical Slip,* by John Beynon Harris; *The Man Who Collected Poe,* by Robert Bloch; *Hector,* by Michael West; *Roman Remains,* by Algernon Blackwood; *A Damsel with a Dulcimer,* by Malcolm Ferguson; *The Suppressed Edition,* by Richard Curle; *The Lonesome Place,* by August Derleth; *The Case of Charles Dexter Ward,* by H.P. Lovecraft.

An anthology of supernatural tales by some of Arkham House's regular contributors, including Bloch, Jacobi, Lovecraft, Wakefield, Wellmann and other writers. The story attributed to J. Sheridan LeFanu, *The Churchyard Yew,* was actually written by August Derleth. This was the second book to be published by Pellegrini & Cudahy, New York, for Arkham House. The binding is grayish-tan with blue lettering on the spine. The usual Arkham House end colophon with printing information is missing. A second printing was published at a later date. This printing is apparently acknowledged on the front dust jacket flap as "Second Printing," and with a new cover price of $3.50. First printing $125/25; second printing $50/10

49. The Curse of Yig, by Zealia B. Bishop. Collection of Lovecraft revisions. (1953.) 175 pp. 1217 copies printed. Jacket art by Ronald Clyne.

Contents: *The Curse of Yig; Medusa's Coil; The Mound; H.P. Lovecraft: A Pupil's View; A Wisconsin Balsaz: A Profile of August Derleth.*

The novelette and two short stories that comprise the main part of this title, are parts of the "Cthulhu Mythos" and to a large extent are revisions by Lovecraft of basic plots. Zealia Bishop was a long-term pupil of Lovecraft. The three pieces were later reprinted in *The Horror in the Museum and Other Revisions* (No. 115 and No. 180). Includes photos of H.P. Lovecraft and August Derleth, and a reproduction of Virgil Finlay's Lovecraft drawing from the rear panel of the dust jacket of the *Selected Letters* series. No other AH reprints. $175/35

50. The Feasting Dead, by John Metcalfe. Short stylish vampire novel. (1954.) 123 pp. 1242 copies printed. Cover price $2.50. Jacket art by Frank Utpatel. The only book by this British author by Arkham House. No AH reprints. $225/50

51. **August Derleth: Thirty Years of Writing 1926–1956,** by August Derleth. A small, promotional pamphlet, bound in wrappers, updating: *Twenty-Five Years of Writing 1926–1951.* (1956.) 32 pp. No print numbers given. No cover price. Contains some brief biographical and bibliographical information on Derleth and was given away free to subscribers. A scarce Arkham House item and the last of three booklets on Derleth's writing career. $500

52. **The Survivor and Others,** by H.P. Lovecraft and August Derleth (ed.). Collection of supernatural stories. (1957.) 161 pp. 2096 copies printed. Cover price $3.00. Jacket art by Ronald Clyne.
Contents: *The Survivor; Wentworth's Day; The Peabody Heritage; The Gable Window; The Ancestor; The Shadow out of Space; The Lamp of Alhazred.*

Most of the stories in this collection were written by August Derleth from plot outlines found in Lovecraft's papers. All the stories were reprinted in *The Watchers Out of Time* (No. 133). No other AH reprints. $125/25

53. Always Comes Evening, by Robert Ervin Howard. Collection of heroic poetry, compiled by Glen Lord. (1957.) 86 pp. 636 copies printed. Cover price $3.00. Jacket art by Frank Utpatel.
    Contents: *Foreword,* by Glenn Lord; *Introduction,* by Dale Hart; *Always Comes Evening; The Poets; The Singer in the Mist; Solomon Kane's Homecom-*

Always Come Evening, by Robert E. Howard (1957). Cover art by Frank Utpatel. No. 53.

76

ing; Futility; The Song of the Bats; The Moor Ghost; Recompense; The Hills of Kandahar; Which Will Scarcely Be Understood; Haunting Columns; The Last Hour; Ships; The King and the Oak; The Riders of Babylon; Easter Island; Moon Mockery; Shadows on the Road; The Soul-Eater; The Dream and the Shadow; The Ghost Kings; Desert Dawn; An Open Window; The Song of a Mad Minstrel; The Gates of Nineveh; Fragment; The Harp of Alfred; Remembrance; Crete; Forbidden Magic; Black Chant Imperial; A Song out of Midian; Arkham; Voices of the Night; Song at Midnight; The Ride of Falume; Autumn; Dead Man's Hate; One Who Comes at Eventide; To a Woman; Emancipation; Retribution; Chant of the White Beard; Rune; The Road of Azrael; Song of the Pict; Prince and Beggar; Hymn of Hatred; Invective; Men of the Shadows; Babylon; Niflheim; The Heart of the Sea's Desire; Laughter in the Gulfs; A Song of the Don Cossacks; The Gods of Easter Island; Nisapur; Moon Shame; The Tempter; Lines Written in the Realization That I Must Die; Chapter Headings.

A slim, but superb volume of the best of Robert E. Howard's poems. The printing of this volume was funded by Glenn Lord, who was Howard's literary executor at the time. On account of its literary merits, the book has become a key Arkham House title, sought by both Arkham House and Howard collectors alike. No AH reprints. $550/100

54. **Spells and Philtres**, by Clark Ashton Smith. Collection of fantasy poetry. (1958.) 54 pp. 519 copies printed. Cover price $3.00. Jacket art by Frank Utpatel.

Contents: *Dedication; Didus Ineptus; Thebaid; Secret Love; The Pagan; Tired Gardener; Nada; High Surf; The Centaur; Said the Dreamer; The Nameless Wraith; The Blindness of Orion; Jungle Twilight; The Phoenix; The Prophet Speaks; Farewell to Eros; Alternative; Only to One Returned; Anteros; No Stranger Dream; Do you Forget, Enchantress?; Necromancy; Dialogue; October; Dominion; Tolometh; Disillusionment; Almost Anything; Parnassus a la Mode; Fence and Wall; Growth of Lichen; Cats in Winter Sunlight; Abandoned Plum-Orchard; Harvest Evening; Willow-Cutting in Autumn; Late Pear-Pruner; Geese in the Spring Night; The Sparrow's Nest; The Last Apricot; Unicorn; Untold Arabian Fable; A Hunter Meets the Martichoras; The Sciapod; The Monacle; Feast of St. Anthony; Paphnutius; Philter; Perseus and Medusa; Essence; Passing of an Elder God; Nightmare of the Lilliputian; Mithridates; Quiddity; "That Motley Drame"* (from Clérigo Herrero); *Rimas XXXIII* (from Gustavo Adolfo Bequer);

Ecclesiastes (from Leconte de Lisle); *Anterior Life* (from Charles Baudelaire); *Song of Autumn* (from Charles Baudelaire); *Lethe* (from Charles Baudelaire); *The Metamorphoses of the Vampire* (from Charles Baudelaire); *Epigrams and Apothegms.*

Another limited edition collection of verse by Clark Ashton Smith, including several translations of poems by Spanish and French writers. No reprints. A slim volume, yet the quality of work and limited print numbers have escalated the value of this title on the rare book market. $750/150

55. **The Mask of Cthulhu,** by August Derleth. Collection of weird stories. (1958.) 201 pp. 2051 copies printed. Cover price $3.50. Jacket art by Richard Taylor.

Contents: *Introduction; The Return of Hastur; The Whippoorwills in the Hills; Something in the Wood; The Sandwin Compact; The House in the Valley; The Seal of R'lyeh.*

The jacket art for this Lovecraft tributary collection was done by the *New Yorker* comic artist Richard Taylor. The majority of stories were first published in *Weird Tales* between the 1930s and 1950s. No AH reprints. $200/40

56. **Nine Horrors and a Dream,** by Joseph Payne Brennan. Author's first collection of weird stories. (1958.) 120 pp. 1336 copies printed. Cover price $3.00. Jacket art by Frank Utpatel.

Contents: *Slime; Levitation; The Calamander Chest; Death in Peru; On the Elevator; The Green Parrot; Canavan's Back Yard; I'm Murdering Mr. Massington; The Hunt; The Mail for Juniper Hill.*

Nine Horrors and a Dream, by Joseph Payne Brennan (1958). Cover art by Frank Utpatel. No. 56.

This is the first collection of horror tales and the first book by the American poet and writer,

Joseph P. Brennan, a Yale University librarian. The stories first appeared in pulp magazines in the 1950s. A key title. No AH reprints $225/50

57. **Arkham House: The First 20 Years,** by August Derleth. A brief history and bibliography of books published by Arkham House since 1939. (1959.) 54 pp. 815 copies printed. Cover price $1.00. Cover design by Frank Utpatel. 80 copies were bounds in boards and 735 copies bound in wrappers. Updated in 1970 (No. 111). No other reprints. Boards $950; wrappers $250

58. **Some Notes on H.P. Lovecraft,** by August Derleth. Biographical notes and other pieces on Lovecraft. (1959.) 42 pp. 1044 copies printed. Cover price $1.25. Cover design by Gary Gore.
   Contents: *The Myths; The Unfinished Manuscripts; The Writing Habits; The Barlow Journal; H.P. Lovecraft: Four Letters.*
   Essays, clarifications and notes on various aspects of H.P. Lovecraft, his life, career and writings. The title was bound in wraps and for unknown reason not copyrighted. Not reprinted by Arkham House, but many other reprints exist. $125

59. **The Shuttered Room and Other Pieces,** by H.P. Lovecraft and Divers Hands. Collection of stories, essays and reflection by various writers, edited by August Derleth. (1959.) 313 pp. 2527 copies printed. Cover price $5.00. Jacket art by Richard Taylor.
   Contents: *Foreword,* by August Derleth; *The Shuttered Room,* by H.P. Lovecraft; *The Fisherman of Falcon Point,* by H.P. Lovecraft and August Derleth; *Juvenilia; Early Tales,* by H.P. Lovecraft (*The Little Glass Bottle; The Secret Cave; The Mystery of the Grave-Yard; The Mysterious Ship; The Alchemist; Poetry and the Gods; The Street); Old Bugs,* by H.P. Lovecraft; *Idealism and Materialism: A Reflection,* by H.P. Lovecraft; *The Commonplace Book of H.P. Lovecraft,* annotated by August Derleth and Donald Wandrei; *Lovecraft in Providence,* by Donald Wandrei; *Lovecraft as Mentor,* by August Derleth; *Out of the Ivory Tower,* by Robert Bloch; *Three hours with H.P. Lovecraft,* by Dorothy C. Walter; *Memories of a Friendship,* by Alfred Galpin; *Homage to H.P. Lovecraft,* by Felix Stefanile; *H.P.L.,* by Clark Ashton Smith; *Lines to H.P. Lovecraft,* by Joseph Payne Brennan; *Revenants,* by August Derleth; *The Barlow Tributes,* by R.H. Barlow; *H.P. Lovecraft: The Books,* by Lin Carter;

H.P. Lovecraft: The Gods, by Lin Carter; *Addendum: Some Observations on the Carter Glossary,* by T.G.L. Cockcroft; *Notes on the Cthulhu Mythos,* by George Wetzel; *Lovecraft's First Book,* by William L. Crawford; *Dagon,* by H.P. Lovecraft; *The Strange High House in the Mist,* by H.P. Lovecraft; *The Outsider,* by H.P. Lovecraft.

Another volume of Lovecraft marginalia and miscellany. Several of the pieces are by Lovecraft, but the majority of material is contributed by other writers. A variant of this title exists, bound in boards, rather than cloth. No other AH reprints. $225/50

60. **The Abominations of Yondo,** by Clark Ashton Smith. Collection of weird stories. (1960.) 227 pp. 2005 copies printed. Cover price $4.00. Jacket art by Ronald Clyne.

Contents: *The Nameless Offspring; The Witchcraft of Ulua; The Devotee of Evil; The Epiphany of Death; A Vintage from Atlantis; The Abominations of Yondo; The White Sybil; The Ice-Demon; The Voyage of King Euvoran; The Master of the Crabs; The Enchantress of Sylaire; The Dweller in the Gulf; The Dark Age; The Third Episode of Vathek; Chinoiserie; The Mirror in the Hall of Ebony; The Passing of Aphrodite.*

The author's fourth collection of weird tales, mostly written in the 1930s. No AH reprints. $200/35

61. **Pleasant Dreams; Nightmares,** by Robert Bloch. Collection of horror stories. (1960.) 233 pp. 2060 copies printed. Cover price $4.00. Jacket art by Gary Gore.

Contents: *Sweets to the Sweet; The Dream-Makers; The Sorcerer's Apprentice; I Kiss Your Shadow-; Mr. Steinway; The Proper Spirit; Catnip; The Cheaters; Hungarian Rhapsody; The Light-House; The Hungry House; Sleeping Beauty; Sweet Sixteen; That Hell-Bound Train; Enoch.*

The author's second collection of horror stories, the majority reprinted from magazine publications in the 1940s and 1950s. No AH reprints. $200/35

62. **Invaders from the Dark,** by Greye La Spina. Werewolf novel originally serialized in *Weird Tales* in 1925. (1960.) 168 pp. 1559 copies printed. Cover price $3.50. Jacket art by Gary Gore. No AH reprints. $150/25

63. Strayers from Sheol, by H. Russell Wakefield. Collection of ghost stories. (1961.) 186 pp. 2070 copies printed. Cover price $4.00. Jacket art by Gary Gore.
Contents: Introduction: *Farewell to All Those!; The Triumph of Death; Ghost Hunt; The Third Shadow; The Gorge of the Churels; Mr. Ash's Studio; Woe Water; A Kink in Space-Time; Messrs. Turkes and Talbot; "Immortal Bird"; The Caretaker; "Four-Eyes"; The Sepulchre of Jasper Sarasen; The Middle Drawer; Monstrous Regiment.*

The second and last Arkham House collection of Wakefield's ghost stories. A few had appeared in *The Arkham Sampler.* No reprints. $85/15

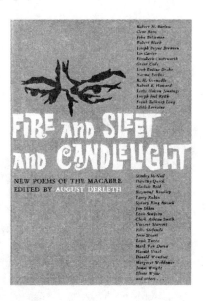

Fire and Sleet and Candlelight, by August Derleth (ed.) (1961). Cover art by Gary Gore. No. 64.

64. Fire and Sleet and Candlelight, by August Derleth (ed.). Collection of weird, fantasy and macabre poems. (1961.) 236 pp. 2026 copies printed. Cover price $4.00. Jacket art by Gary Gore. Contents:

Introduction, by August Derleth; *You Were at the Dead River; Death is a Little Thing; The Clean Gentleman,* by George Abbe; *The Step Mother; The Fair Young Wife,* by Helen Adam; *An Exceeding Great Army,* by Ethan Ayer; *Edgar Allan Poe; Shub-Ad; Warning to Snake Killers; Mythological Episode,* by Robert H. Barlow; *The Panther Possible; The Gourd-Heads; In the Beginning,* by William D. Barney; *Lament for Better or Worse,* by Gene Baro; *Top Hat and Tales; Soft Sell,* by Lorna Beers; *The Rovers; Babylon,* by Laura Benét; *A Lincolnshire Tale,* by John Betjeman; *Nightmare Number Four,* by Robert Bloch; *This Here Is Hell; Roc's Brood,* by Samuel M. Bradley; *One Day of Rain; Ghost-Town Saloon: Winter; The Humming Stair; Recognition of Death; The Scythe of Dreams; The Chestnut Roaster; The Man I Met; The Serpent Waits; Grandfather's Ghost;*

The Last Pagan Mourns for Dark Rosaleen; Ossian; The Wind of Time; Avery Anameer; Nightmare, by Joseph Payne Brennan; *Mr. Ripley Parodies Mr. Nash-or Vice Versa,* by Julian Brown; *Opening Door; Ghosts,* by Winifred Adams Burr; *Grand Finale,* by Sara King Carleton; *Lunae Custodiens; The Dream-Demon; The Sabbath; Carcosa; Dark Yuggoth,* by Lin Carter; *Semi-Private; Addict,* by Mabel MacDonald Carver; *Sorceress; The Stair,* by Gertrude Claytor; *Green Woods; Empty House; The Wind Shrieked Loud; Murder House; Daniel Webster's Horses,* by Elizabeth Coatsworth; *Atlantis; The Watcher,* by Stanton A. Coblentz; *The High Place at Marib; News of My Friends; Highway to Nowhere; The Night Refuses a Dreamer; Playground of the Pixie; Foreboding; Ballad of Two Kings; Building of Sand; Nursery Rhymes for Surrealists (Prayer in Blackout; Nos Moraturi Te Salutamus; Epitaph for a Wooden Soldier),* by Grant Code; *2000 A.D.; Testimony,* by Beverly Connelly; *Room in Darkness,* by Mary Elizabeth Counselman; *Country Lane,* by Margaret Stanion Darling; *From Nothing Strange; Downgoing; Ambushed by Angels,* by Gustav Davidson; *Moon and Fog; Place-Ghost,* by August Derleth; *Invisible Painter; Dark Hotel; Reversions,* by Alfred Dorn; *The Woods Grow Darker; A Warning to Skeptics; The Pool; The Word of Willow; The Gods of the Dana; The Witches,* by Leah Bodine Drake; *The Unexplored; Inbound; Shadowed; Lost Voice on this Hill,* by Burnham Eaton; *Tropes of One Season,* by Charles Edward Eaton; *Unicorns at Harvard; Parkinson and the Octopus; Witching Hour,* by Norma Farber; *Paneled in Pine; Brief Biography; Here I Lie,* by Marguerite George; *The Know,* by Ryah Tumarkin Goodman; *Tenant; Otherwhere; Tapers,* by Frances Angevine Gray; *Devil Doll,* by Lisa Grenelle; *Nightmare; Intuition; Ghost; Borderline,* by R.H. Grenville; *The Brothers,* by Amy Groesbeck; *The Sands of Time; Earth-Born,* by Robert E. Howard; *Arachnida; Female; Party Bird,* by Aletha Humphreys; *Keep Darkness; The Yellow Cat,* by Leslie Nelson Jennings; *A Winter Legend,* by Geoffrey Johnson; *250 Willow Lane; Bedtime Tales; Mr. Lerner; Child Wife; Woman Telephoning; Flogged Child; Sunday Edition; Wolf and Tiger Dining; A.B.; Salems of Oppression; Old Meg of Kitrann; Party Line; Nightmare in Morganza,* by Joseph Joel Keith; *Wilderness Road; Herbs and Simples,* by Martha Keller; *One of the Sidhe,* by Mary Kennedy; *Prenatal Fantasy; The Hanged Thing; Vampire; Trap; The Stone,* by Walter H. Kerr; *Evocation,* by Herman Stowell Link; *Erda,* by Vera Bishop Konrick; *Adjuration; The New Adam; It Is Not Only the Dead,* by Frank Belknap Long; *Since We Are Property; No Escape; Case*

History; It May be Like This; Legend of the Hills, by Lilith Lorraine; *Pause,* by Rosa Zagnoni Marinoni; *Nightmare,* by Anne Marx; *Elsie's House; Lottie Mae; The Secrets of Cisterns; The House on Maple Hill; The Witch,* by Stanley McNail; *Part-Time Tenant,* by Edna Meudt; *Second Sight,* by H.S. Neill; *Aunt Jane,* by Alden A. Nowlan; *Musings of an Insomniac; Premonition,* by Edith Ogutsch; *Legend of Ramapo Mountain,* by Jennie M. Palen; *Dark House in Autumn,* by Conrad Pendleton; *Jim Desterland,* by Hyam Plutzik; *Black Spirit,* by Tom Poots; *The Monster; House of Life; The Forest; Undertone,* by Dorothy Quick; *Enigma,* by Katherine Reeves; *Ghost,* by Alastair Reid; *All Souls,* by Liboria E. Romano; *Vendor; Professor Nocturnal; Black Are the Stars; Where Roots Tangle; In Time of Darkness; The Scissors Grinder; Alan; GI; Tour. In Rain,* by Raymond Roseliep; *Synchronized; For a Poetry Reading to Which No One Came; The Druggist,* by Larry Rubin; *Night Peril; Warning; The Shape of Fear; Forecast; Six Silver Handles; Perennial Mourner; Spectre,* by Sydney King Russell; *Danse Macabre,* by Antonia Y. Schwab; *Prophecy; House of Yesterday,* by Walter Shedlofsky; *Waltz,* by Ruth Forbes Sherry; *Deeply Gone,* by John Silkin; *The Lover's Ghost,* by Louis Simpson; *Stranger Bride; And the Pear Trees Shiver; The Invaders,* by Jocelyn Macy Sloan; *To the Daemon Sublimity; The Incubus of Time; Metaphor; Memorial; Amor Aeternalis; The Horologe,* by Clark Ashton Smith; *Femme Fatale; Romantic Episode; The Death of Santa Claus,* by Vincent Starrett; *A Little Night Music; Praying Mantis; Vampire Bride; That Familiar Stranger; So Separate and Strange,* by Felix Stefanile; *Hawick's Crossing,* by Jane Stuart; *Heart-Summoned; The Gone; Spring Voices; Two Leaves; Extended Invitation,* by Jesse Stuart; *Frail Hands,* by Lucia Trent; *The Seer; Gather These Bones (i. One Song for Old Bones; ii. Sonata for Wind and Wood; iii. Theme for a Dust Devil; iv. Plainchant among the Maidenhair; v. Libretto in White; vi. Epitaph in a Minor Key),* by Lewis Turco; *Oldest Cemetery,* by Mark Van Doren; *Flight; Ghostly Reaper; Sleeping Village; Gentleman in Oils; A Wreath for One Lost; We, the Few Who Believe; Toward Avernus; Heimdall; The Well-Finder,* by Harold Vinal; *Water Sprite; The Woman at the Window; The Prehistoric Huntsman; The Challenger; Forest Shapes; Lyric of Doubt,* by Donald Wandrei; *On the Staircase; A Ballad of Despair,* by Wade Wellman; *Fancy Fishing,* by James L. Weil; *Companions; Ghost to Come,* by Margaret Widdemer; *The Skeptic; Recompense,* by Loring Williams; *The Ghost,* by James Wright; *Atavism,* by Elinor Wylie.

A companion volume to *Dark of the Moon* (No. 24). Like its predecessor, it is a notable book of poetry which includes the work of many distinguished writers. The contents represent works from the 1930s to the 1950s and is listed alphabetically by author. A key title. No AH reprints. $150/30

65. **The Shunned House,** by H.P. Lovecraft. This is not a proper Arkham House title. The printing was done in 1928 by W. Paul Cook, but the printed sheets were not bound in numbers until Arkham House bound 100 sets in 1961 in plain brown wrappers. The binding has the Arkham House imprint on the spine. Cover price $17.50. This is the rarest book associated with Arkham House. About 50 unbound sets were sold by Arkham House in 1959 at a cover price of $15. The story was first published in *Weird Tales* in October 1937. Extremely rare. No reprints. Prospective buyers should beware of counterfeit copies! Unbound signatures $3000; bound signatures $5000

66. **Dreams and Fancies,** by H.P. Lovecraft. Collection of Lovecraft's letters regarding dreams. (1962.) 174 pp. 2030 copies printed. Cover price $3.50. Jacket art by Richard Taylor.
Contents: *Introduction,* by August Derleth; *Dreams and Fancies* (Letters to Rheinhart Kleiner, Maurice W. Moe, The Gallomo, Bernard Austin Dwyer, Donald Wandrei, Clark Ashton Smith, Duane W. Rimel, R.H. Barlow, William Lumley, Willis Conover, Jr., Virgil Finlay); *Recapture; Night-Gaunts; Memory; The Statement of Randolph Carter; Celephais; The Doom That Came to Sarnath; Nyarlathotep; The Evil Clergyman; The Thing in the Moonlight; The Shadow Out of Time.*
Collection of letters from Lovecraft to friends and associates, recounting his dreams, followed by several stories and poems which were supposedly inspired by dreams. Provides an interesting insight into Lovecraft's dream perception susceptibility. No reprints. $225/40

67. **Lonesome Places,** by August Derleth. Collection of weird tales. (1962.) 198 pp. 2201 copies printed. Cover price $3.50. Jacket designed by Gary Gore with C.J. Laughlin photography.
Contents: *The Lonesome Place; Pikeman; Kingsridge 214; The Ebony Stick; "Sexton, Sexton, on the Wall"; The Closing Door; A Room in a House;*

Pott's Triumph; Twilight Play; The Disc Recorder; Hector; "Who Shall I Say Is Calling?"; The Extra Child; The Place in the Wood; Hallowe'en for Mr. Faulkner; House-with Ghost; The Slayers and the Slain; The Dark Boy.
The author's fifth collection of weird tales, mostly reprints of pulp magazine stories of the 1940s and 1950s. No reprints. $125/20

68. **Dark Mind, Dark Heart**, by August Derleth (ed.). Anthology of weird tales. (1962.) 249 pp. 2493 copies printed. Cover price $4.00. Jacket art by Dale Mann with lettering by Gary Gore. Contents: *Foreword*, by August Derleth; *Under the Horns*, by Robert Bloch; *Come Back, Uncle Ben!*, by Joseph Payne Brennan; *The Church in the High Street*, by J. Ramsey Campbell; *Hargrave's Fore-Edge Book*, by Mary Elizabeth Counselman; *Miss Esperson*, by Stephen Grendon; *The Habitants of the Middle Islet*, by William Hope Hodgson; *The Grey God Passes*, by Robert E. Howard; *The Aquarium*, by Carl Jacobi; *The Man Who Wanted To Be in the Movies*, by John Jakes; *In Memoriam*, by David H. Keller; *Witches' Hollow*, by H.P. Lovecraft and August Derleth; *The Ideal Type*, by Frank Mace; *The Firing-Chamber*, by John Metcalfe; *The Green Vase*, by Dennis Roidt; *Xélucha*, by M.P. Shiel; *The Animals in the Case*, by H. Russell Wakefield; *Caer Sidhi*, by George Wetzel.

Dark Mind, Dark Heart, by August Derleth (ed.) (1962). Cover art by Dale Mann. No. 68.

An anthology of new or previously unpublished weird fiction by various writers. The story *The Church in the High Street* introduces J. Ramsey Campbell to Arkham House readers. Campbell was only sixteen at the time and the story was rewritten by August Derleth before publication. However, Ramsey Campbell was on his way to becoming a great horror story writer, who in addition to his work with other publishers, would have five separate collections of stories published by Arkham House. No AH reprints. $175/35

69. 100 Books by August Derleth, by August Derleth. Bibliography, checklist and relevant items. (1962.) 121 pp. 1225 copies printed. Cover price $2.00. Cover design by Gary Gore. Contents: *Foreword,* by Donald Wandrei; Biographical; Bibliographical; A Checklist of Published Books; Awaiting Publication; Work in Progress; Summary; Recordings; Compilations; Anthologies-Textbooks; Publications; Films; Lectures; Appraisals; From the Reviews; Self-Appraisal.

A reference to the works of August Derleth, primarily published for use by editors, libraries, teachers and the news media. The standard edition is bound in wraps, but 200 copies were bound in boards. No AH reprints. Boards $500; wrapper $150

70. The Trail of Cthulhu, by August Derleth. Novel in the Cthulhu Mythos. (1962.) 248 pp. 2470 copies printed. Cover price $4.00. Jacket art by Richard Taylor.

Contents: *The House on Curwen Street; The Watcher from the Sky; The Gorge Beyond Salapunco; The Keeper of the Key; The Black Island; A Note on the Cthulhu Mythos.*

This novel is built on a series of five short stories which first appeared in *Weird Tales* in the 1940s and 1950s. No AH reprints. $175/30

71. The Dunwich Horror and Others, by H.P. Lovecraft. Collection of supernatural and macabre stories. (1963.) 431 pp. 3133 copies printed. Cover price $5.00. No headband. Jacket art by Lee Brown Coye.

The Dunwich Horror and Others, by H. P. Lovecraft (1963). Cover art by Lee Brown Coye. No. 71.

Contents: *H.P. Lovecraft and His Work*, by August Derleth; *In the Vault; Pickman's Model; The Rats in the Wall; The Outsider; The Colour Out of Space; The Music of Eric Zann; The Haunter of the Dark; The Picture in the House; The Call of Cthulhu; The Dunwich Horror; Cool Air; The Whisperer in Darkness; The Terrible Old Man; The Thing on the Doorstep; The Shadow Over Innsmouth; The Shadow Out of Time.* The first of three volumes that reintroduces Lovecraft's supernatural fiction. Because of its popularity, the title was reprinted by Arkham House several times. Second printing in 1966 (2990 copies) $6.50, with headband. Third printing in 1970 (4050 copies) $6.50. Fourth printing in 1974 (4978 copies) $7.50. Fifth printing in 1981 (3084 copies) ($10 raised to $12.95). A revised or "corrected" edition with new cover art was published in 1984 (No. 169). First printing $200/40; second printing $125/10; others cover price

72. Collected Poems, by H.P. Lovecraft. Collection of poetry. (1963.) 134 pp. 2013 copies printed. Cover price $4.00. Jacket art and interior illustrations by Frank Utpatel.

Contents: *Foreword*, by August Derleth; *Providence; On a Grecian Colonnade in a Park; Old Christmas; New-England Fallen; On a New-England Village Seen by Moonlight; Astrophobos; Sunset; To Pan; A Summer Sunset and Evening; To Mistress Sophia Simple, Queen of the Cinema; A Year Off; Sir Thomas Tryout; Phaeton; August; Death; To the American Flag; To a Youth; My Favorite Character; To Templeton and Mount Monadnock; The Poe-et's Nightmare; Lament for the Vanished Spider; Regnar Lodbrug's Epicedium; Little Sam Perkins; Drinking Song from the Tomb; The Ancient Track; The Eidolon; The Nightmare Lake; The Outpost; The Rutted Road; The Wood; The House; The City; Hallowe'en in a Suburb; Primavera; October; To a Dreamer; Despair; Nemesis; Yule Horror; To Mr. Finlay, Upon his Drawing for Mr. Bloch's Tale, "The Faceless God"; Where Once Poe Walked; Christmas Greetings to Mrs. Phillips Gamwell-1925; Brick Row; The Messenger; To Klarkash-Ton, Lord of Averoigne; Psychopompos; Fungi from Yuggoth (The Book; Pursuit; The Key; Recognition; Homecoming; The Lamp; Zaman's Hill; The Port; The Courtyard; The Pigeon-Flyers; The Well; The Howler; Hesperia; Star Winds; Antarktos; The Window; A Memory; The Gardens of Yin; The Bells; Night-Gaunts; Nyarlathotep; Azathoth; Mirage; The Canal; St. Toad's; The Familiars; The Elder Pharos; Expectancy; Nostalgia; Back-*

ground; The Dweller; Alienation; Harbour Whistles; Recapture; Evening Star; Continuity).

A representative selection of Lovecraft's poetry, primarily reprinted from the two previous volumes *Beyond the Wall of Sleep* and *Something About Cats*. Utpatel's interior illustrations add considerable esthetic quality to the book. A key title. No AH reprints. $250/45

73. **Who Fears the Devil?**, by Manly Wade Wellman. Collection of supernatural stories. (1963.) 213 pp. 2058 copies printed. Cover price $4.00. Jacket by Lee Brown Coye.

Who Fears the Devil?, by Manly Wade Wellman (1963). Cover art by Lee Brown Coye. No. 73.

Contents: *John's My Name: O Ugly Bird!; Why They're Named That: One Other; Then I Wasn't Alone: Shiver in the Pines; You Know the Tale of Hoph: Old Devlins Was A-Waiting; Find the Place Yourself: The Desrick on Yandro; The Stars Down There: Vandy, Vandy; Blue Monkey: Dumb Supper; I Can't Claim That: The Little Black Train; Who Else Could I Count On: Walk Like a Mountain; None Wiser for the Trip: On the Hills and Everywhere; Nary Spell: Nine Yards of Other Cloth.*

This collection features the stories of John the Balladeer and his supernatural encounters. They were first published in *The Magazine of Fantasy and Science Fiction* in the 1950s and 1960s. $300/50

74. **Mr. George and Other Odd Persons,** by Stephen Grendon. Collection of weird fiction by August Derleth, writing as Stephen Grendon. (1963.) 239 pp. 2546 copies printed. Cover price $4.00. Jacket art by Robert E. Hubbell.

Contents: *Introduction,* by August Derleth; *Mr. George; Parrington's Pool; A Gentleman from Prague; The Man on B-17; Blessed Are the*

Meek; Mara; The Blue Spectacles; Alannah; Dead Man's Shoes; The Tsantsa in the Parlor; Balu; The Extra Passenger; The Wind in the Lilacs; Miss Esperson; The Night Train to Lost Valley; Bishop's Gambit; Mrs. Manifold. The sixth volume of Derleth's weird fiction, contains mostly stories published in *Weird Tales* in the 1940s and 1950s. Two can be found in *The Arkham Sampler* in 1948. No AH reprints. $100/25

75. **The Dark Man and Others,** by Robert E. Howard. Collection of fantasy stories. (1963.) 284 pp. 2029 copies printed. Cover price $5.00. Jacket art by Frank Utpatel.

Contents: *Introduction,* by August Derleth; *The Voice of El-Lil; Pigeons from Hell; The Dark Man; The Gods of Bal-Sagoth; People of the Dark; The Children of the Night; The Dead Remember; The Man on the Ground; The Garden of Fear; The Thing on the Roof; The Hyena; Dig Me No Grave; The Dream Snake; In the Forest of Villefére; Old Garfield's Heart.* The second collection of Robert E. Howard's fantasy stories, selected by August Derleth and Glenn Lord. The stories first appeared in *Weird Tales* and other pulp magazines in the 1920s and 1930s. A key title. No AH reprints. $250/60

76. **The Horror from the Hills,** by Frank Belknap Long. Short novel. (1963.) 110 pp. 1997 copies printed. Cover price $3.00. Jacket art by Richard Taylor. Originally serialized in *Weird Tales* in 1931 and later expanded for book publication, the novel may be considered part of the "Cthulhu Mythos." No reprints. $175/30

77. **Autobiography Some Notes on a Nonentity,** by H.P. Lovecraft. A brief autobiography by H.P. Lovecraft, first printed in *Beyond the Wall of Sleep* (No. 4). (1963.) 17 pp. 500 copies printed. Cover price $1.00. With extensive annotations by August Derleth. The first Arkham House publication to be printed outside the United States by Villiers Publications, Ltd., in London. $250

78. **AH 1939–1964: 25th Anniversary** A small booklet published to celebrate the 25th anniversary of Arkham House. (1964.) No page or print numbers given. The booklet provides a brief history of Arkham House together with a list of books published through 1964 and those in preparation for publication. Titles under the

Mycroft & Moran and Stanton & Lee imprints are also included. The booklet was distributed free to subscribers. A rare Arkham House item. $200

79. The Inhabitant of the Lake and Less Welcome Tenants, by J. Ramsey Campbell. Collection of weird stories. (1964.) 207 pp. 2009 copies printed. Cover price $4.00. Jacket art by Frank Utpatel.

Contents: *A Word from the Author; The Room in the Castle; The Horror from the Bridge; The Insects from Shaggai; The Render of the Veils; The Inhabitant of the Lake; The Plain of Sound; The Return of the Witch; The Mine on Yuggoth; The Will of Stanley Brooke; The Moon-Lens.*

The first collection of weird fiction by J. Ramsey Campbell, who was only 18 years old at the time. The stories are mostly inspired by Lovecraft's "Cthulhu Mythos," but, on the advice of August Derleth, they are set in a British milieu. Following the publication of this volume, Campbell abandoned the Lovecraft pastiche and found his own style, producing some of the finest fantasy and horror stories in the genre. A key title. No reprints. $200/50

The Inhabitant of the Lake and Less Welcome Tenants, by J. Ramsey Campbell (1964). Cover art by Frank Utpatel. No. 79.

80. Poems for Midnight, by Donald Wandrei. Collection of poems. (1964.) 68 pp. 742 copies printed. Cover price $3.75. Jacket art by Frank Utpatel.

Contents: *Song of Autumn; Song of Oblivion; Lost Atlantis; Phantom; The Corpse Speaks; The Woman at the Window; Shadowy Night; The Worm-King; Water Sprite; Incubus; The Prehistoric Huntsman; Witches Sabbath; Forest Shapes; The Dream That Dies; The Sleeper; The Moon-Glen Altar; Under the Grass; The Whispering Knoll; On Some Drawings; The Plague Ship; The Voyagers' Return to Tyre; The Morning of a Nymph; In Mandrikor; The Woodland Pool; Death and the Traveler; In Memoriam: George Sterling; Red; King of the Shadowland; Borealis; In Memoriam: No Name; Ishmael; Dark Odyssey; Look Homeward, Angel; The Challenger; Sonnets of the Midnight Hours: After Sleep; Purple; The Old Companions; The Head; In the Attic; The Cocoon; The Metal God; The Little Creature; The Pool; The Prey; The Tor-turers; The Statues; The Hungry Flowers; The Eye; The Rack; Escape; Cap-ture; In the Pit; The Unknown Color; Monstrous Form; Nightmare in Green; What Followed Me?; Fantastic Sculpture; The Tree; The Bell; The Ultimate Vision; Somewhere Past Ispahan.*

A small printing of Wandrei's earlier poetry, which first appeared in his collections *Ecstacy and Other Poems* (1928) and *Dark Odyssey* (1931.) No AH reprints. $250/50

81. Over the Edge, by August Derleth (ed.). Anthology of supernatural tales. (1964.) 297 pp. 2520 copies printed. Cover price $5.00. Jacket art by Frank Utpatel.

Contents: *Foreword,* by August Derleth; *The Crew of the Lancing,* by William Hope Hodgson; *The Last Meeting of Two Old Friends,* by H. Russell Wakefield; *The Shadow in the Attic,* by H.P. Lovecraft and August Derleth; *The Renegade,* by John Metcalfe; *Told in the Desert,* by Clark Ashton Smith; *When the Rains Came,* by Frank Belknap Long; *The Blue Flame of Vengeance,* by Robert E. Howard; *Crabgrass,* by Jesse Stuart; *Kincaid's Car,* by Carl Jacobi; *The Patchwork Quilt,* by August Derleth; *The Black Gondolier,* by Fritz Leiber; *The Old Lady's Room,* by J. Vernon Shea; *The North Knoll,* by Joseph Payne Brennan; *The Huaco of Sênor Peréz,* by Mary Elizabeth Counselman; *Mr. Alucard,* by David A Johnstone; *Casting the Stone,* by John Pocsik; *Aneanoshian,* by Michael Bailey; *The Stone on the Island,* by J. Ramsey Campbell.

An anthology of original supernatural tales, mainly by Arkham House authors and published to commemorate the twenty-fifth anniversary of Arkham House. No AH reprints. $125/20

82. At the Mountains of Madness and Other Novels, by H.P. Love-craft. Collection of weird stories and two short novels. (1964.) 432 pp. 3552 copies printed. Cover price $6.50. Jacket art by Lee Brown Coye.

Contents: *H.P. Lovecraft's Novels,* by August Derleth; *At the Mountain of Madness; The Case of Charles Dexter Ward; The Shunned House; The Dreams in the Witch-House; The Statement of Randolph Carter; The Dream Quest of Unknown Kadath; The Silver Key; Through the Gates of the Silver Key.*

The second of three volumes that reintroduce Lovecraft's supernatural fiction. As did *The Dunwich Horror and Others*, it sold out quickly and was reprinted by Arkham House several times. The first edition dust jacket is green and the reprint dust jackets are red/orange. Second printing in 1968 (2987 copies) $6.50, printing stated on page 433. Third printing in 1971 (3082 copies) $7.50 in green jacket, printing stated on page 433 and on dust jacket front flap. Fourth printing in 1975 (4005 copies), same point as for the third printing. A revised or "corrected" edition with new cover art was published in 1985 (No. 171). First printing $225/45; second (1968) $50/10; others cover price

83. **Portraits in Moonlight,** by Carl Jacobi. Collection of weird fiction. (1964.) 213 pp. 1987 copies printed. Cover price $4.00. Jacket art by Frank Utpatel.

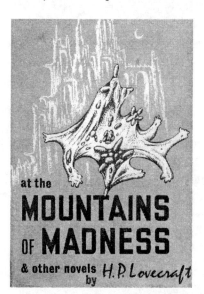

At the Mountains of Madness and Other Novels, by H.P. Lovecraft (1964). Cover art by Lee Brown Coye. No. 82.

Contents: *Portrait in Moonlight; Witches in the Cornfield; The Martian Calendar; The Corbie Door; Tepondicon; Incident at the Galloping Horse; Made in Tanganyika; Matthew South and Company; Long Voyage; The Historian; Lodana; The Lorenzo Watch; The La Prello Paper; The Spanish Camera.*

The author's second collection of weird fiction. The stories are from *Weird Tales* and other pulp magazines, written in the 1940s and 1950s. No reprints. $100/15

84. **Tales of Science and Sorcery,** by Clark Ashton Smith. Collection of fantasy and science fiction stories. (1964.) 256 pp. 2482 copies printed. Cover price $4.00. Jacket art by Frank Utpatel.

Contents: *Clark Ashton Smith: A Memoir,* by E. Hoffmann Price; *Master of the Asteroid; The Seed from the Sepulcher; The Root of Ampoi; The Immortals of Mercury; Murder in the Fourth Dimension; Seedling of Mars; The Maker of Gargoyles; The Great God Awto; Mother of Toads; The Tomb-Spawn; Schizoid Creator; Symposium of the Gorgon; The Theft of Thirty-Nine Girdles; Morthylla.*

The author's fifth collection of fantasy tales, including four science fiction stories, written and published in pulp magazines between the 1930s and 1950s. No AH reprints. $175/30

85. **Nightmare Need,** by Joseph Payne Brennan. Collection of weird and macabre poems. (1964.) 69 pp. 500 copies printed. Cover price $3.50. Jacket art by Frank Utpatel.

Contents: *The Old Man with Tarnished Eyes; The Gods Return; Return of the Young Men; The Guest; Demon's Wood; The Humming Stair; A Chinese Fable; The Snow Wish; Poems Unpleasant; How Shall I Speak of Stored Intemperate Terrors?; The Old Man; The Leopard; The Man with a Pear; The Wild Boars; An Hour After Midnight; Atavism; Confederate Cemetery, 1961; Spruce Stump; When Yellow Leaves; Undertakers; Grandmother's Parlour; Mad Lines; Interment for the Atom Age; On Desolate Streets; Forest Fantastique; In the Night's Cold Passage; Epitaph; Suicide; Somewhere in the Sapphire Winds; Grandfather's Ghost; Nightmare: The Arena; One Winter Afternoon; The Scythe of Dreams; The Knowing Heart; The Black Rent; The Secret Cage; Your God of Harps; Heart of Earth; The Eyes; The Dead Reach Out; Desolation; The Wind of Time; Dream-Land; Wraith on the Wind; The Man I Met; Land of Desolation; Robert Torrell; The Resurrected Skull; The Grey Horror; Nocturne Macabre; Black October; The White Huntress; The Silent Houses; Rehearsal; The Cold Corridors; The Chestnut Roasters; Riddle.*

This title was printed and published for Arkham House by Villiers Publications, Ltd., in London. Apart from *Autobiography Some Notes on a Nonentity* (No. 77), which was a small 17-page booklet, this was the first Arkham House book to be printed outside the United States. The binding is not the customary black Novelex with gold spine lettering, but a reddish cloth. A key title. No AH reprints. $300/75

86. **Selected Letters I: 1911–1924,** by H.P. Lovecraft. Letters by H.P. Lovecraft, collected and edited by August Derleth and Donald

Wandrei. (1965.) 362 pp. 2504 copies printed. Cover price $7.50. Jacket photography by Ronald Rich, illustration by Virgil Finlay and design and lettering by Gary Gore.

Contents: *Preface,* by August Derleth and Donald Wandrei. Letters 1–178.

Throughout his adult life, H.P. Lovecraft maintained a prolific and extensive correspondence, which in sheer magnitude almost superseded his other literary works. This is the first in a series of five volumes that contain selected letters from 1911 through 1937. The jacket design by Ronald Rich and Gary Gore, with Virgil Finlay's illustration on the rear panel, was planned to be used for each volume, with only color variations. The color scheme of the Volume I jacket is blue. Reprinted by Arkham House in 1975 (3045 copies). First printing $125/20; second $50/10

87. **Poems in Prose,** by Clark Ashton Smith. Collection of prose poems. (1965.) 54 pp. 1016 copies printed. Cover price $4.00. Jacket art and illustrations by Frank Utpatel.

Contents: *Clark Ashton Smith, Poet in Prose,* by Donald S. Fryer; *The Traveller; The Flower-Devil; Images (Tears; The Secret Rose; The Wind and the Garden; Offerings; A Coronal); The Black Lake; Vignettes (Beyond the Mountains; The Broken Lute; Nostalgia of the Unknown; Grey Sorrow; The Hair of Circe; The Eyes of Circe); A Dream of Lethe; The Caravan; The Princess Almeena; Ennui; The Statue of Silence; Remoteness; The Memnons of the Night; The Garden and the Tomb; In Cocaigne; The Litany of the Seven Kisses; From a Letter; From the Crypts of Memory; A Phantasy; The Demon, The Angel, and Beauty; The Shadows;*

Selected Letters I: 1911–1924, by H.P. Lovecraft (1965). Cover art by Ronald Rich, Virgil Finlay and Gary Gore. No. 86.

The Crystals; Chinoiserie; The Mirror in the Hall of Ebony; The Muse of Hyperborea; The Lotus and the Moon; The Passing of Aphrodite; To the Daemon; The Forbidden Forest; The Mithridate; Narcissus; The Peril that Lurks Among Ruins; The Abomination of Desolation; The Touchstone; The Image of Bronze and the Image of Iron; The Corpse and the Skeleton; The Sun and the Sepulchre; Sadastor.

A superb collection of the author's prose poems, a literary form in which he transcended his peers. The pieces were mostly written in the 1910s and 1920s, with a few of a later date. A key title. No AH reprints. $200/60

Dagon and Other Macabre Tales, by H.P. Lovecraft (1965). Cover art by Lee Brown Coye. No. 88.

88. Dagon and Other Macabre Tales, by H.P. Lovecraft. Collection of supernatural stories. (1965.) 413 pp. 3471 copies printed. Cover price $6.50. Jacket art by Lee Brown Coye.

Contents: *Introduction,* by August Derleth; *Dagon; The Tomb; Polaris; Beyond the Wall of Sleep; The Doom that Came to Sarnath; The White Ship; Arthur Jermyn; The Cats of Ulthar; Celephais; From Beyond; The Temple; The Tree; The Moon-Bog; The Nameless City; The Other Gods; The Quest of Iranon; Herbert West–Reanimator; The Hound; Hypnos; The Festival; The Unnamable; Imprisoned with the Pharaohs; He; The Horror at Red Hook; The Strange High House in the Mist; In the Walls of Eryx; The Evil Clergyman; The Beast in the Cave; The Alchemist; Poetry and the Gods; The Street; The Transition of Juan Romero; Azathoth; The Descendant; The Book; The Thing in the Moonlight; Supernatural Horror in Literature.*

The third of three volumes that reintroduce Lovecraft's supernatural fiction. As did its predecessors, it sold well and was reprinted by Arkham House several times. Second printing in 1965 (3000 copies), indicates "3000 copies printed" in the end colophon versus "3500 copies" in the first printing. Third printing in 1969 (1988 copies). Fourth printing in 1971 (3045 copies). Fifth printing in 1975 (4024 copies). A revised or "corrected" edition with new cover art was published in 1986 (No. 174). Still in print. First printing $200/40; second (1965) $75/15; others cover price

89. **Something Breathing,** by Stanley McNail. Collection of macabre poetry. (1965.) 44 pp. 500 copies printed. Cover price $3.00. Jacket art by Frank Utpatel.
    Contents: *What the Voice Said; Metamorphoses; Lines to an Unbeliever; Dark Counsel; The Sounds She Knew; The Feast; Night Things; Who Goes There?; After the Rite; Three Sisters; Lights along the Road; The Broken Wall; Merlin's Robe; Lottie Mae; The Gray People; The Covered Bridge; Miss Pinnie's Clothes; The Tall, Spare Summer; Nobody Knows Where Mary Went; The Red Beard of Fascinus; Dialogue; Elsie's House; The Witchmark; Follow the Wind; The Secrets of Cisterns; These Anglers; Old Black Billy Goat; The Witch; Watson's Landing; A Note from Mother; The House on Maple Hill; Uncle Charlie.*

The author's first and only work published by Arkham House. As was *Nightmare Need* (No. 85), the book was printed for Arkham House by Villiers Publications, Ltd., in London and bound in green cloth. No AH reprints. $350/80

Something Breathing, by Stanley McNail (1965). Cover art by Frank Utpatel. No. 89.

90. **The Quick and the Dead,** by Vincent Starrett. Collection of strange tales. (1965.) 145 pp. 2047 copies printed. Cover price $3.50. Jacket by Frank Utpatel.
    Contents: *The Fugitive; The Man in the Cask; The Quick and the Dead; The Sinless Village; The*

Head of Cromwell; Penelope; The Elixer of Death; Coffins for Two; The Tattooed Man; Footsteps of Fear.
The author's only collection of weird fiction published by Arkham House. No reprints. $125/20

91. **Strange Harvest,** by Donald Wandrei. Collection of weird tales. (1965.) 289 pp. 2000 copies printed. Cover price $4.00. Jacket art by Howard Wandrei.
Contents: *Spawn of the Sea; Something from Above; The Green Flame; Strange Harvest; The Chuckler; The Whisperers; The Destroying Horde; Uneasy Lie the Drowned; Life Current; The Fire Vampires; The Atom-Smasher; Murray's Light; The Man Who Never Lived; Infinity Zero; A Trip to Infinity; Giant-Plasm; Nightmare.*
The author's second collection of weird fiction, which first appeared in *Weird Tales* and *Astounding Stories* in the 1930s. No reprints. $125/20

92. **The Dark Brotherhood and Other Pieces,** by H.P. Lovecraft and Divers Hands. Collection of essays, articles and other items by various writers, edited by August Derleth. (1966.) 321 pp. 3460 copies printed. Cover price $5.00 Jacket art by Frank Utpatel.
Contents: *Introduction,* by August Derleth; *The Dark Brotherhood,* by H.P. Lovecraft and August Derleth; *Suggestions for a Reading Guide,* by H.P. Lovecraft; *Alfredo,* by H.P. Lovecraft; *Amateur Journalism: Its Possible Needs and Betterment,* by H.P. Lovecraft; *What Belongs in Verse,* by H.P. Lovecraft; *Bells; A Cycle of Verse (Oceanus; Clouds; Mother Earth); Cindy; On a Battlefield in France,* by H.P. Lovecraft; *The Loved Dead; Deaf, Dumb, and Blind; The Ghost-Eater,* by C.M. Eddy, Jr.; *The Lovecraft "Books": Some Addenda and Corrigenda,* by William Scott Home; *To Arkham and the Stars,* by Fritz Leiber; *Through Hyperspace with Brown Jenkin,* by Fritz Leiber; *Lovecraft and the New England Megaliths,* by Andrew E. Rothovius; *Howard Phillips Lovecraft: A Bibliography,* by Jack L. Chalker; *Walks with H.P. Lovecraft,* by C.M. Eddy, Jr.; *The Cancer of Superstition,* by H.P. Lovecraft and C.M Eddy, Jr.,; *The Making of a Hoax,* by August Derleth; *Lovecraft's Illustrators,* by John E. Vetter; *Final Notes,* by August Derleth.
Another volume of Lovecraft marginalia and miscellany. Contains essays, comments, discussions, elaborations and other pieces by and about Lovecraft. Illustrated. No reprints. $175/30

93. **Colonel Markesan and Less Pleasant People,** by August Derleth and Mark Schorer. Collection of supernatural tales. (1966.) 285 pp. 2405 copies printed. Cover price $5.00. Jacket art by Frank Utpatel.

Contents: *In the Left Wing; Spawn of the Maelstrom; The Carven Image; The Pacer; The Lair of the Star-Spawn; Colonel Markesan; The Return of Andrew Bentley; The Woman at Loon Point; Death Holds the Post; Laughter in the Night; The Vengeance of Aï; Red Hands; They Shall Rise; Eyes of the Serpent; The Horror from the Depths; The Occupant of the Crypt; The House in the Magnolias.*

The stories in this collection were written by August Derleth and Mark Shorer in the summer of 1931 while sharing a cottage near the Wisconsin River. The tales were written for submission to *Weird Tales,* where most of them were published. No reprints. $75/10

94. **Black Medicine,** by Arthur J. Burks. Collection of supernatural tales. (1966.) 308 pp. 1952 copies printed. Cover price $5.00. Jacket art by Lee Brown Coye.

Contents: *Strange Tales of Santo Domingo (A Broken Lamp-Chimney; Desert of the Dead; Daylight Shadows; The Sorrowful Sisterhood; The Phantom Chibo; Faces); Three Coffins; When the Graves Were Opened; Vale of The Corbies; Voodoo; Luisma's Return; Thus Spake the Prophetess; Black Medicine; Bells of Oceana; The Ghosts of Steamboat Coulee; Guatemozin the Visitant.*

The best of the author's supernatural tales, mostly from *Weird Tales* in the 1920s. Burks was a retired USMC colonel and a prolific writer of pulp fiction. No reprints. $75/10

95. **Deep Waters,** by William Hope Hodgson. Collection of supernatural tales. (1967.) 300 pp. 2556 copies printed. Cover price $5.00. Jacket art by Frank Utpatel.

Contents: *Foreword,* by August Derleth; *The Sea Horses; The Derelict; The Thing in the Weeds; From the Tideless Sea; The Island of the Ud; The Voice in the Night; The Adventure of the Headland; The Mystery of the Derelict; The Shamraken Homeward-Bounder; The Stone Ship; The Crew of the Lancing; The Habitants of Middle Islet; The Call in the Dawn.*

Collects some of Hodgson's finest supernatural sea-stories, selected by August Derleth. No reprints. $150/25

96. **Travellers by Night,** by August Derleth (ed.). Collection of strange tales by various writers. (1967.) 261 pp. 2486 copies printed. Cover price $4.00. Jacket art by James Dietrich, with design and lettering by Gary Gore.

Contents: *The Cicerones,* by Robert Aickman; *Episode on Cain Street,* by Joseph Payne Brennan; *The Cellars,* by J. Ramsey Campbell; *The Man Who Rode the Trains,* by Paul A. Carter; *A Handful of Silver,* by Mary Elizabeth Counselman; *Denkirch,* by David Drake; *The Wild Man of the Sea,* by William Hope Hodgson; *The Unpleasantness at Carver House,* by Carl Jacobi; *The Terror of Anerley House School,* by Margery Lawrence; *The Horror from the Middle Span,* by H.P. Lovecraft and August Derleth; *Not There,* by John Metcalfe; *Family Tree,* by Frank D. Thayer, Jr.; *Death of a Bumblebee,* by J. Russell Wakefield; *The Crater,* by Donald Wandrei.

A third anthology of previously unpublished work, by some of the best Arkham House writers and other distinguished contributors. A companion volume to the two previous anthologies *Dark Mind, Dark Heart* (No. 68, 1962) and *Over the Edge* (No. 81, 1964). No reprints. $100/20

97. **The Arkham Collector, Number 1,** by August Derleth (ed.). The first issue of a small periodical containing announcements of upcoming books, news clips, essays, poems and other items. (Summer 1967.) 24 pp. Ca. 2500 copies printed. Cover price $.50.

Contents: The Arkham Collector; About "The Shuttered Room" in Paperback; *Graveyard in April,* by Joseph Payne Brennan; H.P. Lovecraft and Science Fiction; The Mrs. Ann Radcliffe Literature Award; *Someone at the Pasture Gate,* by August Derleth; Nightshade; The Praed Street Irregulars; The Pontine Dossier; *Nightmare,* by Walter Shedlofsky; A Bok Folio; *The Key,* by Duane Rimel; *Nocturne,* by Herman Stowell King; Necrology; Bibliographical Notes; Colin Wilson; Coye Illustrates Lovecraft; The Lovecraft Letters; E. Hoffmann Price; Nightmares and Daydreams; The Art of the Pastiche; The First Solar Pons Novel; The Projected Arkham House Program; *Tintagel,* by L. Sprague de Camp; On Publication Dates.

The purpose of this publication was to replace the free announcements routinely mailed to customers with a paid subscription in order to recover printing costs. Only ten issues were published between 1967 and 1971. A continuation was planned, but with the death of August Derleth in July 1971, publication of *The Arkham Collector* ceased. The remaining complete sets of ten issues were bound in a limited, hardcover edition and published later in 1971 (No. 126). No reprints. $50

98. The Mind Parasites, by Colin Wilson.
Pastiche Lovecraft novel. (1967.) 222 pp. 3045 copies printed. Cover price $4.00. Jacket art by Frank Utpatel. The novel was published in England a few months prior to the American release, which has a new preface. Consequently, the Arkham House book is not a true first edition, but a first American edition. No AH reprints. $150/25

99. 3 Tales of Horror, by H.P. Lovecraft. Collection of three of the best Lovecraft horror tales. (1967.) 134 pp. 1522 copies printed. Cover price $7.50. Jacket art and interior illustrations by Lee Brown Coye.
Contents: *The Colour Out of Space; The Dunwich Horror; The Thing on the Doorstep.*

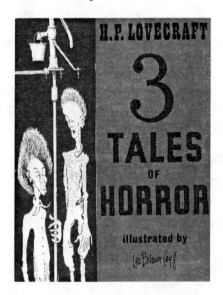

3 Tales of Horror, by H. P. Lovecraft (1967). Cover art by Lee Brown Coye. No. 99.

This slim collection of three Lovecraft horror stories, reprinted from *The Dunwich Horror and Others* (No. 71, 1963), distinguishes itself in a number of ways. It is a beautiful, slightly over-sized book with 15 exceptional drawings by Lee Brown Coye, printed on coated paper. In spite of the repetition of the stories, its format and illustrations make this book a key issue. No reprints. $250/60

100. Strange Gateways, by Edgar Hoffmann Price.
Collection of supernatural tales. (1967.) 208 pp. 2007 copies printed. Cover price $4.00. Jacket art by Lee Brown Coye.

Contents: *The Fire and the Flesh; Graven Image; The Stranger from Kurdistan; The Rajah's Gift; The Girl from Samarcand; Tarbis of the Lake; Bones for China; Well of the Angels; Strange Gateway; Apprentice Magician; One More River; Pale Hands.* A collection of the Author's best work. Price was one of the most prolific of the pulp writers in the 1930s and wrote numerous stories with an Oriental or Middle East theme. No reprints. $175/30

101. The Arkham Collector, Number 2, by August Derleth (ed.). Periodical announcing new books and other items. (Winter 1968.) 28 pp. Ca. 2500 copies printed. Cover price $.50.

H.P. Lovecraft at work, as drawn by Lee Brown Coye (1967).

Contents: The Arkham Program; *Notes on the Writing of Weird Fiction,* by H.P. Lovecraft; *Lorenzo's Visit,* by Raymond Roseliep; *Alas,* by Arthur M. Sampley; *Down Endless Years,* by Joseph Payne Brennan; Old Friends Meet Again; The First PSI Annual Dinner; *No Limits on Hippogrifs,* by David Drake; The Origin of a Lovecraft Essay; *H.P. Lovecraft,* by William Fagan; *More than Twice Told Tales(1. The Valley; 2. Leaves from Family Trees; 3. Once on a Country Road; 4. Frances: Fears That Pinch the Breastbone),* by Edna Meudt; Bibliographical Notes; Hugo Gernsback; Dunwich Productions, Inc.; *The Visitant,* by Wade Wellman; *Connaissance Fatale,* by Donald S. Fryer; Southey's Commonplace Book; Arkham House in London.

See comments for No. 97. Collected and bound in No. 126. No reprints. $40

102. The Green Round, by Arthur Machen. Supernatural novel. (1968.) 218 pp. 2058 copies printed. Cover price $3.75. Jacket art by Ronald Clyne. The novel by the well-known

Welsh, fantasy writer was first published in London in 1933. No reprints. $100/20

103. Selected Letters II: 1925–1929, by H.P. Lovecraft. Letters by H.P. Lovecraft, collected and edited by August Derleth and Donald Wandrei. (1968.) 359 pp. 2482 copies printed. Cover price $7.50. Jacket photography by Ronald Rich, illustration by Virgil Finlay and design and lettering by Gary Gore.

Contents: *Preface,* by August Derleth and Donald Wandrei. Letters 179–359.

See comments for No. 86. The color scheme of the Volume II jacket is red. Reprinted by Arkham House in 1975 (3041 copies). First printing $100/15; second printing $50/10

104. Nightmares and Daydreams, by Nelson Bond. Collection of weird stories and a poem. (1968.) 269 pp. 2040 copies printed. Cover price $5.00. Jacket art by Ronald Clyne.

Contents: *To the People of a New World; A Rosy Future for Roderick; Petersen's Eye; The Abduction of Abner Greer; Bird of Prey; The Spinsters; The Devil to Pay; "Down Will Come the Sky"; The Pet Shop; Al Haddon's Lamb; Last Inning; The Dark Door; Much Ado About Pending; Final Report.*

The author's first Arkham House collection of fantasy stories. Most of these were first published in the *Blue Book* in the 1940s and 1950s. No reprints. $100/15

105. The Arkham Collector, Number 3, by August Derleth (ed.). Periodical announcing new books and other items. (Summer 1968.) 36 pp. Ca. 2500 copies printed. Cover price $.50.

Contents: Arkham House vs Mycroft & Moran; Back to Praed Street; Of Miles Pennoyer; Tales of the Cthulhu Mythos; *Poe,* by Thomas Bailey Aldrich; *The Lemurienne,* by Clark Ashton Smith; Of Brian Lumley; *The Cyprus Shell,* by Brian Lumley; *Edith Miniter,* by H.P. Lovecraft; *Atlas in a Fourth Avenue Bar,* by Arthur M. Sampley; *Revelation,* by Jack Hajdu; "The Shuttered Room" on Film; *Cthulhu in Celluloid,* by J. Ramsey Campbell; *Mary's Ghost,* by Thomas Hood; *Night,* by L. Sprague de Camp; Clifford M. Eddy; Anthony Boucher; Bibliographical Notes; *The Chain,* by Frances May; *The Vampire's Tryst,* by Manly Wade Wellman; Coming Books; POGO cartoon strip.

See comments for No. 97. Collected and bound in No. 126. No reprints. $35

106. The Arkham Collector, Number 4, by August Derleth (ed.). Periodical announcing new books and other items. (Winter 1969.) 36 pp. Ca. 2500 copies printed. Cover price $.50.

Contents: Arkham House in 1969; A Lovecraft Revision(*Till All The Seas*); *Bleak November Days,* by Joseph Payne Brennan; Lovecraft's Last Letter; *The Purple Door,* by Walter Shedlofsky; *The Thing in the Moonlight,* I: by H.P. Lovecraft, II: by Brian Lumley; *To an Infant,* by H.P. Lovecraft; *Memories of Lovecraft*: I. Sonia Haft Lovecraft Davis, II. Helen Sully; *In Memoriam: H.P. Lovecraft,* by James Wade; Bibliographical.

See comments for No. 97. Collected and bound in No. 126. No reprints. $30

107. The Arkham Collector, Number 5, by August Derleth (ed.). Periodical announcing new books and other items. (Summer 1969.) 32 pp. Ca. 2500 copies printed. Cover price $.50.

Contents: An Arkham Warehouse; Dr. Keller's Last Collection; Thirty Years of Arkham House; A Final Collection of Smith's Tales; *A Twist of Frame,* by William D. Barney; *Under the Eaves,* by Lin Carter; *Nightmare Three,* by Joseph Payne Brennan; *Shadow on the Wall,* by Duane Rimel; Of William Hope Hodgson; *Lost,* by William Hope Hodgson; *Shoon of the Dead,* by William Hope Hodgson; *The Crack in the Wall,* by Walter Jarvis; *Ghosts,* by L. Sprague de Camp; *A Fragment from the Atlantean,* by Donald S. Fryer; *The Onlooker,* by Wade Wellman; *A Darker Shade over Innsmouth,* by James Wade; *Carcosa,* by Richard L. Tierney; Bibliographical Notes; *What It Is,* by Roger Mitchell.

See comments for No. 97. Collected and bound in No. 126. No reprints. $30

108. Tales of the Cthulhu Mythos, by H.P Lovecraft and Others. Collection of Lovecraft inspired tales by various writers, edited by August Derleth. (1969.) 407 pp. 4024 copies printed. Cover price $7.50. Jacket art by Lee Brown Coye.

Contents: *The Cthulhu Mythos,* by August Derleth; *The Call of*

Cthulhu, by H.P. Lovecraft; *The Return of the Sorcerer*, by Clark Ashton Smith; *Ubbo-Sathla*, by Clark Ashton Smith; *The Black Stone*, by Robert E. Howard; *The Hounds of Tindalos*, by Frank Belknap Long; *The Space-Eaters*, by Frank Belknap Long; *The Dweller in Darkness*, by August Derleth; *Beyond the Threshold*, by August Derleth; *The Shambler from the Stars*, by Robert Bloch; *The Haunter of the Dark*, by H.P. Lovecraft; *The Shadow from the Steeple*, by Robert Bloch; *Notebook Found in a Deserted House*, by Robert Bloch; *The Salem Horror*, by Henry Kuttner; *The Haunter of the Graveyard*, by J. Vernon Shea; *Cold Print*, by J. Ramsey Campbell; *The Sister City*, by Brian Lumley; *Cement Surroundings*, by Brian Lumley; *The Deep Ones*, by James Wade; *The Return of the Lloigor*, by Colin Wilson; Biographical Data.

The definite anthology of weird fiction inspired by the "Cthulhu Mythos." The tales are written by a variety of the most talented genre writers at the time. A key title. A revised edition was published in 1990 (No. 182). No other AH reprints. $225/80

Tales of the Cthulhu Mythos, by H.P. Lovecraft and others (1969). Cover art by Lee Brown Coye. No. 108.

109. The Folsom Flint and Other Curious Tales, by David H. Keller. Collection of supernatural tales. (1969.) 256 pp. 2031 copies printed. Cover price $5.00. Jacket art by Ronald Clyne.

Contents: *In Memoriam: David Henry Keller*, by Paul Spencer; *Unto Us a Child Is Born; The Golden Key; The Question; The Red Death; The White City; The Pent House; Air Lines; Chasm of Monsters; Dust in the House; The Landslide; The Folsom Flint; The Twins; Sarah; Fingers in the Sky; The Thing in the Cellar; A Piece of Linoleum; The Dead Woman.*

The author's second collection of weird fiction first appeared in pulp magazines in the 1930s to the 1950s. No reprints. $85/15

110. **The Arkham Collector, Number 6,** by August Derleth (ed.). Periodical announcing new books and other items. (Winter 1970.) 24 pp. Ca. 2500 copies printed. Cover price $.50.
Contents: A Near Catastrophe; *Poe's Lake,* by Joseph Payne Brennan; *To Clark Ashton Smith,* by Lin Carter; *A Night for a Shearing Wind,* by William D. Barney; *Nyarlathotep,* by H.P. Lovecraft; *The Gate in the Mews,* by Meade Frierson III; *Star Winds,* by Walter Shedlofsky; *The Edomite Kings,* by Frank D. Thayer, Jr.; *Billy's Oak,* by Brian Lumley; *The Wendigo,* by Richard L. Tierney; *The Hour of the Wolf,* by Viktor R. Kemper; Necrology; Bibliographical Notes.
See comments for No. 97. Collected and bound in No. 126. No reprints. $30

111. **Thirty Years of Arkham House: 1939-1969,** by August Derleth. History and bibliography of the first thirty years of Arkham House publishing, including the titles under the Mycroft & Moran and Stanton & Lee imprints. (1970.) 99 pp. 2137 copies printed. Cover price $3.50. Dust jacket designer not identified. No reprints. $75/15

112. **Demons and Dinosaurs,** by L. Sprague de Camp. Collection of fantasy poetry. (1970.) 72 pp. 500 copies printed. Cover price $4.00. Jacket by Frank Utpatel.
Contents: *About L. Sprague de Camp,* by Lin Carter; *The Powers (Creation; Ziggurat; Reward of Virtue; Transposition; The Gods); Crumbling Ruins (Ruins; Avebury; The Great Pyramid of Giza; Nabonidus; Merôe; Tintagel; Tikal); Far Places (The Little Lion of Font-de Gaume; New Year's Eve in Baghdad; The Jungle Vine; Patnâ; Kaziranga, Assam; A Tale of Two John Carters); Other Times (A Brook in Vermont; The Dragon-Kings; The*

Demons and Dinosaurs, by L. Sprague de Camp (1970). Cover art by Frank Utpatel. No. 112.

Tusk; The Ogre; Sirrush; Progress in Baghdad; Heldendämmerung; Nahr al-Kalb; The Sorcerers; Ghosts); The Storyteller's Trade (A Skald's Lament; Old Heroes; To R.E.H.; Où Sont les Planètes d'Antan?; Heroes; The End of the Lost Race Story; Envy; Daydreams); The Quatrains of Bessas the Bactrian.; Myself(Faunas; First Lake at Midnight; Warriors; Acrophobia; Night; Time).

A slim, limited collection of verse by the well-known fantasy and science fiction writer. Although not indicated in the book and bound in the traditional black binding with gold lettering, the book was printed by Villiers Publications, Ltd., in London. Rare because of the small print numbers. No reprints. $450/100

113. **Other Dimensions,** by Clark Ashton Smith. Collection of supernatural and science fiction tales. (1970.) 329 pp. 3144 copies printed. Cover price $6.50. Jacket art by Lee Brown Coye.

Contents: *Marooned in Andromeda; The Amazing Planet; An Adventure in Futurity; The Immeasurable Horror; The Invisible City; The Dimension of Chance; The Metamorphosis of Earth; Phoenix; The Necromantic Tale; The Venus of Azombeii; The Resurrection of the Rattlesnake; The Supernumerary Corpse; The Mandrakes; Thirteen Phantasms; An Offering to the Moon; Monsters in the Night; The Malay Krise; The Ghost of Mohammed Din; The Mahout; The Raja and the Tiger; Something New; The Justice of the Elephant; The Kiss of Zoraida; A Tale of Sir John Maundeville; The Ghoul; Told in the Desert.*

The author's last collection of weird and science fiction. The contents consist of the remaining of Smith's earlier published fiction not already reprinted by Arkham House. No reprints. $150/30

114. **The Arkham Collector, Number 7,** by August Derleth (ed.). Periodical announcing new books and other items. (Summer 1970.) 40 pp. Ca. 2500 copies printed. Cover price $.50.

Contents: The 1970 Program; The Horror in the Museum and Other Revisions; Demons and Dinosaurs; Selected Letters III; Brian Lumley's First Book; More of Walden West; Other Coming Books; *Marsh Moment,* by Joseph Payne Brennan; *Gary Myers; The House of the Worm,* by Gary Myers; *Judgment Day,* by Joseph Payne Brennan; *Bertrand Russell in Hell,* by William D. Barney; *Moonlight,* by Clark Ashton Smith; *The Sorcerer,* by Wade Wellman; *Miss McWhortle's Weird,* by Donald A. Wollheim; *All Hallow's Eve*, by Lin Carter; *An Item of Supporting Evidence*, by Brian Lumley; *Vapor Fetch*, by Walter Shedlofsky; *Not to Hold*, by Joyce Odam; Necrology; Associational Items; A Map of Arkham; Associational Items; *Two Prose Poems*, by Donald Wandrei *(The Lost Moon; An Epitaph on Jupiter)*. See comments for No. 97. Collected and bound in No. 126. No reprints. $30

115. The Horror in the Museum and Other Revisions, by H.P. Lovecraft. Collection of Lovecraft revisions. (1970.) 383 pp. 4058 copies printed. Cover price $7.50. Jacket art by Gahan Wilson.

Contents: Lovecraft's "Revisions," by August Derleth; *The Crawling Chaos*, by H.P. Lovecraft and Elizabeth Berkeley; *The Green Meadow*, by H.P. Lovecraft and Elizabeth Berkeley; *The Invisible Monster*, by Sonia Greene; *Four O'Clock*, by Sonia Greene; *The Man of Stone*, by Hazel Heald; *Winged Death*, by Hazel Heald; *The Loved Dead*, by C.M. Eddy, Jr.; *Deaf, Dumb and Blind*, by C.M. Eddy, Jr.; *The Ghost-Eater*, by C.M. Eddy, Jr.; "*Till All the Seas,*" by Robert H. Barlow; *The Horror in the Museum*, by Hazel Heald; *Out of the Eons*, by Hazel Heald; *The Dairy of Alonzo Typer*, by William Lumley; *The Horror in the Burying Ground*, by Hazel Heald; *The Last Test*, by Adolphe de Castro; *The Electric Executioner*, by Adolphe de Castro; *The Curse of Yig*, by Zealia Bishop; *Medusa's Coil*, by Zealia Bishop; *The Mound*, by Zealia Bishop; *Two Black Bottles*, by Wilfred Blanch Talman.

A collection of Lovecraft's best known revisions of other authors' works. Some were revised to the point that they are almost entirely written by Lovecraft on the basic of a plot sketch, while others were only lightly redone. Three of the revisions of Zealia Bishop had been reprinted as a separate collection titled *The Curse of Yig* in 1953 (No. 49). Reprinted by Arkham House in 1976 (3958 copies). A revised or "corrected" edition with new cover art was published in 1989 (No. 180). Still in print. First printing $125/25; second printing $40/10

116. The Arkham Collector, Number 8, by August Derleth (ed.). Periodical announcing new books and other items. (Winter 1971.) 36 pp. Ca. 2500 copies printed. Cover price $.50.

Contents: Denis Tiani; Rising Costs; Coming Books; *To His Mistress, Dead and Darkly Return'd*, by Roger Johnson; *The Cocomacaque*, by

Carl Jacobi; *To Howard Phillips Lovecraft*, by Clark Ashton Smith; *Black Thirst*, by Lin Carter; *Enough*, by Brian Lumley; *Yohk the Necromancer*, by Gary Myers; *K'n-Yan*, by Walter C. DeBill, Jr.; *Summer Night*, by Joseph Payne Brennan; Lovecraft on Love; *The Jersey Devil*, by Barbara A. Holland; *Strange Flowers Bloom*, by Duane Rimel; *The Shade in the Old Apple Tree*, by Walter H. Kerr; *A Presentation to George*, by Miki Myrick; Necrology; Associational.

See comments for No. 97. Collected and bound in No. 126. No reprints. $30

117. Selected Poems, by Clark Ashton Smith. Voluminous collection of fantasy and supernatural poems. (1971.) 403 pp. 2118 copies printed. Cover price $10. Jacket art by Gary Gore.

Contents: *Clark Ashton Smith: Emperor of Shadows*, by Benjamin de Casseres; *Nero; Chant to Sirius; The Star-Treader; The Night Forest; The Mad Wind; Medusa; Ode to the Abyss; The Butterfly; The Price; The Meaning; The Last Night; Ode to Imagination; The Maze of Sleep; The Winds;*

The Masque of Forsaken Gods; A Sunset; The Summer Moon; The Return of Hyperion; Lethe; Atlantis; The Unremembered; The Eldritch Dark; The Cherry-Snows; Nirvana; White Death; Retrospect and Forecast; Shadow of Nightmare; The Song of a Comet; The Retribution; To the Darkness; A Dream of Beauty; Pine Needles; To the Sun; Averted Malefice; The Medusa of the Skies; A Dead City; A Song of Dreams; The Balance; Saturn; Finis; The Pursuer; Said the Dreamer; The City of the Titans; In the Wind; Fire of Snow; To Beauty; Decadence; In the Desert; The Blindness of Orion; Somnus; The Nameless Wraith; Dolor of Dreams; The City of Destruction; Luna Aeternalis; To the Daemon of Sublimity; Preface (to Ebony and Crystal), by

The Horror in the Museum and Other Revisions, by H.P. Lovecraft (1970). Cover art by Gahan Wilson. No. 115.

George Sterling; *Arabesque; Beyond the Great Wall; To Omar Khayyam; Strangeness; The Infinite Quest; Rosa Mystica; The Nereid; In Saturn; Impressions; Triple Aspect; Desolation; A Fragment; Crepuscule; Inferno; Mirrors; Belated Love; The Absence of the Muse; Dissonance; To Nora May French; In Lemuria; Recompense; Exotique; Transcendence; Satiety; The Ministers of Law; Coldness; The Crucifixion of Eros; The Exile; Ave Atque Vale; Song of Sappho's Arabian Daughter; Solution; The Tears of Lilith; A Precept; Remembered Light; Song; Haunting; The Hidden Paradise; Cleopatra; Ecstacy; A Psalm to the Best Beloved; Symbols; The Hashish-Eater; The Sorrow of the Winds; Artemis; Love Is Not Yours,*

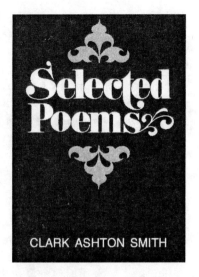

Selected Poems, by Clark Ashton Smith (1971). Cover art by Gary Gore. No. 117.

Love Is Not Mine; The City in the Desert; The Melancholy Pool; The Mirrors of Beauty; Winter Moonlight; To the Beloved; Requiescat; Mirage; Inheritance; Chant of Autumn; Nevermore; Echo of Memnon; Twilight on the Snow; Image; The Refuge of Beauty; Nightmare; Forgetfulness; Flamingoes; The Chimera; The Incubus of Time; Satan Unrepentant; The Abyss Triumphant; The Motes; The Medusa of Despair; Laus Mortis; Nocturne; The Ghoul and the Seraph; Metaphor; Sea-Memory; At Sunrise; The Land of Evil Stars; The Harlot of the World; Amor Aeternalis; The Hope of the Infinite; Palms; Memnon at Midnight; Eidolon; The Kingdom of Shadows; Requiescat in Pace; Alexandrines; Alexandrins; Ashes of Sunset; November Twilight; Sepulture; Quest; Beauty Implacable; A Vision of Lucifer; Desire of Vastness; Antepast; The Witch in the Graveyard; Memorial; The Horologe; "The Last Infirmity"; The Orchid of Beauty; The Last Goddess; The Flight of Azrael; Semblance; The Song of Aviol; We Shall Meet; Forgotten Sorrow; You Are Not Beautiful; Lemurienne; Dissidence; Sestet; Change; Query; Enigma; Incognita; The Secret; The End of Autumn; The Love-Potion; The Song of Cartha; Afterwards; Contradiction; The Last Oblivion; Autumn Orchards; Remembrance; The Wingless Archangels; Moon-Dawn; Lunar Mystery; Enchanted Mirrors; Duality; A Valediction; Selenique; Alienage;

Adventure; On the Canyon Side; Song; Minatory; Maya; Interrogation; Consolation; The Barrier; Apologia; Estrangement; Loss; A Catch; Don Juan Sings; On Re-reading Baudelaire; To the Chimera; A Parisian Dream (by Charles Baudelaire; tr. Smith); *Hymn to Beauty* (by Charles Baudelaire; tr. Smith); *The Ideal* (by Charles Baudelaire; tr. Smith); *Semper Eadem* (by Charles Baudelaire; tr. Smith); *The Giantess* (by Charles Baudelaire; tr. Smith); *Examination at Midnight* (by Charles Baudelaire; tr. Smith); *Doubtful Skies* (by Charles Baudelaire; tr. Smith); *The Sick Muse* (by Charles Baudelaire; tr. Smith); *Moesta et Errabunda* (by Charles Baudelaire; tr. Smith); *The Fountain of Blood* (by Charles Baudelaire; tr. Smith); *Evening Harmony* (by Charles Baudelaire; tr. Smith); *The Spiritual Dawn* (by Charles Baudelaire; tr. Smith); *The Wine of Lovers* (by Charles Baudelaire; tr. Smith); *The Death of Lovers* (by Charles Baudelaire; tr. Smith); *Obsession* (by Charles Baudelaire; tr. Smith); *Alchemy of Sorrow* (by Charles Baudelaire; tr. Smith); *Sympathetic Horror* (by Charles Baudelaire; tr. Smith); *The Owls* (by Charles Baudelaire; tr. Smith); *The Phantom* (by Charles Baudelaire; tr. Smith); *Mists and Rains* (by Charles Baudelaire; tr. Smith); *Sed Non Satiata* (by Charles Baudelaire; tr. Smith); *Spleen* (by Charles Baudelaire; tr. Smith); *Song of Autumn* (by Charles Baudelaire; tr. Smith); *Anterior Life* (by Charles Baudelaire; tr. Smith); *Lethe* (by Charles Baudelaire; tr. Smith); *Irremediable* (by Charles Baudelaire; tr. Smith); *Beatrice* (by Charles Baudelaire; tr. Smith); *The Voice* (by Charles Baudelaire; tr. Smith); *The Poison* (by Charles Baudelaire; tr. Smith); *The Two Kind Sisters* (by Charles Baudelaire; tr. Smith); *The Metamorphoses of the Vampire* (by Charles Baudelaire; tr. Smith); *Moonlight* (by Paul Verlaine; tr. Smith); *The Faun* (by Paul Verlaine; tr. Smith); *En Sourdine* (by Paul Verlaine; tr. Smith); *IX (Ariettes Oubliées)* (by Paul Verlaine; tr. Smith); *Crimen Amoris* (by Paul Verlaine; tr. Smith); *The Wheel of Omphale* (by Victor Hugo; tr. Smith); *Oblivion* (by José-Maria Heredia; tr. Smith); *Ecclesiastes* (by Charles-Marie-René Leconte de Lisle; tr. Smith); *The Sleep of the Condor* (by Charles-Marie-René Leconte de Lisle; tr. Smith); *Elysian Landscape* (by Pierre Lièvre; tr. Smith); *The Pagan; Madrigal; The Nymph; Chansonette; An Old Theme; Classic Epigram; Exotic Memory; By the River; Moments; Tempus; Tristan to Iseult; Concupiscence; Heliogabalus; Secret Love; Psalm; In Alexandria; Satiety; The Whisper of the Worm; The Funeral Urn; Mors; Where?* (By Gustavo Adolfo Bécquer; tr. Smith); *The Cypress* (by José A Calca_o; tr. Smith); *"That Motley Drama"* (by Clérigo Herrero; tr. Smith); *La Fortresse; Outlanders; Envoys; Shadows; Nyctalops; On a Chinese Vase; Jungle Twilight; The Phoenix; The Thralls of Circe Climb Parnassus; To George Sterling: A Valediction; To George Sterling; La Mare; Vaticinations; The Hill-Top; The Old Water-Wheel; Lichens; Cumuli; October; December; Necromancy; The Witch with Eyes of Amber; Lamia; Dialogue; In Slumber; Warning; The Nightmare Tarn; Cambion; Tolometh; Desert Dweller; The Prophet Speaks; A Fable; Au Bord du Léthé; L'Espoir du Néant; Farewell to Eros; Alternative; Moly; Paysage Paien; The Outer Land; A Dream of the Abyss; To Howard Phillips Lovecraft; After Armageddon; Chance; Ennui; Apostrophe; Sonnet; The Saturnienne; Revenant; Une Vie Spectrale; Song of the Necromancer; In Thessaly; Lines on a Picture; Hellenic Sequel; Refuge; Only to One Returned; But Grant, O Venus; Town Lights; Strange Girl; Some Blind Eidolon; If Winter Remain; Pour Chercher du Nouveau; Anteros; Attar of the Past; Passing of an Elder God; Nightmare of the Lilliputian; Poets in Hades; Mummy of the Flower; The Heron; Bird of Long Ago; Mithridates; Someone; Late November Evening; Quiddity; Epitaph for an Astronomer; Copyist; Love and Death; Unicorn; Untold Arabian Fable; A Hunter Meets the Mantichoras; The Limniad; The Sciapod; The Monacle; Feast of St. Anthony; Paphnutius; Philtre; Borderland; Lethe; Perseus and Medusa; Odysseus in Eternity; The Ghost of Theseus; Fence and Wall; Growth of Lichen; Cats in Winter Sunlight; Abandoned Plum-Orchard; Harvest Evening; Willow-Cutting in Autumn; Declining Moon; Late Pear-Pruner; Nocturnal Pines; Phallus Impudica; Stormy Afterglow; Geese in the Spring Night; Foggy Night; Reigning Empress; The Sparrow's Nest; The Last Apricot; Mushroom-Gatherers; Spring Nunnery; Nuns Walking in the Orchard; Improbable Dream; Crows in Spring; Slaughter-House in Spring; High Mountain Juniper; Storm's End; Pool at Lobos; Poet in a Barroom; Fallen Grape-Leaf; Slaughter-House Pasture; Gopher-Hole in Orchard; Basin in Boulder; Indian Acorn-Mortar; Old Limestone Kiln; Love In Dreams; Night of Miletus; Tryst at Lobos; Prisoner in Vain; Mountain Trail; Future Meeting; Classic Reminiscence; Goats and Manzanita-Boughs; Picture by Piero di Cosimo; Garden of Priapus; Bed of Mint; Chainless Captive; January Willow; Snowfall on Acacia; Flight of the Yellow-Hammer; Sunset over Farm-Land; Flora; Windows at Lamplighting Time; Old Hydraulic Diggins; Hearth on Old Cabin-Site; Builder of Deserted Hearth; Aftermath of Mining Days; River-Canyon; School-Room Pastime; Boys Telling Bawdy Tales; Water-Fight; Boys Rob a Yellow-Hammer's Nest; Grammar School Vixen; Girl of Six; Snake, Owl, Cat or Hawk;*

Cattle Salute the Psychopomp; Field Behind the Abatoir; Plague from the Abatoir; La Morts des Amants; Vultures Come to the Ambarvalia; For the Dance of Death; Berries of the Deadly Nightshade; Water Hemlock; Felo-de-se of the Parasite; Disillusionment; Almost Anything; To Whom It May Concern; Tin Can on the Mountain Top; Surrealist Sonnet; Sonnet for Psychoanalysts; Parnassus à la Mode; The Nevermore-to-Be; Fantasie d'Antan; One Evening; Trope; Canticle; Venus; November; Le Miroir des Blanches Fleurs; Les Marées; The Autumn Lake; Winter Moonlight; To Antares; Connaissance; Exorcism; Calendar; Madrigal of Evanescence; September; Indian Summer; The Dragon-Fly; Touch; Sufficiency; Ineffability; Mystery; Dominion; Dancer; Bacchante; Wizard's Love; Resurrection; Witch Dance; Paean; The Knoll; Interim; Reverie in August; Wine in Summer; Ode; For an Antique Lyre; Silent Hour; To One Absent; Bond; The Mime of Sleep; Madrigal of Memory; Fragment; Humors of Love; Grecian Yesterday; Yerba Buena; Sonnet; "All is Dross That Is Not Helena"; Amor; The Sorcerer to his Love; Twilight Song; Before Dawn; Amor Hesternalis; Supplication; Erato; The Hill of Dionysus; Anodyne of Autumn; Nocturne: Grant Avenue; Future Pastoral; Postlude; Midnight Beach; Even in Slumber; De Profundis; Illumination; Omniety; From Arcady; Sea Cycle; Do You Forget, Enchantress?; No Stranger Dream; On the Mount of Stone; Calenture; Awowal.

The ultimate collection of Smith's poems, with translations of the works of other poets such as Baudelaire and Paul Verlaine. A cardinal piece of genre literature; the collection was prepared by Smith as early as the late 1940s, but for various delays was not published until eight years after his death. A key title and, because of Smith's popularity and the literary merit of the work, it was the first Arkham House poetry title to be issued in a larger printing. No reprints. $225/50

118. The Face in the Mirror, by Denys Val Baker. Collection of weird tales. (1971.) 113 pp. 2045 copies printed. Cover price $3.75. Jacket art by Gary Gore.

Contents: *The Face in the Mirror; The Inheritance; The Anniversary; Voice from the Past; Passenger to Liverpool; The Trees; A Woman of Talent; The Cruise of the Morweena; A Tall Tale; The Old Man of the Towans; The Tune; The Last Laugh.*

The only Arkham House collection of stories by the British novelist. No reprints. $40/15

119. **The Arkham Collector, Number 9,** by August Derleth (ed.). Periodical announcing new books and other items. (Spring 1971.) 44 pp. Ca. 2500 copies printed.Cover price $.50.

Contents: Two New Spring Books; Eight Tales; Songs and Sonnets Atlantean; *To Great Cthulhu*, by Richard L. Tierney; *Passing of a Dreamer*, by Gary Myers; *May-Eve*, by Steve Eng; *The Aphids*, by William D. Barney; *The Waiting Room*, by Robert Aickman; *Ghost Stories, Fairy Tales and Riddles*, by Joyce Odam; *Dream for a Windy Night*, by Caryl Porter; *When the Moon is Pale*, by Wade Wellman; *The Relic*, by Roger Johnson; *After You, Montagu*, by Donald Wandrei; *In Pressure-Pounded Chasms*, by Brian Lumley; Necrology; Bibliographical Notes; Schedule Changes; *Panels for a Nativity*, by James Wade; *Atlantic City: 5:30 P.M.*, by W.P. Ganley.

See comments for No. 97. Collected and bound in No. 126. No reprints. $30

120. **Eight Tales,** by Walter de la Mare. Collection of weird tales. (1971.) 108 pp. 2992 copies printed. Cover price $4.00. Jacket art by Gary Gore.

Contents: *Introduction*, by Edward Wagenknecht; *Kismet; The Hangman's Luck; A Mote; The Village of Old Age; The Moon's Miracle; The Giant; De Mortuis; A: B: O.*

The only Arkham House title by this British poet and fiction writer. No reprints. $50/8

121. **Dark Things,** by August Derleth (ed.). Collection of original weird tales by various writers. (1971.) 330 pp. 3051 copies printed. Cover price $6.50. Jacket art by Herb Arnold and Gary Gore.

Contents: *The Funny Farm*, by Robert Bloch; *The Eyes of Mme. Dupree*, by P.H. Booth; *"The Perils That Lurks Among Ruins,"* by Joseph Payne Brennan; *Napier Court*, by Ramsey Campbell; *The Dweller in the Tomb*, by Lin Carter; *Shaggai*, by Lin Carter; *The House by the Tarn*, by Basil Copper; *The Knocker at the Portico*, by Basil Copper; *Lord of the Depths*, by David Drake; *Omega*, by Alice R. Hill; *The House in the Oaks*, by Robert E. Howard and August Derleth; *The Singleton Barrier*, by Carl Jacobi; *The Case of the Double Husband*, by Margery Lawrence; *Innsmouth Clay*, by H.P. Lovecraft and August Derleth; *Rising with Surtsey*, by Brian Lumley; *The Deep-Sea Conch*, by Brian Lumley; *Company in the*

113

Orchard, by Frances May; *"Beyondaril,"* by John Metcalfe; *The Man-terfield Inheritance*, by Charles Partington; *The Storm King*, by Emil Petaja; *The Elevator*, by James Wade; *Appointment with Fire*, by H. Russell Wakefield; *The Rings of the Papaloi*, by Donald J. Walsh, Jr.; *Requiem for Earth*, by Donald Wandrei; Biographical.

The fourth and last anthology of unpublished weird fiction, edited by August Derleth, who died in July 1971. No reprints. $75/10

122. The Arkham Collector, Number 10, by August Derleth (ed.). Periodical announcing new books and other items. (Summer 1971.) 48 pp. Ca. 2500 copies printed. Cover price $.50.

Contents: Looking Ahead; *III Samuel*, by William D. Barney; *The Mass Media Horror*, by James Wade; *The Crest of Satan*, by Sara Lindsay Rath; *Where They Rule*, by Meade Frierson III; *The Doom of Yakthoob*, by Lin Carter; *In Intricate Magicks*, by Walter H. Kerr; *To My Masters*, by Roger Johnson; *Notes Concerning a Green Box*, by Alan Dean Foster; *Night Sounds*, by Walter C. DeBill; Lovecraft in France; *Shadow Game*, by George Wetzel; Bibliographical; Index.

The final issue. See comments for No. 97. Collected and bound in No. 126. No reprints. $30

123. Songs and Sonnets Atlantean, by Donald S. Fryer. Collection of poems and prose poems. (1971.) 134 pp. 2045 copies printed. Cover price $5.00. Jacket art by Gordon R. Barnett.

Contents: *Introduction*, by Dr. Ibid M. Andor (i.e. Donald S. Fryer); *Avalonessys; The Crown and the Trident Imperial; Atlantis; The Rose and the Thorn; Rose Escarlate; "O Ebon-Colored Rose"; Your Mouth of Pomegranate; As Buds and Blossoms in the Month of May the Rose; To Clark Ashton Smith; Pavane; When We Were Prince and Princess; The Crown and Trident; Song; "Thy Spirit Walks the Sea"; Recompense; To a Youth; Spenserian Stanza-Sonnet Empourpré; A Symbol for All Splendor Lost; The Ashes in the Rose Garden; To Edmind Spencer; Rose Verdastre; Ave Atque Vale; Thaïs and Alexander in Persepolis; A Fragment; O fair dark eyes, O glances turned aside; The Cydnus; Golden Mycenae; Lullaby; Minor Chronicles of Atlantis:(Proem; The Hippokamp; The Alpha Huge; The River Called Amphus; The Amphus Delta; The Imperial Crown Jewels of Atlantis; The Atlantean Obelisk; The Garden of the Jealous Roses; The Tale of an Olden Love; The Shepherd and the Shepherdess; Reciprocity; The Iffinnix; A Vision of Strange Splendor); Kilcoman Castle: 20*

August 1965; Aubade; The Lilac Hedge at Cassell Prairie: 27 May 1967; Black Poppy and Black Lotus; The House of Roses; "The Musical Note of Swans...before their Death"; Green Sleeves; O Beautiful Dark-Amber Eyes of Old; The Forsaken Palace; For the "Shapes of Clay" of Ambrose Bierce; Connaissance Fatale; For the "Black Beetles in Amber" of Ambrose Bierce; Offrande Exotique; Sonnets on an Empire of Many Waters:(I. Here, where the fountains of the deep sea flows; II. Atlantis; III. Gades; IV. Atlantigades; V. Atkantharia; VI. Iffrikonn-Yssthia; VII. Atlantessys; VIII. Atlantillia; IX. Attatemthessys; X. At-Thulonn; XI. Avalonessys; XII. Poseidonis; XIII. The Merchant-Princes; XIV. An Argosy of Trade; XV. Memories of Astazhan; XVI. A Letter From Valoth; XVII. No, not until the final age of Earth); Notes, by Dr. Ibid M. Andor (i.e. Donald S. Fryer).

An important collection of poems and the author's only Arkham House title. Fryer was greatly inspired by the works of Clark Ashton Smith and later wrote several essays, monographs and a superior bibliography on Smith's writings. No reprints. $50/8

124. **Selected Letters III: 1929–1931,** by H.P. Lovecraft. Letters by H.P. Lovecraft, collected and edited by August Derleth and Donald Wandrei. (1971.) 451 pp. 2513 copies printed. Cover price $10. Jacket photography by Ronald Rich, illustration by Virgil Finlay and design and lettering by Gary Gore.

Contents: *Preface,* by August Derleth and Donald Wandrei. Letters 360–516.

The most important of the five volumes of Lovecraft's letters and the last one edited by Derleth and Wandrei. Also, see comments for No. 86. The color scheme of the Volume III jacket is dark green. Reprinted by Arkham House in 1997 (2531 copies). Still in print. First printing $225/60; Second printing $26/8

125. **The Caller of the Black,** by Brian Lumley. Collection of Lovecraft inspired weird tales. (1971.) 235 pp. 3606 copies printed. Cover price $5.00. Jacket art by Herb Arnold.

Contents: *A Thing about Cars!; The Cypress Shell; Billy's Oak; The Writer in the Garret; The Caller of the Black; The Mirror of Nitocris; The Night Sea-Maid Went Down; The Thing from the Blasted Heath; An Item of Supporting Evidence; Dylath-Leen; De Marigny's Clock; Ambler's Inspiration; In the Vaults Beneath; The Pearl.*

The author's first book. Several of the tales included are inspired by the "Cthulhu Mythos." Brain Lumley would write two more books for Arkham House and numerous other books of weird fiction for other publishers. No reprints. $125/25

126. The Arkham Collector, Volume I, by August Derleth (ed.). This volume collects 'The Arkham Collector' issues 1–10 in a hard cover binding. (1971.) 348 pp. 676 copies printed. Cover price $10. No dust jacket issued. No reprints. $250

127. Disclosures in Scarlet, by Carl Jacobi. Collection of fantasy and science fiction tales. (1972.) 181 pp. 3127 copies printed. Cover price $5.00. Jacket art by Frank Utpatel.

Contents: *The Aquarium; The Player at Yellow Silence; The Unpleasantness at Carver House; The Cocomacaque; The Gentleman Is an Epwa; The Royal Opera House; Strangers to Straba; Exit Mr. Smith; Gentlemen, the Scavengers; Round Robin; The White Pinnacle; Mr. Iper of Hamilton; The War of the Weeds; Kincaid's Car; The Random Quantity; Sequence; The Singleton Barrier.*

The author's third and last Arkham House collection, which consists mainly of science fiction and fantasy tales. No reprints. $50/15

128. The Rim of the Unknown, by Frank Belknap Long. Collection of weird tales and science fiction. (1972.) 291 pp. 3650 copies printed. Cover price $7.50. Jacket art by Herb Arnold.

Contents: *The Spiral Intelligence; The World of Wulkins; The Man with a Thousand Legs; Humpty Dumpty Had a Great Fall; Guest in the House; The Trap; Fuzzy Head; The House of the Rising Winds; Mr. Caxton Draws a Martian Bird; The Critters; The Cottage; The Man from Time; Cones; Preview; Lesson in Survival; Good To Be a Martian; Filch; Little Men of Space; The Spectacles; Man of Distinction; The Great Cold; Green Glory; The Last Men.*

The author's second Arkham House title. A mixture of weird tales and science fiction. Many of the stories first appeared in magazines between the 1930s and 1950s. No AH reprints. $150/25

129. Stories of Darkness and Dread, by Joseph Payne Brennan. Collection of supernatural tales. (1973.) 173 pp. 4138 copies printed. Cover price $6.00. Jacket art by Denis Tiani.

Contents: *City of the Seven Winds; The Keeper of the Dust; Zombique; The Seventh Incantation; Delivery at Erdmore Street; The Way to the Attic; Mr. Octbur; Episode on Cain Street; Killer Cat; In the Very Stones; The House at 1248; Black Thing at Midnight; Monton; Apprehension; The House on Hazel Street; The Man in Grey Tweeds; The North Knoll; The Dump.*
The author's second collection of weird tales, mostly written between the 1950s and 1970s. No reprints. $75/18

130. Demons by Daylight, by Ramsey Campbell. Collection of weird tales. (1973.) 153 pp. 3472 copies printed. Cover price $5.00. Jacket art by Eddie Jones.
Contents: *Potential; The End of a Summer's Day; At First Sight; The Franklyn Paragraphs; The Interloper (*as by Errol Undercliffe); *The Sentinels; The Guy; The Old Horns; The Lost; The Stocking; The Second Staircase; Concussion; The Enchanted Fruit; Made in Goatswood.*
An important key title that brings the works of the talented J. Ramsey Campbell back to Arkham House, after a nine year absence. Most of the stories were written in the 1960s and show considerable promise. No AH reprints. $75/20

131. From Evil's Pillow, by Basil Copper. Collection of horror tales. (1973.) 177 pp. 3468 Copies printed. Cover price $6.00. Jacket art by Frank Utpatel.
Contents: *Amber Print; The Grey House; The Gossips; A Very Pleasant Fellow; Charon.*
The British author's first collection of weird fiction published in the United States. More were to follow under the Arkham House imprint. No reprints. $60/18

From Evil's Pillow, by Basil Copper (1973). Cover art by Frank Utpatel. No. 131.

132. **Beneath the Moors,** by Brian Lumley. Cthulhu inspired novel. (1974.) 145 pp. 3842 copies printed. Cover price $6.00. Jacket art by Herb Arnold. No reprints. $75/20

133. **The Watchers out of Time and Others,** by H.P. Lovecraft and August Derleth. Collection of supernatural tales. (1974.) 405 pp. 5070 copies printed. Cover price $8.50. Jacket art by Herb Arnold. Contents: *Foreword,* by August Derleth; *The Lurker at the Threshold; The Survivor; Wentworth's Day; The Peabody Heritage; The Gable Window; The Ancestor; The Shadow Out of Space; The Lamp of Alhazred; The Shuttered Room; The Fisherman at Falcon Point; Witches Hollow; The Shadow in the Attic; The Dark Brotherhood; The Horror from the Middle Span; Innsmouth Clay; The Watchers Out of Time.*

The stories in the collection are primarily compiled from other previous appearances in anthologies and magazines. Second printing in 1984 (1974 copies). Third printing in 1988 (3000 copies). First printing $125/20; second printing $30/5; third printing cover price

134. **Collected Ghost Stories,** by Mary E. Wilkins-Freeman. Collec-

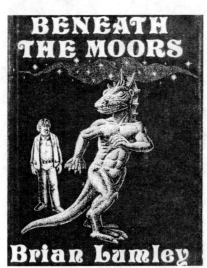

Beneath the Moors, **by Brian Lumley (1974). Cover art by Herb Arnold. No. 132.**

tion of New England ghost stories. (1974.) 189 pp. 4155 copies printed. Cover price $6.00. Jacket art by Frank Utpatel.

Contents: *Introduction,* by Edward Wagenknecht; *The Shadow on the Wall; The Hall Bedroom; Luella Miller; The Vacant Lot; A Far-Away Melody; A Symphony in Lavender; The Wind in the Rose-bush; A Gentle Ghost; The Southwest Chamber; The Lost Ghost; The Jade Bracelet.*

The only Arkham House title by this American writer who was best known for her New England regional writings. No reprints. Still in print. $40/ 10

135. **Howard Phillips Lovecraft: Dreamer on the Nightside,** by Frank Belknap Long. Lovecraft biography and memoir. (1975.) 237 pp. 4991 copies printed. Cover price $8.50. Jacket art by Frank Utpatel.
A personal look at Lovecraft, his life and work, through the eyes of a writer who was a close friend of H.P.L. for nearly twenty years. Edited by James Turner. No reprints. $65/10

136. **The House of the Worm,** by Gary Myers. Dunsany/Lovecraft inspired collection of fantasy stories. (1975.) 77 pp. 4144 copies printed. Cover price $5.50. Jacket art by Allan Servos.
Contents: *Introduction; The House of the Worm; Yohk the Necromancer; Xiurhn; Passing of a Dreamer; The Return of Zhosph; The Three Enchantments; Hazuth-Kleg; The Loot of Golthoth; The Four Sealed Jars; The Maker of Gods.*
The author's first book. No reprints. $50/10

137. **Nameless Places,** by Gerald W. Page (ed.). Collection of horror and fantasy stories by various authors. (1975.) 279 pp. 4160 copies printed. Cover price $7.50. Jacket art by Tim Kirk.
Contents: *Foreword,* by Gerald W. Page; *Glimpses,* by A.A. Attanasio; *The Night of the Unicorn,* by Thomas Burnett Swann; *The Warlord of Kul Satu,* by Brian Ball; *More Things,* by G.N. Gabbard; *The Real Road to the Church,* by Robert Aickman; *The Gods of Earth,* by Gary Myers; *Walls of Yellow Clay,* by Robert E. Gilbert; *Businessman's Lament,* by Scott Edelstein; *Dark Vintage,* by Joseph F. Pumilia; *Simaitha,* by David A. English; *In the Land of Angra Mainyu,* by Stephen Goldin; *Worldsong,* by Gerald W. Page; *What Dark God?,* by Brian Lumley; *The Stuff of Heroes,* by Bob Maurus; *Forringer's Fortune,* by Joseph Payne Brennan; *Before the Event,* by Denys Val Baker; *In 'Ygiroth,* by Walter C. DeBill, Jr.; *The Last Hand,* by Ramsey Campbell; *Out of the Ages,* by Lin Carter; *Awakening,* by David Drake; *In the Vale of Pnath,* by Lin Carter; *Chameleon Town,* by Carl Jacobi; *Botch,* by Scott Edelstein; *Black Iron,* by David Drake; *Selene,* by E. Hoffmann Price; *The Christmas Present,* by Ramsey Campbell; *Lifeguard,* by Arthur Byron Cover; Biographical.
An anthology of previously unpublished work that introduces several new writers to Arkham House readers. The book was intended as

a continuation of August Derleth's earlier anthologies of unpublished weird fiction. No reprints. $45/10

138. The Purcell Papers, by J. Sheridan LeFanu. A collection of weird fiction. (1975.) 241 pp. 4288 copies printed. Cover price $7.00. Jacket art by Frank Utpatel.

Contents: *Introduction,* by August Derleth; *The Ghost and the Bone-Setter; The Fortunes of Sir Robert Ardagh; The Drunkard's Dream; The Quare Gander; The Child That Went with the Fairies; The White Cat of Drumgunniol; Ghost Stories of Chapelizod (I. The Village Bully; II. The Spectre Lovers); Stories of Lough Guir; A Night in the Bell Inn* (by Henry Ferris); *The Dead Sexton; The Legend of Dunblane; The Mysterious Lodger; The Churchyard Yew* (by August Derleth).

The second Arkham House collection of LeFanu's short stories, containing work published between the 1830s and 1870s. The stories in this collection are of lesser literary merit and not as successful as the author's first collection *Green Tea and Other Stories* (No. 12, 1945.) No reprints. Still in print. $45/10

139. Dreams from R'lyeh, by Lin Carter. Collection of fantasy poetry. (1975.) 72 pp. 3152 copies printed. Cover price $5.00. Jacket art by Tim Kirk.

Contents: *Merlin on the Queens Express,* by L. Sprague de Camp; *Dreams from R'lyeh: A Sonnet Cycle: I. Remembrances; II. Arkham; III. The Festival; IV. The Old Wood; V. The Locked Attic; VI. The Shunned Church; VII. The Last Ritual; VIII. The Library; IX. Black Thirst; X. The Elder Age; XI. Lost R'lyeh; XII. Unknown Kadath; XIII. Abdul Alhazred; XIV. Hyperborea; XV. The Book of Eibon; XVI. Tsathoggua; XVII. Black Zimbabwe; XVIII. The Return; XIX. The Sabbat; XX. Black Lotus; XXI. The Unspeakable; XXII. Carcosa; XXIII. The Candidate; XXIV. The Dream-Daemon; XXV. Dark Yuggoth; XXVI. The Silver Key; XXVII. The Peaks Beyond Throk; XXVIII. Spawn of the Black Goat; XXIX. Beyond; XXX. The Accursed; XXXI. The Million Favored Ones; Lunae Custodiens; Merlin, Enchanted; To Clark Ashton Smith; Once in Fabled Grandeur; The Night Kings; All Hallow's Eve; Shard; The Wind in the Rigging; Diombar's Song of the Last Battle; The Elf-King's Castle; To Lord Dunsany; The Forgotten; Golden Age; Lines Written to a Painting by Hannes Bok; Death Song of Conan the Cimmerian;* Author's Note.

Poetry inspired by the works of Lovecraft, Clark Ashton Smith, Robert E. Howard, and James Branch Cabell, among others. No reprints. $50/10

140. Harrigan's File, by August Derleth. Collection of weird, science fiction stories. (1975.) 256 pp. 4102 copies printed. Cover price $6.50. Jacket art by Frank Utpatel.

Contents: *Mellvaine's Star; A Corner for Lucia; Invaders from the Microcosm; Mark VII; The Other Side of the Wall; An Eye for History; The Maugham Obsession; A Traveller in Time; The Detective and the Senator; Protoplasma; The Mechanical House; By Rocket to the Moon; The Man Who Rode the Saucer; Ferguson's Capsules; The Penfield Misadventure; The Remarkable Dingdong; The Martian Artifact.*

Another volume of Derleth's stories, this one featuring Tex Harrigan, a reporter with a knack for finding himself in impossible and weird situations. Some stories are science fiction. No reprints. Still in print. $50/10

141. Xélucha and Others, by M.P. Shiel. Collection of weird tales. (1975.) 243 pp. 4283 copies printed. Cover price $6.50. Jacket art by Frank Utpatel. Contents: *Introduction; Xélucha; The Primate of the Rose; Dark Lot of One Saul; The House of Sounds; The Globe of Gold-fish* (with John Gawsworth); *Many a Tear; The Bride; The Tale of Henry and Rowena; The Bell of St. Sepulcre; Huguenin's Wife; The Pale Ape; The Case of Euphemia Raphash.*

The author's first collection of supernatural stories in the United States. No reprints. $65/15

Xélucha and Others, by Matthew P. Shiel (1975). Cover art by Frank Utpatel. No. 141.

142. Literary Swordsmen and Sorcerers, by L. Sprague de Camp. Essays on various fantasy writers. (1976.) 313 pp. 5431 copies printed. Cover price $10. Jacket art by Tim Kirk.

Contents: *Introduction: Neomythology*, by Lin Carter; *The Swords of Faërie; Jack of All Arts: William Morris; Two Men in One: Lord Dunsany; Eldritch Yankee Gentleman: H.P. Lovecraft; Superman in a Bowler: E.R. Eddison; The Miscast Barbarian: Robert E. Howard; Parallel Worlds: Fletcher Pratt; Sierran Shaman: Clark Ashton Smith; Merlin in Tweeds: J.R.R. Tolkien; The Architect of Camelot: T.H. White; Conan's Compeers;* Notes; Index.

A non-fiction reference title, containing informal essays and other pieces on various fantasy and weird fiction writers. No reprints. $40/8

143. **The Height of the Scream**, by Ramsey Campbell. Collection of horror stories. (1976.) 229 pp. 4348 Copies printed. Cover price $7.50. Jacket art by Ron Fendel.

Contents: *Introduction and Allergies; The Scar; The Whining; The Dark Show; Missing; Reply Guaranteed; Jack's Little Friend; Beside the Seaside; The Cellars; The Height of the Scream; Litter; Cyril; Smoke Kiss; The Words That Count; Ash; The Telephones; In the Shadows; Second Chance; Horror House of Blood.*

The author's third Arkham House collection of psychological horror stories, written in the 1960s and 1970s. No AH reprints. $60/18

144. **Dwellers in the Darkness**, by August Derleth. Collection of weird fiction. (1976.) 203 pp. 3926 copies printed. Cover price $6.50. Jacket art by Frank Utpatel.

Contents: *The Ghost Walk; The Ormolu Clock; A Knocking in the Wall; The Lost Path; The Place of Desolation; The Patchwork Quilt; The Island Out of Space; The Night Road; Come to Me; Memoir for Lucas Payne; The Passing of Eric Holm; Man in the Dark; The Song of the Pewee; Open, Sesame!; Ghost Lake; The Element of Chance; Fool Proof.*

This is the eighth and last Arkham House collection of August Derleth's weird fiction. Most of the stories were first published between the 1930s and 1950s. No reprints. $35/8

145. **Selected Letters IV: 1932–1934**, by August Derleth and James Turner (eds.). Collection of letters by H.P. Lovecraft. (1976.) 424 pp. 4978 copies printed. Cover price $12.50. Jacket photography

by Ronald Rich, illustration by Virgil Finlay and design and lettering by Gary Gore.

Contents: *Preface,* by James Turner. Letters 517–710.

See comments for No. 86. The color scheme of the Volume IV jacket is yellow. No reprints. $45/10

146. **Selected Letters V: 1934–1937,** by August Derleth and James Turner (eds.). Final collection of letters by H.P. Lovecraft. (1976.) 437 pp. 5138 copies printed. Cover price $12.50. Jacket photography by Ronald Rich, illustration by Virgil Finlay and design and lettering by Gary Gore.

Contents: *Preface,* by James Turner. Letters 711–930.

See comments for No. 86. The color scheme of the Volume V jacket is reddish-maroon. No reprints. Still in print. $45/10

147. **Kecksies and Other Twilight Tales,** by Marjorie Bowen. Collection of ghost and fantasy stories. (1976.) 207 pp. 4391 copies printed. Cover price $7.50. Jacket art by Stephen E. Fabian.

Contents: *Preface; The Hidden Ape; Kecksies; Raw Material; The Avenging of Ann Leete; The Crown Derby Plate; The Sign Painter and the Crystal Fishes; Scoured Silk; The Breakdown; One Remained Behind; The House by the Poppy Field; Florence Flannery; Half-Past Two.*

The only Arkham House title by Marjorie Bowen, a pseudonym of the British writer Gabrielle Margaret Vere Campbell, who was best known for her historical novels. The dust jacket illustration is the first Arkham House cover by Stephen E. Fabian, an exceptional and talented fantasy artist with no formal training. No reprints. Still in print. $40/10

148. **The Horror at Oakdeene and Others,** by Brian Lumley. Collection of weird stories. (1977.) 229 pp. 4162 copies printed. Cover price $7.50. Jacket art by Stephen E. Fabian.

Contents: *The Viking's Stone; Aunt Hester; No Way Home; The Horror at Oakdeene; The Cleaner Woman; The Statement of Henry Worthy; Darghud's Doll; Born of the Winds.*

The author's third Arkham House title, with another of Stephen E. Fabian's gorgeous jacket illustrations. No reprints. $55/15

149. **And Afterwards, the Dark,** by Basil Copper. Collection of weird stories. (1977.) 222 pp. 4259 copies printed. Cover price $7.50. Jacket art by Stephen E. Fabian.

Contents: *Introduction,* by Edward Wagenknecht; *The Spider; The Cave; Dust to Dust; Camera Obscura; The Janissaries of Emilion; Archives of the Dead; The Flabby Men.*

The author's second Arkham House collection of weird fiction. No reprints. $40/10

150. **In Mayan Splendor,** by Frank Belknap Long. Collection of fantasy poems. (1977.) 66 pp. 2947 copies printed. Cover price $6.00. Jacket art by Stephen E. Fabian.

Contents: *In Mayan Splendor; A Knight of La Mancha; Sonnet; A Man from Genoa; Advice; Pirate-Men; On Icy Kinarth; The Magi; On Reading Arthur Machen; Stallions of the Moon; In Hospital; Ballad of Saint Anthony; The White People; An Old Tale Retold; Prediction; The Rebel; Two Stanzas for Master François Villon; The Goblin Tower; West Indies; The Hashish Eater; When We Have Seen; The Marriage of Sir John Mandeville; Manhattan Skyline & W.W.; The Horror on Dagoth Wold; In the Garden of Eros; The Prophet; Night-Trees; Florence; When Chaugnar Wakes; In Antique Mood; The Abominable Snow Men; A Sonnet for Seamen; Ballad of Mary Magdalene; Great Ashtaroth; Subway; An Old Wife Speaketh It; A Time Will Come; The Inland Sea; Exotic Quest; H.P. Lovecraft.*

And Afterward the Dark, by Basil Copper (1977). Cover art by Stephen Fabian. No. 149.

A slim volume of superior poetry, illustrated with five haunting images by the talented Stephen E. Fabian. No reprints. $75/15

151. **Half in Shadow,** by Mary Elizabeth Counselman. Collec-

tion of supernatural stories. (1978.) 212 pp. 4288 copies printed. Cover price $8.95. Jacket art by Tim Kirk. Contents: *The Three Marked Pennies; The Unwanted; The Shot-Tower Ghost; Night Court; The Monkey Spoons; The Smiling Face; A Death Crown for Mr. Hapworthy; The Black Stone Statue; Seventh Sister; Parasite Mansion; The Green Window; The Tree's Wife; Twister; A Handful of Silver.* The author's only Arkham House title. The collection consists mostly of stories written for *Weird Tales* from the 1930s to 1950s. No reprints. Still in print. $40/10

Born to Exile, by Phyllis Eisenstein (1978). Cover art by Stephen Fabian. No. 152.

152. **Born to Exile,** by Phyllis Eisenstein. Fantasy novel. (1978.) 202 pp. 4148 copies printed. Cover price $8.95. Jacket art by Stephen E. Fabian. The American author's first book. No AH reprints. $50/12

153. **The Black Book of Clark Ashton Smith,** by Clark Ashton Smith. Collection of notes, essays, ideas and thoughts. (1979.) 143 pp. 2588 copies printed. Cover price $6.00. Paperback with no dust jacket issued.

Contents: *Foreword,* by Marvin R. Hiemstra; *A Note on the Text,* by Donald Sidney-Fryer; *Explanation of Editorial Devices; Index by Title; The Black Book; Excerpts from The Black Book; Appendix of Finished Poems: (Song of the Necromancer; Dominium in Excelsis; Shapes in the Sunset; Don Quixote on Market Street; Soliloquy in an Ebon Tower; The Isle of Saturn; The Centaur; Ye Shall Return; Thebaid); Appendix of Published Epigrams and Pensées; As I Remember Klarkash-Ton,* by George F. Haas; *Memories of Klarkash-Ton,* by George F. Haas; *Cycles.*

The first Arkham House paperback edition. An interesting "note-book" that contains a number of items related to Smith's writings. Black cover with gold spine lettering and design. Interior illustrations by Andrew Smith. No reprints. $85

154. **The Princess of All Lands,** by Russell Kirk. Collection of fantasy stories. (1979.) 228 pp. 4120 copies printed. Cover price $8.95. Jacket art by Joe Wehrle.
Contents: *Prologue; Sorworth Place; Behind the Stumps; The Princess of All Lands; The Last God's Dream; The Cellar of Little Egypt; Ex Tenebris; Balgrummo's Hell; There's a Long, Long Trail A-Winding; Saviourgate.*
The author's first collection of fantasy stories published by Arkham house. No reprints. $65/15

155. **In the Mist and Other Uncanny Encounters,** by Elizabeth Walter. Collection of weird stories. (1979.) 202 pp. 4053 copies printed. Cover price $8.95. Jacket art by Stephen E. Fabian.
Contents: *Preface; The Concrete Captain; The Sin Eater; In the Mist; Come and Get Me; The Island of Regrets; The Hare; Davy Jones's Tale*
The only Arkham House title by this British writer. The author's selection of her best stories, mostly written in the 1960s and 1970s. A key title. No AH reprints. $50/12

156. **New Tales of the Cthulhu Mythos,** by Ramsey Campbell (ed.). Collection of Cthulhu-inspired tales. (1980.) 257 pp. 3647 copies printed. Cover price $11.95. Jacket art by Jason Van Hollander.
Contents: *Introduction,* by Ramsey Campbell; *Crouch End,* by Stephen King; *The Star Pools,* by A.A. Attanasio; *The Second Wish,* by Brian Lumley; *Dark Awakening,* by Frank Belknap Long; *Shaft Number 247,* by Basil Copper; *Black Man with a Horn,* by T.E.D. Klein; *The Black Tome of Alsophocus,* by H.P. Lovecraft and Martin S. Warnes; *Than Curse the Darkness,* by David Drake; *The Faces at Pine Dunes,* by Ramsey Campbell; Notes on Contributors.
An anthology of newer Cthulhu inspired tales, different from previously published stories, by various writers, including Stephen King. From 1980, the end colophons were eliminated and "First Edition" designations were identified by that term on the copyright page. No AH reprints. $125/25

157. **Necropolis,** by Basil Copper. Stylish Gothic novel. (1980.) 352 pp. 4050 copies printed. Cover price $12.95. Great jacket art by Stephen E. Fabian. A key title. Second printing in 1981 (1539 copies). First printing $75/20; second printing $30/8

158. **The Third Grave,** by David Case. Egyptian archeology horror novel. (1981.) 184 pp. Jacket art by Stephen E. Fabian. 184 pp. 4158 copies printed. Cover price $10.95. No reprints. Still in print. $45 /10

Necropolis, by Basil Copper (1980). Cover art by Stephen Fabian. No. 157.

159. **Tales from the Nightside,** by Charles L. Grant. Collection of horror stories. (1981.) 228 pp. 4121 copies printed. Cover price $11.95. Jacket art by Michael Whelan.

Contents: *Foreword,* by Stephen King; *Coin of the Realm; Old Friends; Home; If Damon Comes; A Night of Dark Intent; The Gentle Passing of a Hand; When All the Children Call My Name; Needle Song; Something There Is; Come Dance with Me on My Pony's Grave; The Three of Tens; Digging; From All the Fields of Hail and Fire; The Key to English; White Wolf Calling*

The only Arkham House title by this author. Most of the stories were published in magazines in the 1970s. Interior illustrations by Andrew Smith. No AH reprints. $50/10

160. **Collected Poems,** by Richard L. Tierney. Collection of poetry. (1981.) 82 pp. 1030 copies printed. Cover price $6.95. No dust jacket.

Contents: *A Man in the Crowd; The Altar; Sabbat; In Halls of Fantasy; To Gorice XII, King in Carcë; Night Visitant; The Nereid; The Dread-*

*ful City; The Madness of the Oracle; The Moon of Endless Night; Hate; The
Scrolls; Jack the Ripper; Moubata; The Garret-Room; In Evil Dreams; The
Hills; The Volcano; Demon-Star; The Pinnacles; Zarria; The Shadow; Star-
Dreams; The Mountain; The Sleeper; The Pilgrimage; The Vengeance of
Earth; The Evil House; Homesickness; A Vision on a Midsummer Night;
Fulfillment; The Doom Prophet; Found in a Storm-Destroyed Lighthouse;
Gods; Tahuantin-Suyu; Sonnet to a Box Elder Bug; The Legend; Yahweh;
Mountains of Madness; Carcosa; The Wendigo; The Great Cthulhu;
Carpathian Dream; The Swamp Dweller; To Mount Sinai; Dream; Escape;
Beyond the Maze; Zora Rach Nam Psarrion; The Image; The Great City;
Optimism; The Jewels; Giantess; The Cat; The Balcony; To a Girl Who Is
Too Gay; Minas Morgul; Mordor; Hope; Illusion; A Glimpse of Hell; Con-
tempt; The Serpent-Men; Enchantress; Prayer to Zathog; To the Hydrogen
Bomb.*

A premier collection of weird poems by a leading writer in the
genre. The second Arkham House paperback edition. Black cover with
gold spine lettering and signature. Interior illustrations by Jason Van
Hollander. No reprints. $75

161. **Blooded on Arachne,** by Michael Bishop. Collection of science
fiction stories. (1981.) 338 pp. 4081 copies printed. Cover price
$13.95. Jacket art by Ron Walotsky.

Contents: *Preface; Among the Hominids at Olduvai; Blooded on
Arachne; Cathadonian Odyssey; Effigies; The House of the Compassionate
Sharers; In Chinstrex Fortronza the People Are Machines; Leaps of Faith;
On the Street of the Serpents; Piñon Fall; Rogue Tomato; Spacemen and
Gypsies; The White Otter of Childhood; For the Lady of a Physicist.*

The author's first short story science fiction collection. Interior
illustrations by Glenn Ray Tutor. No AH reprints. $45/10

162. **The Darkling,** by David Kesterton. Fantasy novel. (1982.) 259
pp. 3126 copies printed. Cover price $12.95. Jacket art by Ray-
mond Bayless. The Canadian author's first book. No reprints. Still
in print. $45/10

163. **The Wind from a Burning Woman,** by Greg Bear. Collection of
science fiction stories. (1982.) 270 pp. 3046 copies printed. Cover
price $13.95. Jacket art by Vincent Di Fate.

Contents: *Preface; The Wind from a Burning Woman; The White Horse Child; Petra; Scattershot; Mandala; Hardfought.*

A superb first short story collection of science fiction by an author who is considered a leading science fiction writer today. Greg Bear's first hardcover book and the fastest selling Arkham House title. Interior illustrations by Dennis Neal Smith. Second printing in 1983 (1503 copies). Still in print. First printing $150/30; second printing $30/5

The Wind from a Burning Woman, by Greg Bear (1982). Cover art by Vincent Di Fate. No. 163.

164. **The House of the Wolf,** by Basil Copper. Victorian werewolf novel. (1983.) 298 pp. 3578 copies printed. Cover price $14.95. Jacket art by Stephen E. Fabian.

No reprints. Another gothic novel from Copper's pen. Not quite the same caliber as *Necropolis,* but the Stephen Fabian jacket painting and interior drawings makes this a very attractive book. $50/12

165. **The Zanzibar Cat,** by Joanna Russ. Collection of vampire, ghost and science fiction stories. (1983.) 244 pp. 3526 Copies printed. Cover price $13.95. Jacket art by James C. Christiansen.

Contents: *Foreword,* by Marge Piercy; *When It Changed; The Extraordinary Voyage of Amélie Bertrand; The Soul of a Servant; Gleepsite; Nobody's Home; My Dear Emily; The New Men; My Boat; Useful Phrases for the Tourist; Corruption; There is Another Shore, You Know, Upon the Other Side; A Game of Vlet; How Dorothy Kept Away the Spring; Poor Man, Beggar Man; Old Thoughts, Old Presences; The Zanzibar Cat.*

The well-known American author's first science fiction short story collection, with interior illustrations by Dennis Neal Smith. No reprints. $75/20

166. One Winter in Eden, by Michael Bishop. Collection of fantasy stories. (1984.) 273 pp. 3596 copies printed. Cover price $13.95. Jacket art by Raymond Bayless.

Contents: *Introduction,* by Thomas M. Disch; *One Winter in Eden; Seasons of Belief; Cold War Orphans; The Yukio Mishima Cultural Association of Kudzu Valley, Georgia; Out of the Mouth of Olympus; Patriots; Collaborating; Within the Walls of Tyre; The Monkey's Bride; Vernalfest Morning; Saving Face; The Quickening.*

The author's second Arkham House short story collection, with interior illustrations by Andrew Smith. No reprints. $35/10

167. Watchers at the Strait Gate, by Russell Kirk. Collection of supernatural stories. (1984.) 256 pp. 3459 copies printed. Cover price $14.95. Jacket art by Renée Redell.

Contents: *A Cautionary Note on the Ghostly Tale; The Invasion of the Church of the Holy Ghost; The Surly Sullen Bell; The Peculiar Demesne of Archvicar Geronion; Uncle Isaiah; The Reflex Man in Whinnymuir Close;*

What Shadows We Pursue; Lex Talionis; Fate's Purse; An Encounter by Mortstone Pond; Watchers at the Strait Gate.

The author's second Arkham House short story collection, with most of the stories written in the 1960s. No reprints. $40/10

168. Who Made Stevie Crye?, by Michael Bishop. Southern horror novel. (1984.) 309 pp. 3591 copies printed. Cover price $15.95. Jacket art by Glennray Tutor. Interior illustrations by Jeffrey K. Potter. The author's first Arkham House novel. Still in print. No AH reprints. $35/8

The Zanzibar Cat, by Joanna Russ (1983). Cover art by James C. Christiansen. No. 165.

169. The Dunwich Horror and Others, by H.P. Lovecraft. Cor-

rected sixth printing of No. 71, edited by S.T. Joshi. (1984.) 433
pp. 4124 copies printed. Cover price $15.95. Jacket art by Ray-
mond Bayless.

Contents: *A Note on the Texts*, by S.T. Joshi; *Heritage of Horror*, by
Robert Bloch; *In the Vault; Pickman's Model; The Rats in the Wall; The
Outsider; The Colour Out of Space; The Music of Eric Zann; The Haunter
of the Dark; The Picture in the House; The Call of Cthulhu; The Dunwich
Horror; Cool Air; The Whisperer in Darkness; The Terrible Old Man; The
Thing on the Doorstep; The Shadow over Innsmouth; The Shadow Out of
Time*.

The first of four revised and corrected new editions of Lovecraft's
tales, competently edited by Joshi on the basis of consultation of original manuscripts and other sources. Reprints are as follows: Seventh
printing in 1985 (3675 copies). Eighth printing in 1988 (4783 copies).
Ninth printing in 1992 (4973 copies). Tenth printing in 1997 (2945
copies). Eleventh printing in 2000 (no print numbers given). Still in
print. 1984 printing $75/15; others cover price

170. **Lovecraft's Book**, by Richard A. Lupoff. Fictionalized historical
novel about H.P. Lovecraft. (1985.) 260 pp. 3544 copies printed.
Cover price $15.95. Jacket art by Jeffrey K. Potter. Photo by Ansel
Weston. The story centers around Lovecraft's involvement in an
unlikely Nazi plot to overthrow the United States government.
Not a convincing or realistic portrayal of either persons or course
of events. No AH reprints. $60/15

171. **At the Mountains of Madness and Other Novels**, by H.P. Lovecraft. Corrected fifth printing of No. 82, edited by S.T. Joshi.
(1985.) 458 pp. 3990 copies printed. Cover price $16.95. Jacket art
by Raymond Bayless.

Contents: *A Note on the Texts*, by S.T. Joshi; *A Mythos in His Own
Image*, by James Turner; *At the Mountain of Madness; The Case of Charles
Dexter Ward; The Shunned House; The Dreams in the Witch House; The
Statement of Randolph Carter; The Dream Quest of Unknown Kadath; The
Silver Key; Through the Gates of the Silver Key* (with E. Hoffmann Price).

The second of four revised and corrected new editions of Lovecraft's tales, competently edited by Joshi on the basis of consultation of
original manuscripts and other sources. Reprints are as follows: Sixth

printing in 1987 (4077 copies). Seventh printing in 1991 (4461 copies). Eight printing in 1997 (3032). Ninth printing in 2001 (no print numbers given). Still in print. 1985 printing $75/15; others cover price

172. **Tales of the Quintana Roo,** by James Tiptree, Jr. Collection of three linked stories. (1986.) 101 pp. 3673 copies printed. Cover price $11.95. Jacket art by Glenn Ray Tutor.

Contents: *What Came Ashore at Lirios; The Boy Who Waterskied to Forever; Beyond the Dead Reef.*

A slim volume of science fiction stories by the prominent American writer Alice Hastings Bradley Sheldon, writing under the above pseudonym. No reprints. $35/10

173. **Dreams of Dark and Light,** by Tanith Lee. Collection of fantasy and science fiction stories. (1986.) 507 pp. 3957 copies printed. Cover price $21.95. Jacket art by Max Ernst.

Contents: *Foreword,* by Rosemary Hawley Jarman; *Because Our Skins Are Finer; Bite-Me-Not, or, Fleur de Fur; Black as Ink; Bright Burning Tiger; Cyrion in Wax; A Day in the Skin (or, The Century We Were out of Them); The Dry Season; Elle Est Trois (La Mort); Foreign Skins; The Gorgon; La Reine Blanche; A Lynx with Lions; Magritte's Secret Agent; Medra; Nunc Dimittis; Odds Against the Gods; A Room with a Vie; Sirriamnis; Southern Lights; Tamastara; When the Clock Strikes; Wolfland; Written in Water.*

A premier collection of the best works of the noted and prolific American fantasy and science fiction writer. Interior illustrations by Douglas Smith. No reprints. $75/18

174. **Dagon and Other Macabre Tales,** by H.P. Lovecraft. Corrected fifth printing of No. 88, edited by S.T. Joshi. (1986.) 448 pp. 4023 Copies printed. Cover price $18.95. Jacket art by Raymond Bayless.

Contents: *A Note on the Texts,* by S.T. Joshi; *A Dreamer's Tales,* by T.E.D. Klein; *The Tomb; Dagon; Polaris; Beyond the Wall of Sleep; The White Ship; The Doom That Came to Sarnath; The Tree; The Cats of Ulthar; The Temple; Facts Concerning the Late Arthur Jermyn and His Family; Celephaïs; From Beyond; The Nameless City; The Quest of Iranon; The Moon-Bog; The Other Gods; Herbert West-Reanimator; Hypnos; The*

Hound; The Lurking Fear; The Unnameable; The Festival; Under the Pyramids (with Harry Houdini); *The Horror at Red Hook; He; The Strange High House in the Mist; The Evil Clergyman; In the Walls of Eryx* (with Kenneth Sterling); *The Beast in the Cave; The Alchemist; The Transition of Juan Romero; The Street; Poetry and the Gods* (with Anna Helen Crofts); *Azathoth; The Descendant; The Book; Supernatural Horror in Literature;* Index to "Supernatural Horror in Literature"; Chronology of the Fiction of H.P. Lovecraft, by S.T. Joshi.

The third of four revised and corrected new editions of Lovecraft's tales, competently edited by Joshi on the basis of consultation of original manuscripts and other sources. Reprints are as follows: Sixth printing in 1987 (3932 copies). Seventh printing in 1991 (3996 copies). Eighth printing in 1997 (3025) Ninth printing in 2001 (no print numbers given). Still in print. 1986 printing $65/12; others cover price

175. **The Jaguar Hunter**, by Lucius Shepard. Collection of horror and science fiction stories. (1987.) 404 pp. 3194 copies printed. Cover price $21.95. Jacket art and interior illustrations by Jeffrey K. Potter.

Contents: *Foreword,* by Michael Bishop; *The Jaguar Hunter; The Night of the White Bhairab; Salvador; How the Wind Spoke at Madaket; Black Coral; R & R; The End of Life as We Know It; A Traveler's Tale; Mengele; The Man Who Painted the Dragon Griaule; A Spanish Lesson.*

An outstanding collection of stories by a very talented American novelist and poet. First Arkham House title by the author. The majority of stories first appeared in science fiction magazines in the mid–1980s. Second printing in 1987 (1508 copies). First printing $125/25; second printing $50/12

The Jaguar Hunter, by Lucius Shepard (1987). Cover art by jeffrey K. Potter. No. 175.

176. **Polyphemus,** by Michael Shea. Collection of horror and science fiction stories. (1987.) 245 pp. 3528 copies printed. Cover price $16.95. Jacket art by Harry O. Morris.

Contents: *Foreword,* by Algis Budrys; *Polyphemus; The Angel of Death; Uncle Tuggs; The Pearls of the Vampire Queen; The Horror on the #33; The Extra; The Autopsy.*

The author's first hardcover book. Most stories in the collection first appeared in *The Magazine of Fantasy and Science Fiction* in the 1970s and 1980s. Interior illustrations by John Stewart. No AH reprints. $100/20

177. **A Rendezvous in Averoigne,** by Clark Ashton Smith. Collection of fantasy and supernatural stories. (1988.) 472 pp. 5025 copies printed. Cover price $22.95. Jacket art and interior illustrations by Jeffrey K. Potter.

Contents: *Introduction,* by Ray Bradbury; *The Holiness of Azédarac; The Colossus of Ylourgne; The End of the Story; Atlantis; The Last Incantation; The Death of Malygris; A Voyage of Sfanomoë; The Weird of Avoosl Wuthoqquan; The Seven Geases; The Tale of Satampra Zeiros; The Coming of the White Worm; The City of the Singing Flame; The Dweller in the Gulf; The Chain of Aforgomon; Genius Loci; The Maze of Maal Dweb; The Vaults of Yoh-Vombis; The Uncharted Isle; The Planet of the Dead; Master of the Asteroid; The Empire of the Necromancers; The Charnel God; Xeethra; The Dark Eidolon; The Death of Ilalotha; The Last Hieroglyph; Necromancy in Naat; The Garden of Adompha; The Isle of the Torturers; Morthylla.*

A collection of reprints of the author's best and best known stories, drawn from many of Smith's series. Second printing, with new cover art, in 2003 (No. 204). $75/15

178. **Memories of the Space Age,** by J.G. Ballard. Collection of science fiction stories. (1988.) 216 pp. 4903 copies printed. Cover price $16.95. Jacket art is a reproduction of Max Ernst's painting "Europe after the Rain."

Contents: *The Cage of Sand; A Question of Re-entry; The Dead Astronaut; My Dream of Flying to Wake Island; News from the Sun; Memories of the Space Age; Myths of the Near Future; The Man Who Walked on the Moon.*

A sterling collection of interrelated science fiction stories by one of Britain's greatest contemporary writers of fantasy and science fiction. Interior illustrations by Jeffrey K. Potter. No reprints. $35/8

MEMORIES OF THE SPACE AGE

179. Crystal Express, by Bruce Sterling. Collection of science fiction stories. (1989.) 264 pp. 4231 copies printed. Cover price $18.95. Jacket art by Rick Lieder.

Contents: *Swarm; Spider Rose; Cicada Queen; Sunken Gardens; Twenty Evocations; Green Days on Brunei; Spook; The Beautiful and the Sublime; Telliamed; The Little Magic Shop; Flowers of Edo; Dinner in Audoghast.*

The only Arkham House collection of stories to date by one of the American authors commonly associated with the "cyberpunk" movement in science fiction writing. No AH reprints. $50/10

J. G. BALLARD

Memories of the Space Age, by J.G. Ballard (1988). Cover art by Max Ernst. No. 178.

180. The Horror in the Museum and Other Revisions, by H.P. Lovecraft. Corrected third printing of No. 115, edited by S.T. Joshi. (1989.) 450 pp. 5062 copies printed. Cover price $18.95. Jacket art by Raymond Bayless.

Contents: *A Note on the Texts*, by S.T. Joshi; *Lovecraft's "Revisions,"* by August Derleth; *The Green Meadow* (with Elizabeth Berkeley; *The Crawling Chaos* (with Elizabeth Berkeley); *The Last Test* (with Adolphe de Castro); *The Electric Executioner* (with Adolphe de Castro); *The Curse of Yig* (with Zealia Bishop); *The Mound* (with Zealia Bishop); *Medusa's Coil* (with Zealia Bishop); *The Man of Stone* (with Hazel Heald); *The Horror in the Museum* (with Hazel Heald); *Winged Death* (with Hazel Heald); *Out of the Aeons* (with Hazel Heald); *The Horror in the Burying-Ground* (with Hazel Heald); *The Diary of Alonzo Typer* (with William Lumley); *The Horror at Martin's Beach* (with Sonia Green); *Ashes* (with C.M. Eddy, Jr.); *The Ghost-Eater* (with C.M. Eddy, Jr.); *The Loved Dead* (with C.M. Eddy, Jr.); *Deaf, Dumb, and Blind* (with C.M. Eddy, Jr.); *Two Black Bottles* (with Wilfred B. Talman); *The Trap* (with Henry S. Whitehead); *The Tree on the Hill* (with Duane W. Rimel); *The Disinterment* (with Duane W. Rimel); *"Till All the Seas"* (with R.H. Barlow); *The Night Ocean* (with R.H. Barlow).

The final volume of four revised and corrected new editions of Lovecraft's tales and revisions, competently edited by Joshi on the basis of consultation of original manuscripts and other sources. Reprints as follows: Fourth printing in 1992 (4994 copies). Fifth printing in 2002 (no print numbers given). Still in print. 1989 printing $45/10; others cover price

181. Her Smoke Rose Up Forever, by James Tiptree, Jr. Collection of fantasy and supernatural stories. (1990.) 520 pp. 4108 copies printed. Cover price $25.95. Jacket art by Andrew Smith.

Contents: *Introduction,* by John Clute; *The Last Flight of Dr. Ain; The Screwfly Solution; And I Awoke and Found Me Here on the Cold Hill's Side; The Girl Who was Plugged In; The Man Who Walked Home; And I Have Come Upon This Place by Lost Ways; The Women Men Don't See; Your Faces, O my Sisters! Your Faces Filled of Light!; Houston, Houston, Do You Read?; With Delicate Mad Hands; A Momentary Taste of Being; We Who Stole the Dream; Her Smoke Rose Up Forever; Love is the Plan the Plan Is Death; On the Last Afternoon; She Waits for All Men Born; Slow Music; And So On, and So On.*

A posthumous collection of the author's best science fiction stories, primarily written during the 1970s. A premium collection showing great talent and imagination. No AH reprints. $60/15

182. Tales of the Cthulhu Mythos, by H.P. Lovecraft and Divers Hands. Revised edition of title No. 108, edited by James Turner. (1990.) 529 pp. 7015 copies printed. Cover price $23.95. Jacket art and illustrations by Jeffrey K. Potter.

Contents: *Iä! Iä! Cthulhu fhtagn!,* by James Turner; *The Call of Cthulhu,* by H.P. Lovecraft; *The Return of the Sorcerer,* by Clark Ashton Smith; *Ubbo-Sathla,* by Clark Ashton Smith; *The Black Stone,* by Robert E, Howard; *The Hounds of Tindalos,* by Frank Belknap Long; *The Space-Eaters,* by Frank Belknap Long; *The Dweller in Darkness,* by August

Derleth; *Beyond the Threshold,* by August Derleth; *The Shambler from the Stars,* by Robert Bloch; *The Haunter of the Dark,* by H.P. Lovecraft; *The Shadow from the Steeple,* by Robert Bloch; *Notebook Found in a Deserted House,* by Robert Bloch; *The Salem Horror,* by Henry Kuttner; *The Terror from the Depths,* by Fritz Leiber; *Rising with Surtsey,* by Brian Lumley; *Cold Print,* by J. Ramsey Campbell; *The Return of the Lloigor,* by Colin Wilson; *My Boat,* by Joanna Russ; *Sticks,* by Karl Edward Wagner; *The Freshman,* by Philip José Farmer; *Jerusalem's Lot,* by Stephen King; *Discovery of the Ghooric Zone,* by Richard A. Lupoff.

A fiftieth anniversary edition, which contains much of the same material as its predecessor, but with some new stories added. Although this title had the largest printing in the history of Arkham House, a second printing was done in 2000 (no print numbers given). Still in print. First printing $45/10; second printing cover price

183. **Gravity's Angels,** by Michael Swanwick. Collection of science fiction stories. (1991.) 302 pp. 4119 copies printed. Cover price $20.95. Jacket art by Pablo Picasso.

Contents: *A Midwinter's Tale; The Feast of Saint Janis; The Blind Minotaur; The Transmigration of Philip K; Covenant of Souls; The Dragon Line; Mummer Kiss; Trojan Horse; Snow Angels; The Man Who Met Picasso; Foresight; Ginungagap; The Edge of the World.*

The author's first collection of science fiction. Interior illustrations by Janet Aulisio. No reprints. Still in print. $35/8

184. **The Ends of the Earth,** by Lucius Shepard. Collection of science fiction. (1991.) 484 pp. 4655 copies printed. Cover price $24.95. Jacket art by Jeffrey K. Potter.

Contents: *The Ends of the Earth; Delta Sly Honey; Bound for Glory; The Exercise of Faith; Nomans Land; Life of Buddha; Shades; Aymara; A Wooden Tiger; The Black Clay Boy; Fire Zone Emerald; On the Border; The Scalehunter's Beautiful Daughter; Surrender.*

The second Arkham House collection of the author's science fiction stories which first appeared in magazines in the mid to late 1980s. No AH reprints. Still in print. $50/15

185. **Lord Kelvin's Machine,** by James P. Blaylock. Fantasy/science fiction novel. (1992.) 262 pp. 4015 copies printed. Cover price

$19.95. Jacket art and interior illustrations by Jeffrey K. Potter. No AH reprints. Still in print. $45/10

186. **Meeting in Infinity,** by John Kessel. Collection of allegories and extrapolations. (1992.) 309 pp. 3547 copies printed. Cover price $20.95. Jacket art by Edward Munch. Contents:
Meeting in Infinity; The Pure Product; Mrs. Shummel Exits a Winner; The Big Dream; The Lecturer; Hearts Do Not in Eyes Shine; Faustfathers; A Clean Escape; Not Responsible! Park and Lock It!; Man; Invaders; Judgment Call; Buddha Nostril Bird; Another Orphan; Buffalo.
The first short story collection by the American science fiction author. Most stories were published in science fiction magazines between 1982 and 1992. No reprints. Still in print. $30/8

187. **The Aliens of Earth,** by Nancy Kress. Collection of science fiction stories. (1993.) 327 pp. 3520 copies printed. Cover price $20.95. Jacket art by Ed Paschke.
Contents: *The Price of Oranges; Glass; People Like Us; Cannibals; To Scale; Touchdown; Down Behind Cuba Lake; In a World Like This; Philippa's Hands; Inertia; Phone Repairs; The Battle of Long Island; Renaissance; Spillage; The Mountains to Mohammed; Craps; And Wild for to Hold; In Memoriam.*
The author's first Arkham House collection of science fiction stories. Interior illustrations by Jane Walker. No reprints. Still in print. $25/8

188. **Alone with the Horrors,** by Ramsey Campbell. Collection of ghost and horror stories. (1993.) 515 pp. 3834 copies printed. Cover price $26.95. Jacket art and interior illustrations by Jeffrey K. Potter.
Contents: *So Far* (introduction); *The Room on the Castle; Cold Print; The Scar; The Interloper; The Guy; The End of a Summer's Day; The Man in the Underpass; The Companion; Call First; Heading Home; In the Bag; Baby; The Chimney; Stages; The Brood; Loveman's Comeback; The Gap; The Voice of the Beach; Out of Copyright; Above the World; Mackintosh Willy; The Show Goes On; The Ferries; Midnight Hobo; The Depths; Down There; The Fit; Hearing is Believing; The Hands; Again; Just Waiting; Seeing the World; Old Clothes; Apples; The Other Side; Where the Heart Is; Boiled Alive; Another World; End of the Line.*

The ultimate Ramsey Campbell collection of horror and super-natural stories. This hefty volume includes stories representing Campbell's entire writing career, including some of his early stories in previous Arkham House titles and also, new unpublished works. A key title. No AH reprints. $50/10

189. The Breath of Suspension, by Alexander Jablokov. Collection of science fiction stories. (1994.) 318 pp. 3496 copies printed. Cover price $20.95. Jacket art and illustrations by Jeffrey K. Potter.

Contents: *The Breath of Suspension; Living Will; Many Mansions; The Death Artist; At the Cross-Time Jaunter's Ball; Above Ancient Seas; Deathbinder; The Ring of Memory; Beneath the Shadow of Her Smile; A Deeper Sea.*

The author's first short story collection, including some stories published in *Asimov's Science Fiction Magazine* in the 1980s and 1990s. No reprints. Still in print. $25/8

190. Cthulhu 2000, by James Turner (ed.). Cthulhu inspired stories by various writers. (1995.) 413 pp. 4927 copies printed. Cover price $24.95. Jacket art and illustrations by Bob Eggleton.

Contents: *Cthulhu 2000,* by James Turner; *The Barrens,* by F. Paul Wilson; *Pickman's Modem,* by Lawrence Watt-Evans; *Shaft Number 247,* by Basil Copper; *His Mouth Will Taste of Wormwood,* by Poppy Z. Brite; *The Adder,* by Fred Chappell; *Fat Face,* by Michael Shea; *The Big Fish,* by Kim Newman; *"I Had Vacantly Crumpled It into My Pocket... But by God, Eliot, It was a Photograph from Life!",* by Joanna Russ; *H.P.L.,* by Gahan Wilson; *The Unthinkable,* by Bruce Sterling; *Black Man with a Horn,* by T.E.D. Klein; *Love's Eldritch Ichor,* by Esther M. Friesner; *The Last Feast of Harlequin,* by Thomas Ligotti; *The Shadow on the Doorstep,* by James P. Blaylock; *Lord of the Land,* by Gene Wolf; *The Faces at Pine Dunes,* by Ramsey Campbell; *On the Slab,* by Harlan Ellison; *24 Views of Mt. Fuji, by Hokusai,* by Roger Zelazny.

A collection of "Cthulhu" inspired future stories by various writers. A landmark edition of forward and alternate treatments of the Lovecraftian created "Mythos." No reprints. Still in print. $30/10

191. Miscellaneous Writings, by H.P. Lovecraft. Essays, collaborations, critics and other writings, edited by S.T. Joshi and James

Turner. (1995.) 568 pp. 4959 copies printed. Cover price $29.95.
Jacket design by James Turner.
Contents: *Introduction*, by S.T. Joshi; *The Little Glass Bottle; The
Secret Cave; The Mystery of the Grave Yard; The Mysterious Ship; A Rem-
iniscence of Dr. Samuel Johnson; Old Bugs; Memory; Nyarlathotep; Ex
Oblivione; What the Moon Brings; Sweet Ermengarde; The Very Old Folk;
History of the Necronomicon; Ibid; Discarded Draft of "The Shadow over
Innsmouth"; The Battle That Ended the Century* (with R.H. Barlow); *Col-
lapsing Cosmoses* (with R.H. Barlow); *The Challenge from Beyond* (with
C.L. Moore, A Merritt, Robert E. Howard, and Frank Belknap Long);
*Commonplace Book; Lord Dunsany and His Work; Notes on Writing Weird
Fiction; Some Notes on Interplanetary Fiction; In Memoriam: Robert Ervin
Howard; Idealism and Materialism; Life for Humanity's Sake; In Defense
of Dagon; Nietzscheism and Realism; The Materialist Today; Some Causes
of Self-Immolation; Heritage or Modernism: Common Sense in Art Forms;
Metrical Regularity; The Vers Libre Epidemic; The Case for Classicism; Lit-
erary Composition; Ars Gratis Artis; The Poetry of Lillian Middleton; Rudis
Indigestaque Moles; In the Editor's Study; The Professional Incubus; The
Omnipresent Philistine; What Belongs in Verse; The Crime of the Century;
More Chain Lightning; Old England and the "Hyphen"; Revolutionary
Mythology; Americanism; The League; Bolshevism; Some Repetitions on the
Times; Vermont—A First Impression; Observations on Several Parts of
America; Travels in the Provinces of America; An Account of Charleston;
Some Dutch Footprint in New England; Homes and Shrines of Poe; In a
Major Key; The Dignity of Journalism; Symphony and Stress; United Ama-
teur Press Association: Exponent of Amateur Journalism; A Reply to the Lin-
gerer; Les Mouches Fantastiques; For What Does the United Stand?; Amateur
Journalism: Its Possible Needs and Betterment; What Amateurdom and I
Have Done for Each Other; Lucubrations Lovecraftian; A Matter of Unit-
eds; Mrs. Miniter-Estimates and Recollections; Some Current Motives and
Practices; Trans-Neptunian Planets; The Earth Not Hollow; To the All-
Story Weekly; Science versus Charlatanry; The Fall of Astrology; To Edwin
Baird; To Edwin Baird; The Old Brick Road; To Nils H. Frome; The Brief
Autobiography of an Inconsequential Scribbler; Within the Gates; A Con-
fession of Unfaith; Commercial Blurbs; Cats and Dogs; Some Notes on a
Nonentity;* Bibliography.

A large volume of Lovecraft's miscellaneous writings, divided into
nine specific sections, each covering particular aspects of Lovecraft's

material. Some items are reprinted from earlier Arkham House titles. Several essays are published here for the first time and other items are Lovecraft contributions to the amateur press. No reprints. Still in print. $35/10

192. Synthesis & Other Virtual Realities, by Mary Rosenblum. Collection of science fiction stories. (1996.) 280 pp. 3515 copies printed. Cover price $21.95. Jacket design by Bob Eggleton.

Contents: *Water Bringer; Entrada; The Centaur Garden; Second Chance; Bordertown; Synthesis; Flood Tide; The Rain Stone; Stairway.*

The author's first collection of short stories, previously published in *Asimov's Science Fiction Magazine* in the early 1990s. Interior illustrations by Elizabeth Lawhead Bourne. No reprints. Still in print. $25/5

193. Voyages by Starlight, by Ian R. MacLeod. Collection of horror and science fiction stories. (1996.) 269 pp. 2542 copies printed. Cover price $21.95. Jacket art by Nicholas Jainschigg.

Contents: *Foreword,* by Michael Swanwick; *Ellen O'Hara; Green; Starship Day; The Giving Mouth; The Perfect Stranger; Tirkiluk; Papa; 1/72 Scale; Marnie; Grownups.*

The author's first book, a collection of stories published in science fiction magazines in the early 1990s. No reprints. Still in print. $25/5

194. Flowers from the Moon and Other Lunacies, by Robert Bloch. Collection of weird, horror and science fiction stories. (1998.) 296 pp. 2565 copies printed. Cover price $22.95. Jacket art and design by Tony Patrick and Martin Hertzel.

Contents: *Introduction,* by Robert M. Price; *The Druidic Doom; Fangs of Vengeance; Death is an Elephant; A Question of Identity; Death Has Five Guesses; The Bottomless Pool; The Dark Isle; Flowers from the Moon; He Waits Beneath the Sea; Power of the Druid; Be Yourself; A Sorcerer Runs for Sheriff; Black Bargain; A Bottle of Gin; Wine of the Sabbat; Soul Proprietor; Satan's Phonograph; The Man Who Told the Truth; The Night They Crashed the Party; Philtre Tip.*

After a long absence, Robert Bloch returns with a volume of previously uncollected stories from *Weird Tales* and other pulp magazines, published from the 1930s to the 1950s. No reprint. Still in print. $30/8

195. Lovecraft Remembered, by Peter Cannon (ed.). Collection of memoirs, letters, essays and other items by various writers. (1998.) 486 pp. 3579 copies printed. Cover price $29.95. Jacket art by Jason C. Eckhardt.

Contents: *Introduction,* by Peter Cannon; *His Own Most Fantastic Creation,* by Winfield Townley Scott; *Miscellaneous Impressions of H.P.L.,* by Marian F. Bonner; *A Glimpse of H.P.L.,* by Mary V. Dana; *Lovecraft's Sensitivity,* by August Derleth; *Three Hours with H.P. Lovecraft,* by Dorothy Walter; *A Gentleman from Angell Street,* by Muriel Eddy; *Lovecraft, My Childhood Friend,* by Harold W. Munro; *Little Journeys to the Homes of Prominent Amateurs,* by Andrew Francis Lockhart; *Amateur Writings,* by Edith Miniter; *Amateur Writings,* by George Julian Houtain; *Howard Phillips Lovecraft: The Sage of Providence,* by Maurice W. Moe; *A Tribute from the Past,* by Ira Cole; *Idiosyncrasies of H.P.L.,* by E.A. Edkins; *Ave Atque Vale!,* by Edward H. Cole; *In Memoriam: Howard Phillips Lovecraft: Recollections, Appreciations, Estimates,* by W. Paul Cook; *Discourse on H.P.L.,* by Rheinhart Kleiner; *Memories of a Friendship,* by Alfred Galpin; *Young Man Lovecraft,* by L. Sprague de Camp; *A Few Memories,* by James F. Morton; *Some Random Memories of H.P.L.,* by Frank Belknap Long; *Bards and Bibliophiles,* by Rheinhart Kleiner; *A Memoir of Lovecraft,* by Rheinhart Kleiner; *Howard Phillips Lovecraft,* by Samuel Loveman; *Lovecraft as a Conversationalist,* by Samuel Loveman; *The Normal Lovecraft,* by Wilfred B. Talman; *Walkers in the City: George Willard Kirk and Howard Phillips Lovecraft in New York City, 1924-1926,* by Mara Kirk Hart.; *In Memoriam,* by Hazel Heald; *Lovecraft as I Knew Him,* by Sonia H. Davis; *H.P. Lovecraft: A Pupil's View,* by Zealia Bishop; *Memories of Lovecraft: I,* by Sonia H. Davis; *Memories of Lovecraft: II,* by Helen V. Sully; *Letter to Weird Tales,* by Robert Bloch; *Letter to Weird Tales,* by Clark Ashton Smith; *A Tribute to Lovecraft,* by Robert W. Lowndes; *The Genius of Lovecraft,* by Henry George Weiss (Francis Flagg); *The Man Who Was Lovecraft,* by E. Hoffmann Price; *My Correspondence with Lovecraft,* by Fritz Leiber; *Lovecraft in Providence,* by Donald Wandrei; *Out of the Ivory Tower,* by Robert Bloch; *H.P.L.: A Reminiscence,* by H. Warner Munn; *Recollections of H.P. Lovecraft,* by Vrest Orton; *The Barlow Journal,* by R.H. Barlow; *The Wind That Is in the Grass: A Memoir of H.P. Lovecraft in Florida,* by R.H. Barlow; *Lovecraft's First Book,* by William Crawford; *H.P. Lovecraft: The House and the Shadows,* by J. Vernon Shea; *Caverns Measure-*

less to Man, by Kenneth Sterling; *Autumn in Providence: Harry K Brobst on Lovecraft,* by Will Murray; *A Note on Howard P. Lovecraft's Verse,* by Rheinhart Kleiner; *"Variety" Column,* by Howard Wolf; *Letter to Weird Tales,* by Robert E. Howard; *A Weird Writer Is in our Midst,* by Vrest Orton; *H.P. Lovecraft, Outsider,* by August Derleth; *Lovecraft and Benefit Street,* by Dorothy C. Walter; *H.P. Lovecraft: An Appreciation,* by T.O Mabbott; *Lovecraft and Science,* by Kenneth Sterling; *H.P. Lovecraft,* by Vincent Starrett; *The Lovecraft Legend,* by Vincent Starrett; *A Parenthesis on Lovecraft as Poet,* by Winfield Townley Scott; *The Lord of R'lyeh,* by Matthew H. Onderdonk; *Charon-in Reverse; or, H.P. Lovecraft versus the "Realists" of Fantasy,* by Matthew H. Onderdonk; *A Literary Copernicus,* by Fritz Leiber; *H.P. Lovecraft: An Evaluation,* by Joseph Payne Brennan; *Through Hyperspace with Brown Jenkin: Lovecraft's Contribution to Speculative Fiction,* by Fritz Leiber; *Epilogue: Lovecraft and Poe,* by Frank Belknap Long.

A voluminous tribute and probably the definite collection of Lovecraft memoirs by writers and other people who knew him. Much of the material has been reprinted from earlier Arkham House titles, but new tributes, essays and other items from other sources have been added. No reprints. Still in print. $30/8

196. **New Horizons,** by August Derleth (ed.). Yesterday's Portraits of Tomorrow. Collection of science fiction stories by various writers. (1999.) 299 pp. 2917 copies printed. Cover price $24.95. Jacket art and design by Stephen E. Fabian and Joseph Wrzos.

Contents: *Introduction,* by Joseph Wroz; *The Runaway Skyscraper,* by Murray Leinster; *A Dream of Armageddon,* by H.G. Wells; *Willie,* by Frank Belknap Long; *The Purblind Prophet,* by David H. Keller and Paul Spencer; *The Feline Light and Power Company,* by Jacque Morgan; *Solander's Radio Tomb,* by Ellis Parker Butler; *The Perambulating Home,* by Henry Hugh Simmons; *Countries in the Sea,* by August Derleth and Mark Schorer; *The Ultra-Elixir of Youth,* by A. Hyatt Verrill; *The Book of Worlds,* by Miles J. Breuer; *The Truth About The Psycho-tector,* by Stanton A. Coblentz; *Raiders of the Universe,* by Donald Wandrei; *The Planet Entity,* by E.M. Johnston and Clark Ashton Smith; Appendix: August Derleth's Science Fiction Anthologies, by Joseph Wroz.

The last science fiction anthology edited by August Derleth, with introduction and biographical notes by Joseph Wrzos. It contains a series of stories that Derleth had prepared in the 1960s, but never had printed. The stories spans the range of science fiction story-telling from 1900 to the 1940s. No reprints. Still in print. $25/5

197. **Dragonfly,** by Frederic S. Durbin. Fantasy, horror novel. (1999.) 300 pp. 4000 copies printed. Cover price $22.95. Jacket art and interior illustrations by Jason Van Hollander. The author's first published book. No reprints. Still in print. $25/5

198. **Sixty Years of Arkham House,** by S.T. Joshi (ed.). Biography and bibliography of Arkham House. (1999.) 281 pp. 3500 copies printed. Cover price $25.95. Jacket art and illustrations by Allen Koszowski.
Contents: *Preface; Arkham House: 1939–1969*, by August Derleth; *Arkham House: 1970–1999*, by S.T. Joshi; Bibliography; *Arkham House; Mycroft & Moran; Stanton & Lee;* Appendix: *The "Lost" Arkhams;* Reference Bibliography; Index of Names; Index of Titles.

A comprehensive work and an invaluable reference. The book updates August Derleth's *Thirty Years of Arkham House* (No. 111), and lists all titles (including Mycroft & Moran and Stanton & Lee) from 1939 to 1999. It is much more than an update, however, with extensive biographical and bibliographical notes on each title, and exhaustive indexes of names and titles. A must have book for any Arkham House collector. A key title. No reprints. Still in print. $28/5

Sixty Years of Arkham House, by S.T. Joshi (ed.) (1999). Cover art by Allen Koszowski. No. 198.

199. **Arkham's Masters of Horror,** by Peter Ruber (ed.). A sixtieth anniversary collection of weird stories and essays by some of the principal Arkham House writers.

(1999.) 443 pp. 4000 copies printed. Cover price $32.95. Jacket art and design by Tony Patrick and Martin Hertzel.

Contents: *Foreword*, by Peter Ruber; *Introduction: The Un-Demonizing of August Derleth*, by Peter Ruber; *Excerpts from the H.P. Lovecraft Letters to August Derleth*, by H.P. Lovecraft.; *Prince Alcouz and the Magician*, by Clark Ashton Smith; *Man-Hunt*, by Donald Wandrei; *The Valley of the Lost*, by Robert E. Howard; *The Bat Is My Brother*, by Robert Bloch; *The Latch-Key*, by H. Russell Wakefield; *Dyak Reward*, by Carl Jacobi; *Sea Tiger*, by Henry S. Whitehead; *The Dog-Eared Dog*, by Frank Belknap Long; *The Beautiful Lady*, by David H. Keller; *Sweetheart from the Tomb*, by E. Hoffmann Price; *Wolf of the Steppes*, by Greye La Spina; *Rhythmic Formula*, by Arthur J. Banks; *The Small Assassins*, by Ray Douglas Bradbury; *George Is All Right*, by Howard Wandrei; *Something Old*, by Mary Elizabeth Counselman; *Property of the Ring*, by John Ramsey Campbell; *Bon Voyage, Michele*, by Seabury Quinn; *The Master of Cotswold*, by Nelson Bond; *The Open Window*, by Vincent Starret; *A Visitor from the Outside*, by August Derleth & Mark Schorer.

A different anthology that features representative short stories by many of Arkham House's star writers, with each story preceded by a brief essay by the editor about the author. No reprints. Still in print. $33/8

200. In the Stone House, by Barry N. Malzberg. Collection of horror and science fiction stories. (2000.) 247 pp. 2500 copies printed. Cover price $25.95. Jacket art by Allan C. Servoss. Jacket design by Martin Hertzel.

Contents: *Heavy Metal; Turpentine; Quartermain; The Prince of the Steppes; Andante Lugubre; Standards & Practices; Darwinian Facts; Allegro Marcato; Something from the Seventies; The High Purpose; All Assassins; Understanding Entropy; Ship Full of Jews; Amos; Improvident Excess; Hitler at Nuremberg; Concerto Academico; The Intransigents; Hierartic Realignment; The Only Thing You Learn; Police Actions; Fugato; Major League Triceratops; In the Stone House.*

The first Arkham House collection of horror, fantasy and science fiction by a well-known American author with more than 90 novels and 350 short stories to his credit. All of the stories in this collection first appeared in *Fantasy and Science Fiction, Omni, Science Fiction Age* and other magazines in the late 1980s and early 1990s. No reprints. Still in print. $30/8

201. **Book of the Dead,** by E. Hoffman Price. Friends of Yesteryear: Fictioneers & Others. Collection of essays, memoirs and introductions of the early years of fantasy writing and its best known practitioners. (2001.) 423 pp. 4000 copies printed. Cover price $34.95. Jacket photography by Eric Carlson.

Contents: *E. Hoffmann Price: Introduction,* by Jack Williamson; *Some Notes on EHP and the Book of the Dead,* by Peter Ruber; Friends of Yesteryear: Fictioneers and Others; *Prologue; I Farnsworth Wright; II Otis Adelbert Kline; III Howard Phillips Lovecraft; IV Robert Ervin Howard; V Clark Ashton Smith; VI W.K. Mashburn, Jr.; VII Ralph Milne Farley (Roger Sherman Hoar); VIII Seabury Grandin Quinn; IX Hugh Doak Rankin; X The Varnished Vultures & Spider Bites; XI Barsoom Badigan; XII Harry Olmsted; XIII Albert Richard Wetjen; XIV Norbert W. Davis; XV Milo Ray Phelps; XVI William S. Bruner; XVII Henry Kuttner; XVIII August W. Derleth; XIX Edmond Hamilton; Epiloque;* Other Memories; *The Lovecraft Controversy; Why?,* by E. Hoffmann Price; *Five Million Words,* by Monte Lindsey; *Seabury Quinn: An Appreciation,* by E Hoffman Price; *Mortonius (James Ferdinand Morton),* by E. Hoffmann Price; *A Conversation with E. Hoffmann Price,* by Gregorio Montejo; *One Man's View of the Death of the Pulp Era,* by E. Hoffmann Price; *EHP: A Bibliography,* by Virgil Utter; Index.

A memorial book by one of America's best known pulp magazine writers. Illustrated with photos, the book contains biographical sketches of many of the prominent writers from the 'golden age of pulp'. The book concludes with a section of memories and essays written by Hoffmann and other writers of the time. No reprints. Still in print. $35/10

202. **The Far Side of Nowhere,** by Nelson Bond. Collection of weird stories selected by the author. (2001.) 423 pp. 2500 copies printed. Cover price $34.95. Jacket art and design by Alan Fore and Jen-Graph.

Contents: "Its About Time": *Command Performance; Parallel in Time; Time Exposure; Private Line to Tomorrow; The Castaway; The Message from the Void;* "Odds Without End": *The Battle of Blue Trout Basin; The Unusual Romance of Ferdinand Pratt; The Ballad of Blaster Bill; Case History; Herman and the Mermaid; Double, Double, Toil and Trouble; Proof of the Pudding; Pawns of Tomorrow;* "Family Circle": *Magic City; The*

Masked Marvel; The Scientific Pioneer Returns; Miracles Made Easy; "In Uffish Thought": *The Amazing Invention of Wilberforce Weems; Brother Michel; Pipeline to Paradise; The World Within; The Geometrics of Johnny Day;* "Wild Talents": *Mr. Snow White; The Unpremeditated Wizard; The Secret of Lucky Logan; The Fertility of Dalrymple Todd; The Man Who Weighed Minus Twelve; Occupation: Demigod;* Epilogue. The second Arkham House collection of weird fiction by the author. The stories first appeared in *Amazing Stories, Blue Book, Fantastic Adventures, Weird Tales* and other pulp magazines from 1937 to 1958. No reprints. Still in print $35/10

203. **The Cleansing,** by John D. Harvey. Fantasy novel. (2002.) The tale about an American wolf god who comes to Earth every century, to wreak retribution on humans for their abuse of nature. $35/8

204. **A Rendezvous in Averoigne,** by Clark Ashton Smith. Collection of fantasy stories. Reprint of No. 177. (2003.) $33/8

5

Mycroft & Moran Bibliography, (1945–1998)

The Arkham House imprint Mycroft & Moran was introduced in 1945, primarily for the publication of weird detective and mystery stories, many written by August Derleth and inspired by the Sherlock Holmes tales. The name of the imprint was derived from the names of Sherlock Holmes' brother, Mycroft Holmes, and that of Colonel Sebastian Moran, "the second most dangerous man in London." The imprint colophon, a deerstalker, was designed by Ronald Clyne and used from the beginning.

Titles are listed in chronological order as published. The majority of Mycroft & Moran titles are out of print; the few titles which are still in print are noted accordingly. The term "No reprints" indicates that the title has not been reprinted by any publisher. The term "No MM reprints" indicates that the title has not been reprinted by Mycroft & Moran, but may have been reprinted by other publishers.

The suggested values listed for books published from 1945 through 1974 are for titles in "fine/fine" condition. Books in better condition will demand higher prices, and books in lesser condition will cost less. Values listed for books published from 1975 through 1998 are for books in "very fine" to "near mint" condition. Books in lower grades will sell for less. The first noted value is for books in the original dust jacket; the second is for books without dust jacket or with facsimile jacket.

148

BIBLIOGRAPHY

M1. "In Re: Sherlock Holmes," by August Derleth. The Adventures of Solar Pons. The first collection of Solar Pons stories. (1945.) 238 pp. 3604 copies printed. Cover price $3.00. Jacket art by Ronald Clyne.

Contents: *In Re: Solar Pons*, by Vincent Starrett; *A Word from Dr. Lyndon Parker; The Adventure of the Frightened Baronet; The Adventure of the Late Mr. Faversham; The Adventure of the Black Narcissus; The Adventure of the Norcross Riddle; The Adventure of the Retired Novelist; The Adventure of the Three Red Dwarfs; The Adventure of the Sotheby Salesman; The Adventure of the Purloined Periapt; The Adventure of the Limping Man; The Adventure of the Seven Passengers; The Adventure of the Lost Holiday; The Adventure of the Man with the Broken Face.*

In Re: Sherlock Holmes, by August Derleth (1945). Cover art by Ronald Clyne. No. M1.

The first title published under the Mycroft & Moran imprint. It contains the first collection of August Derleth's Sherlock Holmes pastiches, featuring the Holmesian sleuth Solar Pons and his companion Dr. Lyndon Parker. The earliest of the stories were written in 1929. Stories are reprinted in No. 17. No other MM reprints. $225/80

M2. Carnacki, the Ghost-Finder, by William Hope Hodgson. Collection of supernatural detective stories. (1947.) 241 pp. 3050 copies printed. Cover price $3.00. Jacket art by Frank Utpatel.

Contents: *The Thing Invisible; The Gateway of the Monster; The House Among the Laurels; The Whistling Room; The Searcher of the End*

House; The Horse of the Invisible; The Haunted "Jarvee"; The Find; The Hog.
An significant collection of psychic/supernatural detective stories. Originally published in London in 1913, the Mycroft & Moran edition contains three more stories obtained by Derleth from the Hodgson family. No MM reprints. $150/40

M3. The Memoirs of Solar Pons, by August Derleth. Collection of Solar Pons stories. (1951.) 245 pp. 2038 copies printed. Cover price $3.00. Jacket art by Frank Utpatel.
Contents: *Introduction*, by Ellery Queen; *The Adventure of the Circular Room; The Adventure of the Perfect Husband; The Adventure of the Broken Chessman; The Adventure of the Dog in the Manger; The Adventure of the Proper Comma; The Adventure of Ricoletti of the Club Foot; The Adventure of the Six Silver Spiders; The Adventure of the Lost Locomotive; The Adventure of the Tottenham Werewolf; The Adventure of the Five Royal Coachmen; The Adventure of the Paralytic Mendicant.*

The second collection of Solar Pons adventures. Stories are reprinted in No. 17. No other MM reprints. $200/50

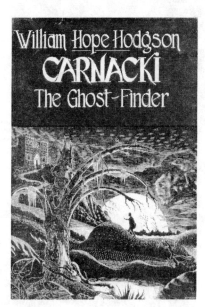

Carnacki, the Ghost Finder, by William Hope Hodgson (1947). Cover art by Frank Utpatel. No. M2.

M4. Three Problems for Solar Pons, by August Derleth. Three Solar Pons stories. (1952.) 112 pp. 996 copies printed. Cover price $2.50. Jacket art by Ronald Clyne.
Contents: *A Note for the Aficionado; The Adventure of the Rydberg Numbers; The Adventure of the Remarkable Worm; The Adventure of the Camberwell Beauty.*
A slim interim volume, with a small printing. All three stories were reprinted in the following title, *The Return of Solar Pons* and also reprinted in No. 17. No other MM reprints. $350/100

M5. The Return of Solar Pons, by August Derleth. Collection of Solar Pons stories. (1958.) 261 pp. 2079 copies printed. Cover price $4.00. Jacket art by Frank Utpatel.

Contents: *Introduction,* by Edgar W. Smith; *The Adventure of the Lost Dutchman; The Adventure of the Devil's Footprints; The Adventure of the Dorrington Inheritance; The Adventure of the "Triple Kent"; The Adventure of the Rydberg Numbers; The Adventure of the Grice-Paterson Curse; The Adventure of the Stone of Scone; The Adventure of the Remarkable Worm; The Adventure of the Penny Magenta; The Adventure of the Trained Cormorant; The Adventure of the Camberwell Beauty; The Adventure of the Little Hangman; The Adventure of the Swedenborg Signatures.*

The third collection of Solar Pons adventures. Stories are reprinted in No. 17. No other MM reprints. $175/50

M6. The Reminiscences of Solar Pons, by August Derleth. Collection of Solar Pons stories. (1961.) 199 pp. 2052 copies printed. Cover price $3.50. Jacket art by Frank Utpatel.

Contents: *Introduction,* by Anthony Boucher; *The Adventure of the Mazarine Blue; The Adventure of the Hats of M. Dulac; The Adventure of the Mosaic Cylinders; The Adventure of the Praed Street Irregulars; The Adventure of the Cloverdale Kennels; The Adventure of the Black Cardinal; The Adventure of the Troubles Magistrate; The Adventure of the Blind Clairaudient; A Chronology of Solar Pons,* by Robert Patrick.

The fourth collection of Solar Pons adventures. Stories are reprinted in No. 17. No other MM reprints. $125/60

M7. The Casebook of Solar Pons, by August Derleth. Collection of Solar Pons stories. (1965.) 281 pp. 3020 copies printed. Cover price $5.00. Jacket art by Frank Utpatel.

Contents: *Foreword,* by Vincent Starrett; *(Cuthbert) Lyndon Parker,* by Michael Harrison; *The Adventure of the Sussex Archers; The Adventure of the Haunted Library; The Adventure of the Fatal Glance; The Adventure of the Intarsia Boy; The Adventure of the Spurious Tamerlane; The Adventure of the China Cottage; The Adventure of the Ascot Scandal; The Adventure of the Crouching Dog; The Adventure of the Missing Huntsman; The Adventure of the Amateur Philologist; The Adventure of the Whispering Knights; The Adventure of the Innkeeper's Clerk; Afterword;* Endpaper map, by Luther Norris.

The fifth collection of Solar Pons adventures. Stories are reprinted in No. 17. No other MM reprints. $150/40

M8. The Phantom Fighter, by Seabury Quinn. Collection of detective stories. (1966.) 263 pp. 2022 copies printed. Cover price $5.00. Jacket art by Frank Utpatel.

Contents: *By Way of Explanation; Terror on the Links; The Dead Hand; Children of Ubasti; The Jest of Warburg Tantavul; The Corpse-Master; The Poltergeist; The Wolf of Saint Bonnot; Restless Souls; The Silver Countess; The Doom of the House of Phipps.*

An important volume of detective tales by a distinguished American pulp fiction writer, featuring Jules de Grandin, the psychic detective. The stories were originally published in *Weird Tales* in the 1920s and 1930s. No reprints. $125/35

M9. A Praed Street Dossier, by August Derleth. Collection of Solar Pons marginalia. (1968.) 108 pp. 2904 copies printed. Cover price $3.00. Jacket art by Frank Utpatel.

Contents: *The Beginnings of Solar Pons; The Sources of the Tales; Concerning Dr. Parker's Background; The Favorite Pastiches; From the Notebooks of Dr. Lyndon Parker; The Adventure of the Bookseller's Clerk; Solar Pons, Off Trail; The Adventure of the Snitch in Time* (with Mack Reynolds); *The Adventure of the Ball of Nostradamus* (with Mack Reynolds).

A mixture of Solar Pons marginalia, miscellany and two new collaborative adventure stories. Three of the stories are reprinted in No. 17. No other MM reprints. $75/20

The Phantom Fighter, by Seabury Quinn (1966). Cover art by Frank Utpatel. No. M8.

M10. The Exploits of the Chevalier Dupin, by Michael Harri-

son. Collection of Auguste Dupin stories. (1968.) 138 pp. 1917 copies printed. Cover price $3.50. Jacket art by Ronald Clyne. Contents: *Introduction*, by Ellery Queen; *Dupin: The Reality Behind the Fiction; The Vanished Treasure; The Mystery of the Fulton Document; The Man in the Blue Spectacles; The Mystery of the Gilded Cheval-Glass; The Fires in the Rue St. Honoré; The Murder in the Rue Royale; The Facts in the Case of the Missing Diplomat.*
The British author's only Mycroft & Moran title. The stories feature Edgar Allan Poe's detective C. Auguste Dupin and appeared first in *Ellery Queen's Mystery Magazine* in the 1960s. No reprints. $75/ 15

M11. Wisconsin Murders, by August Derleth. Wisconsin crime stories. (1968.) 222 pp. 1958 copies printed. Cover price $4.00. Jacket art by Ronald Clyne.
Contents: *Foreword; Caffee Was a Gallowbird; An Affair in Council; A Jury of His Peers; A Way with the Ladies; Coincidence and Dr. Garner; The Tribulations of Sarah Ingersoll; A Rival to Xantippe; A Slight Case of Perjury; "Hell Hath No Fury…"; A Village Borgia; La Follette for the Prosecution; The Dog in the Night-Time; Dear Grace; Hart Gets His Man; Christmas Package; The Wolf at the Church Social.*
A collection of Wisconsin true crime stories, and one of the few non-fiction books published by Arkham House (Mycroft & Moran). Three of these accounts had been published previously in the *Saint Mystery Magazine* and *American Weekly* in the 1950s and 1960s. No reprints. $50/10

M12. The Adventure of the Unique Dickensians, by August Derleth. A single Solar Pons story published in wraps. (1968.) 38 pp. 2012 copies printed. Cover price $1.50. Cover art and interior illustrations by Frank Utpatel. A delightful short Christmas detective story, which was reprinted in No. 15 and No. 17. $45

M13. Mr. Fairlie's Final Journey, by August Derleth. Short Solar Pons novel. (1968.) 131 pp. 3493 copies printed. Cover price $3.50. Jacket art by Frank Utpatel. Reprinted in No. 17. $45/10

M14. Number Seven, Queer Street, by Margery Lawrence. Collection of detective stories. (1969.) 236 pp. 2027 copies printed. Cover price $4.00. Jacket art by Frank Utpatel.

Contents: *Foreword; The Case of the Bronze Door; The Case of the Haunted Cathedral; The Case of Ella McLeod; The Case of the White Snake; The Case of the Moonchild.*

The British author's only Mycroft & Moran title. A collection of stories featuring the psychic detective Miles Pennoyer, the creation of Mrs. Arthur Edward Towle, here writing under her maiden name. No reprints. $100/25

M15. The Chronicles of Solar Pons, by August Derleth. Collection of Solar Pons stories. (1973.) 237 pp. 4176 copies printed. Cover price $6.00. Jacket art by Frank Utpatel.

Contents: *Introduction*, by Allen J. Hubin; *The Adventure of the Red Leech; The Adventure of the Orient Express; The Adventure of the Golden Bracelet; The Adventure of the Shaplow Millions; The Adventure of the Benin Bronze; The Adventure of the Missing Tenants; The Adventure of the Aluminium Crutch; The Adventure of the Seven Sisters; The Adventure of the Bishop's Companion; The Adventure of the Unique Dickensians.*

The sixth collection of Solar Pons adventures. Stories are reprinted in No. 17. $50/15

M16. Prince Zaleski and Cummings King Monk, by M.P. Shiel. Collection of fantasy detective tales. (1977.) 220 pp. 4036 copies printed. Cover price $7.50. Jacket art by Joe Wehrle, Jr.

Contents: *The Race of Orwen; The Stone of the Edmundsbury Monks; The S.S.; The Return of Prince Zaleski; He Meddles with Women; He Defines "Greatness of Mind"; He Wakes an Echo.*

A long-delayed collection of the author's supernatural adventure/ detective stories, featuring Prince Zaleski and Cummings King Monk. An agreement had been reached with August Derleth to publish this volume as early as 1945. No reprints. Still in print. $35/8

M17. The Solar Pons Omnibus, by August Derleth. The complete collection of Solar Pons stories published in a two bound volume edition in slip case. (1982.) No dust jacket issued. 1306 pp. 3031 copies printed. Cover price $39.95.

Contents: Volume One: *Foreword*, by Robert Bloch; *From the*

Notebook of Dr. Lyndon Parker; The Adventure of the Sotheby Salesman; The Adventure of Ricoletti of the Club Foot; The Adventure of the Unique Dickensians; The Adventure of the Haunted Library; The Adventure of the Aluminium Crutch; The Adventure of the Circular Room; The Adventure of the Purloined Periapt; The Adventure of the Lost Locomotive; The Adventure of the Five Royal Coachmen; The Adventure of the Frightened Baronet; The Adventure of the Missing Huntsman; The Adventure of the Amateur Philologist; The Adventure of the Seven Sisters; The Adventure of the Limping Man; The Adventure of the Shaplow Millions; The Adventure of the Innkeeper's Clerk; The Adventure of the Crouching Dog; The Adventure of the Perfect Husband; The Adventure of the Dog in the Manger; The Adventure of the Swedenborg Signatures; The Adventure of the Spurious Tamerlane; The Adventure of the Rydberg Numbers; The Adventure of the Praed Street Irregulars; The Adventure of the Penny Magenta; The Adventure of the Remarkable Worm; The Adventure of the Retired Novelist; The Adventure of the Missing Tenants; The Adventure of the Devil's Footprints; The Adventure of the Sussex Archers; The Adventure of the Cloverdale Kennels; The Adventure of the Lost Dutchman; The Adventure of the Grice-Paterson Curse; The Adventure of the Dorrington Inheritance; The Adventure of the Norcross Riddle; The Adventure of the Late Mr. Faversham; The Adventure of the Black Narcissus. Volume Two:; *The Adventure of the Three Red Dwarfs; The Adventure of the Broken Chessman; The Adventure of the China Cottage; The Adventure of the Black Cardinal; The Adventure of the Hats of M. Dulac; The Adventure of the Little Hangman; The Adventure of the Man with the Broken Face; The Adventure of the Benin Bronze; The Adventure of the Seven Passengers; The Adventure of the Whispering Knights; The Adventure of the Intarsia Box; The Adventure of the Six Silver Spiders; The Adventure of the Stone of Scone; The Adventure of the Mazarine Blue; The Adventure of the Red Leech; The Adventure of the Lost Holiday; The Adventure of the Blind Clairaudient; The Adventure of the Proper Comma; The Adventure of the Bishop's Companion; The Adventure of the Ascot Scandal; The Adventure of the "Triple Kent"; The Adventure of the Paralytic Mendicant; The Adventure of the Trained Cormorant; The Adventure of the Camberwell Beauty; The Adventure of the Tottenham Werewolf; The Adventure of the Troubled Magistrate; The Adventure of the Mosaic Cylinders; The Adventure of the Fatal Glance; The Adventure of the Orient Express; Mr. Fairlie's Final Journey; The Adventure of the Golden Bracelet;*

The Adventure of the Snitch in Time (with Mack Reynolds); *The Adventure of the Ball of Nostradamus* (with Mack Reynolds).
Although the spine of both volumes bear the Arkham House name, the half title page indicates this to be a Mycroft & Moran book. Reprinted in a new format in No. 20. $125

M18. The Final Adventures of Solar Pons, by August Derleth. The last collection of Solar Pons stories, edited by Peter Ruber. (1998.) 202 pp. No print numbers given. Cover price $28.00. Jacket art by Jean-Pierre Cagnat.
Contents: *Introduction*, by Peter Ruber; *"Reception in Elysium"* (poem), by Mary F. Lindsley; *The Terror Over London; The Adventure of Gresham Old Place; The Adventure of the Burlstone Horror; The Adventure of the Viennese Musician; The Adventure of the Muttering Man; The Adventure of the Two Collaborators*, by Peter Ruber; *The Adventure of the Nosferatu* (with Mack Reynolds); *The Adventure of the Extra Terrestrial* (with Mack Reynolds); *More from Dr. Parker's Notebook.*
The final collection of Solar Pons stories. It was published by George Vanderburgh in Ontario, Canada, under a lease of the Mycroft & Moran imprint. The collection includes some unpublished, recently discovered stories, the best of which is the short novel *Terror over London*. No reprints. Still in print. $30/8

M19. In Lovecraft's Shadow, by August Derleth. The Cthulhu Mythos stories of August Derleth. Collection of August Derleth's Cthulhu inspired stories, poems and other material, edited by Joseph Wrzos. (1998.) Folio-sized book. 351 pp. No print numbers given. Cover price $59.95. Jacket art and 23 interior illustrations by Stephen Fabian.
Contents: *Introduction*, by Joseph Wrzos; *A Few Words about the Artist*, by Joseph Wrzos; *Providence: Two Gentlemen Meet at Midnight; The Thing That Walked the Wind; Ithaqua; Beyond the Threshold; The Dweller in Darkness; Lair of the Star-Spawn* (with Mark Schorer); *Spawn of the Maelstrom* (with Mark Schorer); *The Horror from the Depths* (with Mark Schorer); *The House in the Oaks* (with Robert E. Howard); *Those Who Seek; The God Box; Something from Out There; Incubus* (poem); *The Return of Hastur; The Passing of Eric Holm; The Sandwin Compact; Something in the Wood; The Whippoorwills in the Hill; The House in the Val-*

ley; The Seal of R'lyeh; The House on Curwen Street; The Watcher from the Sky; The Gorge Beyond Salapunco; The Keeper of the Key; The Black Island; On Reading Old Letters: For H.P.L.; A Note on the Cthulhu Mythos; Notes, by Joseph Wrzos; Appendix: The Derleth Cthulhu Mythos Series.

A collection of August Derleth's Cthulhu stories, published by George Vanderburgh in Ontario, Canada, under a lease of the Mycroft & Moran imprint. The book includes several collaborations with Mark Schorer previously published by Arkham House. The atmospheric interior illustrations by Stephen Fabian adds greatly to the quality of the book and makes it a very desirable volume. No reprints. Still in print. $75/18

M20. The Original Text: Solar Pons Omnibus Edition, by August Derleth. A new format reprint of No. 17. (2001.) This edition was printed as a Mycroft & Moran title, in a two-volume, folio-sized set without the slip case. The wrap-around dust jackets show the jackets of all the original Solar Pons titles. New text has been added, including recently discovered, unpublished Solar Pons material. Cover price $130. Jacket art and design by Jean Pierre Cagnat. No reprints. Still in print. $130/60

6

Stanton & Lee
Bibliography
(1945–1970)

The Arkham House imprint Stanton & Lee was introduced in 1945. It was intended for the publication of comic cartoons, primarily by Clare Victor Dwiggins, and reprints, poems and regional writings by August Derleth. The name of the imprint was derived from the names of two of Derleth's friends, one of whom was an employee at Arkham House. The imprint colophon for the second title, *Evening in Spring*, was designed by Howard Wandrei, while the colophon for the later Stanton & Lee titles, a stylized whippoorwill, was designed by Ronald Clyne.

Titles are listed in chronological order as published. All Stanton & Lee titles are out of print. The term "No reprints" indicates that the title has not been reprinted by any publisher. The term "No SL reprints" indicates that the title has not been reprinted by Stanton & Lee, but may have been reprinted by other publishers.

The suggested values listed are for titles in "fine/fine" condition. Books in better condition will demand higher prices, and books in lesser condition will cost less. The first listed value is for books in the original dust jacket; the second is for books without dust jacket or in facsimile jacket.

BIBLIOGRAPHY

S1. Bill's Diary, by Clare Victor Dwiggins. Collection of cartoons by Dwiggins and poems by August Derleth. (1945.) 288 pp. 2002 copies printed. Cover price $2.00. Jacket art and illustrations by the author.

Contents: *Dwig and Bill, Eternal Boy,* by August Derleth— *Bill's Diary* (cartoons)—*Night-Haunt—Spring Rain—Woods Music—Leaf Burning Time—Snow,* by August Derleth.

A delightful romp through a boy's rural America as it once was, as seen through the eyes of a distinguished cartoonist. August Derleth had always been an admirer of Dwiggins cartoons and founded the Stanton & Lee imprint partially for the publication of some of Dwiggins' work. No reprints. $125 /40

Bill's Diary, by Clare Victor Dwiggins (1945). Cover art by Clare Victor Dwiggins. No. S1.

S2. **Evening in Spring,** by August Derleth. Reprint of Derleth's 1941 novel. (1945.) 308 pp. 2990 copies printed. Cover price $1.49, changed to $2.50 and later $3.50. Early jacket art by Frank Utpatel and later by Ronald Clyne. No SL reprints. $150/40

S3. **Oliver, the Wayward Owl,** by August Derleth. A cartoon fantasy. (1945.) 84 pp. 3089 copies printed. Cover price $1.50. Jacket art and illustrations by Clare Victor Dwiggins. No Reprints. $95/25

S4. **A Boy's Way,** by August Derleth. Collection of poems and cartoons for children. (1947.) 109 pp. 1990 copies printed. Cover price $2.00. Jacket art and illustrations by Clare Victor Dwiggins.

Contents: *The Ambush; Houseboat; Screech Owls; Fox and Hounds; Down to the Sea in Ships; Rowing at Night; Jew's Harp Music; My Dog Spot; Bullheading; Smokewood; Book Review; Spring; First Kiss; Whistling in the Dark; Spring Fever; Sunfishing; Haunted House; The Collectors; Timber!; Doughnuts; Woods at Night; The Old Frog Pond; The Stereopticon in Grandma's Parlor; Nighthawk; The Recital; The Lamp; Night Mail; Fire-*

bell in the Night; Turtling; The Piano Lesson; Fish Rising; Rain on the Attic Roof; The Day After the Circus; Moonrise; Clouds; Night Train; The Scissor-Grinder; Dwelllers in the Dark; Box-Social; Treasure; Playing at Dusk; New Moon; Horsehair Chair; Damming the Brook; Hallowe'en; Leaf-Burning; O Ye of Little Faith; Nutting; Ice Skating; Sherlock Holmes; Hawk.
A collection of cartoons by Dwiggins, accompanied by poems by August Derleth. A charming depiction of everyday events in the life of a young boy in rural America. No reprints. $150/45

S5. Wisconsin Earth: A Sac Prairie Sampler, by August Derleth. Reprint of Derleth's 1935, 1941 and 1943 collections of regional writings. (1948.) 314 pp. 1186 copies printed. Cover price $5.00. Jacket art by Ronald Clyne. Wood-engravings by George Barford and Frank Utpatel.
Contents: *Shadow of Night; Place of Hawks (Five Alone; Faraway House; Nine Strands in a Web; Place of Hawks); Village Year: A Sac Prairie Journal.*

A collection of some of the best regional writings by August Derleth. End paper map by Hjalmar Skuldt. No SL reprints. $85/20

S6. Sac Prairie People, by August Derleth. Collection of regional stories and character studies. (1948.) 322 pp. 2131 copies printed. Cover price $3.00. Jacket art by Ronald Clyne.
Contents: *Kleine Nachtmusik; Expedition to the North; Ellie Butts; A Little Quiet in the Evening; McCrary's Wife; The Sisters; Moonlight in the Apple Tree; Valse Oubliée; Where the Worms Dieth Not; Now Is the Time for All Good Men; Nella; The Night Light at Vorden's; Aunt May and the*

Sac Prairie People, by August Derleth (1948). Cover art by Ronald Clyne. No. S6.

160

Refugees; Stuff of Dream; Rendezvous; The Lost Kiss; "That Fellow Oates";
One Against the Dead; Light Again; I Was Walking Helen Home.
A collection of short sketches of daily events, personalities and
happenings in a small Wisconsin town. Premier regional writing. No
reprints. $125/20

S7. **It's a Boy's World,** by August Derleth. Collection of poems and
cartoons for children. (1948.) 107 pp. 1244 copies printed. Cover
price $2.00. Jacket art and illustrations by Clare Victor Dwiggins.
Contents: *First Crocus; The Bobbing Cork; Streetlight Shadows; The*
Locomotive Engineer; The Customer; The Raft; The Millpond Terror; School
Play; Roller-Skating; Tadpoles; The Bat; The Old Swimming Hole; Hay-
ing; My Owl; Peewee's Ride; The Cabin in the Woods; The Old Covered
Bridge; The Baseball Game; The Belfry; The Unexplored Island; The Soap-
Coupon Telescope; The Waterfall; Glowworms; Heaven's Gate; Old Speck;
Potato Bugs and Weeds; The Hanging Tree; Dogs Barking; The Long Trail;
The Cellar Dweller; Otter; The Wind in the Leaves; Acorns on the Roof;
The Sparrow in the Willows; Cornshocks; Elerberry Syrup; Pumpkin Faces;
Deer; Torch Signals; Leaf-Painter; Bonfire in the Woods; Witch Hazel on
Hallowe'en; The Dance; Snowstorm; Bob-Sledding; The Long Ride; The
Harness Shop; Drying Hickory Nuts; The Mystery Picture at the Old Elec-
tric; The Caboose on the Train.
Another delightful collection of cartoons and poems by Dwiggins
and Derleth. No reprints. $150/30

S8. **Bright Journey,** by August Derleth. Reprint of Derleth's 1940
regional historical novel. (1953.) 424 pp. 1021 copies printed. Cover
price $3.50. Jacket art by Haberstock. Second printing in 1955
(1567 copies). Third printing in 1960 (2005 copies). Fourth printing in 1968 (1938 copies). 1953 printing $90/20; Others $25/5

S9. **Wind Over Wisconsin,** by August Derleth. Reprint of Derleth's
1938 regional historical novel. (1957.) 391 pp. 1032 copies printed.
Cover price $3.50. Jacket art by Haberstock. Second printing in
1965 (1011 copies). 1957 printing $75/15; 1965 printing $25/5

S10. **Wilbur, the Trusting Whippoorwill,** by August Derleth. Cartoon fantasy. (1959.) 64 pp. 990 copies printed. Cover price $2.00.

Jacket art and illustrations by Clare Victor Dwiggins. No Reprints. $75/25

S11. Restless is the River, by August Derleth. Reprint of Derleth's 1939 regional historical novel. (1965.) 514 pp. 1021 copies printed. Cover price $4.50. Jacket art by Haberstock. No reprints. $60/15

S12. A Wisconsin Harvest, by August Derleth (ed.). Collection of poetry, prose and plays by regional writers. (1966.) 338 pp. 3532 copies printed. Cover price $5.00. Jacket art by Frank Utpatel.
Contents: *Introduction,* by August Derleth; *Morning in March; Old Carriage Block; Old Lumberjack Hotel,* by Dana Kneeland Akers; *No Time for Enchantment; William Morrison Tallman,* by Jo Bartels Alderson; *Medical Remedies of Grandmother's Day,* by Neva Argue; *Spring Tonic,* by May Augustyn; *Popcorn Night,* by Lenore Benedict; *The Birds,* by Wilma Fritz Black; *The Bobbinet Cap,* by Irene Bowman; *Island Winds,* by Louise H. Briesemeister; *The Inheritors,* by Sam Bryan; *The Seven Passenger Nash,* by Ruth Burmester; *Can You Can It?,* by Arlene S. Buttles; *Farmstead on a Winter Night; Terminal Moraine; The Farmer's Wife; Irony,* by Inga Gilson Caldwell; *The Dependable Man,* by Dorothy Carey; *This I Know,* by Marie Cornell; *Short, Sweet Summer of a Tomboy,* by Margarita Cuff; *Two Haiku,* by Magdalene M. Douglas; *Big Ernie,* by Clarice Chase Dunn; *Requiem for Turtles, Etc.,* by Don Eulert; *Memorial for Mathew Grace,* by Arthur L. Fischer; *The Blue Flowers,* by Iris Elizabeth Ford; *Wind,* by Beatrice Frackelton; *A Sturdy People,* by Robert Gard; *Winter Panes,* by Wilhelmina Geurink; *The Old Country Store,* by Winifred Gleason; *Star of Bethlehem,* by Stan Gores; *Antietam in the Lower Forty,* by Erma Graber; *The Celebrity,* by Topsy Gregory; *The Patchwork Quilt,* by Dorothy House Guilday; *Hot Weather Cooking,* by Elizabeth Herritz; *The Doll,* by Marjorie Yourd Hill; *Feeding and Care of the Husband,* by Rusty Hoffland; *Strays,* by Violette Jahnke; *The Saga of Kidd Winchell,* by Verge Karow; *A Hard Nut to Crack,* by Edythe L. Kazda; *Playing Musical Chair with the County Seat,* by Edgar J. Kezeli; *At the P.N.A.,* by Patricia Kieckhefer; *Another Statistic,* by Charlotte Knechtges; *Sweet Applewood Burning,* by Ruby Kuenzli; *In Prima Luce,* by William M. Lamers; *The Bell,* by Julius Landau; *Catalpa Leaf to Church...,* by Hazel Latour; *The Long Voice; Autumn Psalm,* by Louise Leighton; *Mother's Verbal Velvet Glove,* by Florence Lindemann; *A*

Blasters' Blaster, by Dorothy Litersky; *Cherries Are Ripe,* by Hazel Maryan; *Jupon and the Woodpecker; Such a Child's Waiting; Yesterdays,* by Edna Meudt; *Winds of April; Bonniedale,* by Elizabeth Faulkner Nolan; *Honey to Be Savored; The Birthing Place,* by Marian Paust; *Triple Ridge Farm,* by Ruth Fouts Pochmann; *Dens, Dams, La Pointe, Waldorf-Astoria,* by Greta Lagro Potter; *There Are Times; Pearl Harbor Anniversary; Perhaps;* by Star Powers; *Cemetery; Two Empty Bottles,* by Sara Lindsay Rath; *Quail; Old Fence; Land Measure,* by Anne C. Rose; *Ploughman,* by Belle Schacht; *Farm Auction,* by Janet M. Schlatter; *So Much Can Be Done in the Mornings,* by Jean Bunker Schmith; *The Mill Road,* by Dorothy C. Schrader; *Tony's Funeral,* by Isadore Brothers Schwartz; *Paid in Full,* by Laila E. Skagen; *Prelude to Spring; Self-Portrait; Not Yet; Into a Nowhere; Sharp Like an Illusion,* by Helen C. Smith; *George Washington Carver,* by Henry C. Spear; *With a Whetstone Scratch; Late Autumn,* by Charles W. Stonebarger; *Prelude to a Wedding,* by Loretta Strehlow; *Blackberry Harvest,* by Anne Stubbe; *When Frost Stepped Out,* by Cecile Houghton Stury; *Pre-Fabricated Funeral,* by Fidelia Van Antwerp; *The Grocer With One Good Eye,* by George Vukelich; *An Ordinary Couple,* by Michael Warlum; *March; Grandfather,* by Joyce W. Webb; *Skin Game,* by Grace Van Antwerp Woodard; *The Day I Told God Myself,* by Ruby Yarber; *Tradem's Squaw?,* by Mary H. Zimmerman.

A representative collection of poetry by the Wisconsin Regional Writer's Association. No reprints. $35/10

S13. The House on the Mound, by August Derleth. Reprint of Derleth's 1958 regional historical novel. (1966.) 333 pp. 2557 copies printed. Cover price $4.50. Jacket art by Marjorie Auerbach. Title page unchanged. No SL reprints. $60/15

S14. Eyes of the Mole, by Jane Stuart. Slim collection of poetry. (1967.) 48 pp. No print numbers given. Cover price $3.50. Jacket art by Ronald Clyne.

Contents: *The Moon Maker; Flower with Lavender Eyes; The Taste of Spring; Faisal; I Took Your Flowers; To Night; This Night is Beauty; Yellow Roses; Shadows; Red Raspberries; Aegean; On Leaving the Aegean; Evelyn Brown; Memory of May; The Gone; Who Will Hide You?; Maenad; The City of the Dead Blue Wind; Praemorta Sum; Daedalu's Waxen Wings;*

Meleager; Song of the Blackbirds; Where Stuarts Lie; Corn Shuck Dolls; The Beggar in the Trees; Roots; The Chicken House; Eyes of the Mole; August 31ˢᵗ; Willow World; Where Will the Autumn Find Me?; September Song; Woman of Autumn; Purple Fish; Imagination; Apostate; I Who Begin Life; Hollow Music; Julian; Wild Oats.

A small collection of poetry by the daughter of Jesse Stuart, a friend of August Derleth. No reprints. $45/10

S15. New Poetry Out of Wisconsin, by August Derleth (ed.). Collection of poetry by regional writers. (1969.) 300 pp. 2547 copies printed. Cover price $5.00. Jacket art simulating a wood-engraving by Frank Utpatel.

Contents: *Introduction,* by August Derleth; *Summer People,* by Bernice Kreitz Abrahamson; *Historic Site: Gordon; Sonnet for Old Bivouacs; Weather-Wise,* by Dana Kneeland Akers; *Analogy,* by James Michael Alderson; *Phoenix; Night Song,* by Jo Bartels Alderson; *Lament,* by Robert Andrews; *Father; Iceboat,* by Antler; *Old House,* by Orel Barker;

The Red Dress; Beyond the Storm; Biblic Appendix, by James Bertolino; *Transcends; The Vine,* by Joyce Bertolino; *Ripe; March: Wisconsin; O To Write a Poem; After Crickets,* by Louis Bertolino; *After Reading Archibald MacLeish,* by Doris J. Bettin; *On Fishing with Dad; Elegy from Japan,* by Edmund J. Binsfield; *Gunther's Mountain,* by Wilma Fritz Black; *A Song in Wantonness; Of Ideas; Middle of the Night and Morning,* by Carl Bode; *Death,* by Robert C. Broderick; *Approach,* by Sam Bryan; *Campsite; Temporary Home,* by Gene Burd; *Silent Music,* by Dennis Burke; *Old Barn,* by Ruth Burmeister; *Into Night; Indian Valley Pioneer; Retired Farmer,* by Inga Gilson Caldwell; *Beneath the*

New Poetry Out of Wisconsin, by August Derleth (ed.) (1969). Cover art by Frank Utpatel. No. S15.

Snow, by Ruth Bunker Christiansen; *Last Night; A Silver Sleek Car Streaked,* by Wladyslaw Cieszynski; *Return at Evening; In the Fields; Just Spring; Nobody Owns the Weather,* by Grant Hyde Code; *The Cocktail Party; Winter Night Music; Summer Student's Distraction,* by Wayne Cody; *Christmas Contrast,* by F. Roger Constance; *Morning School Bus; My Enemy; Teachers,* by Victor Contoski; *The Lost Peak,* by Frances Crewes; *For Now the Evening,* by Leslie Cross; *The Sisters; Stoned to Death,* by Dorothy Dalton; *Hearsay,* by Marilyn Denham; *Apologia; Thoreau: A Different Drummer; Lines with a Book; Three for Caitlin (i. Lines with a Book, ii. Gem Opal, iii. Moonlight),* by August Derleth; *Reflections,* by Norma L. Edinger; *Retirement,* by George Ellis; *Letter; Picnics; Poem for Fall,* by John Engels; *Femininity,* by Ruth Everts; *Kite Dreams,* by Erna Fenton; *Fits and Dreams,* by Ellison Ferrall; *Cinquains; Words Were Your Beauty; Pushkin Dying,* by Russel Ferrall; *Mountains,* by Arthur L. Fischer; *May Morning,* by Alvina Floistad; *No Girls Allowed!,* by Joan Foley; *River Song,* by Iris Ford; *To Ruth; Some Did Return; Through Spring Has Come,* by Ruth Mary Fox; *The House on Church Street,* by Mardi Fries; *Baudelaire in Clontarf Minnesota; The Proper Authorities,* by Philip Gallo; *Prairie Acre,* by Robert Gard; *Cosi Fan Tutte; You, You; The Spring of the Great Elm Street Harvest,* by Barbara Gibson; *Snow Sequence; Into Evening; October; Acanaemia,* by Morgan Gibson; *April; Mother; Quarry,* by Barbara Goska; *Reading Your Letter,* by George Gott; *A Wreath for Margery; Emerson: Last Days at Concord; Chorus for Survival; The Postman's Bell Is Answered Everywhere,* by Horace Gregory; *Land of Enchantment,* by Suzanne Gross; *Orange Horizon; I Barbara,* by Ruth Guillaume; *In My Seventeenth Year; Partings,* by Jeffrey Ham; *Plain Jane,* by Eddy Hanson; *Mother,* by Elayne Clipper Hanson; *On A Line by Gary Snyder; I Am the Father,* by James Hazard; *A Young Girl's Birthday; Gifts,* by Joseph Heinzkill; *Ash Wednesday; Warning for Spring; For Psyche Marketed; Crossed Dreams,* by Sister Mary Hester; *Housework; Beginnings; Poem Irrelevant of Motive; Calendar,* by Philip H. Hey; *The Moustache Cup,* by Edith H. Hill; *The Beginning; January Night; Remembering; Where?,* by Robert Hillebrand; *Finals in Reno,* by Beryl E. Hoyt; *It Hurts Sometimes; A Fallen Tree,* by Jerold J. Jackson; *The Hills of Home,* by Myrtle Cook Jackson; *Love's Patience; The Old Pas de Deux; The Patchwork Quilt,* by Violette Jahnke; *Codicil; A Forest Strange and Lovely,* by Margaret Fraser Jarnagin; *The Sweetest Singer,* by Russell W. Jones; *House; October; Western; Fisherman: Below*

Genoa; January Poem for Henry Thoreau; Song for a Late Spring; Midnight in America; Drury Pond, by John Judson; *Song of Laughter,* by Paul L. Kegel; *Spring Cleaning,* by Lucille Kleist; *October,* by Caroline S. Kotowicz; *Our Golden Spring; Prayer for a Husbandman,* by Ruby G. Kuenzli; *The Wind in the Defile; April: The Mist, the Moon; April Snowfall; Before November Can Be All,* by Raymond E. F. Larsson; *Humility,* by Louise Leighton; *Sonnet; Dream Fragments,* by Becky Leidner; *Haiku; A Tree and a Prayer,* by Marcia Leitzke; *Girl of the Sea,* by Lucille Lembrich; *Splendor Returns to Lafayette Place,* by Florence Lindeman; *Plea for the City-Bound,* by Margaret Krebs Lohr; *Young White-Tailed Deer,* by Arlyle Mansfield Losse; *In Passing,* by Mary Frances Marburg; *Nettie Laude; No Stranger to This Land; Night Letter to Uncle Willie; The Chain,* by Frances May; *Sultry Gloaming,* by Ralph Alan McCanse; *Farmer's Wife; On Being No Longer Seen; Itinerary,* by Edna Meudt; *Saxifrage; A Morning in Winter; For Mrs. James,* by William Minor; *Games; What It Is?; Across the Way; Saturday Night with Briefcase; Natty Bumppo,* by Roger Mitchell; *Watching a Potter,* by Lucinda Morken; *Terese; The Silver Path,* by Harriet Elizabeth Mott; *From the Bridge; You Didn't Knock; We Sat Twelve Children,* by Nick Nebel; *I Walked; "Shelter"; My Life by Water,* by Lorine Niedecker; *A Goodbye; Like the Grass; 'Til Comes the Sun; The Green Grass Remembers,* by Diane F. Niemer; *Snow; Helix of Heredity,* by Marj Nienstaedt; *The Idyll of the Waiting Wife; Memento Mori: An Elegiac for My Father; May: Moving Between Beloit and Monroe; September: Scene with Cows; Wisconsin,* by Bink Noll; *A Boy's Will,* by Michael O'Connell; *Timberline; Kinsey; The Desert,* by Theodore V. Olson; *Reconnaissance; Contemporary,* by C.B. Oppenheimer; *Country Song; A Word to Someone with Growing To Do; The Challenge,* by Marian Paust; *Waiting for the Quickening; Fog as Prologue,* by Eleanor Pautz; *Teen Glow; Reaction to New Habits for Nuns,* by Jeri Peterson; *Music Eternal; Space Age Moon; Too Close Is Time; The Singing of April,* by Alice Phelps-Rider; *Mohl; Circus; Of Love; Sunday Morning Dialogue; Brown Spring; Coup; Conversation Piece: International; Waiting Line; Truncated Villanelle; Astronaut; Cinderella Revisited,* by Felix Pollak; *Stigmata; My First Dragon,* by Jefry Poniewaz; *Appointment with April,* by Star Powers; *Illusion; The Spark and the Fire; Darcy,* by Kay Price; *City at Dusk; Pine Cone Country,* by Lisa Proctor; *Let's Play; Could April Sing,* by Sara Lindsay Rath; *Oedipus: Untaught by Birds; To Man: January 1,* by Ruby Riemer; *Haiku,* by Victoria Rinelli; *They Go on Hallowe'en,* by Harland

Ristau; *Anonymity; Forgotten Sign; Prairie Born; Upland Plover; Morning,* by Anne C. Rose; *Stay; Roses; Bouquet,* by Nancy A. Rose; *Sharon; In an Early Incarnation I Must Have Been Aquatic; Thoughts on the Primitive Methodist Cemetery in Leadmine, Wisconsin,* by L. Bruce Rowe; *Tree of Life,* by H. Rala Scheel; *As I Am; A Value; Spring Lemonade,* by Jeffrey Schmitt; *Violets,* by Dorothy Cole Schrader; *The Mute Blade,* by Gwen Schultz; *This Was Love; Jesse Calvin; You Come Too,* by Isadore Brothers Schwartz; *Thoreau; Wild Geese; The Chinese; Lone Wolf,* by R.E. Sebenthall; *Sweet Kalliope,* by Gerti H. Sennet; *For Mike in Jail; Some Images,* by Maxine Shaw; *The Snowhawk; Persuasion; This Land,* by Mary Shumway; *Evolutions,* by Roger Skrentny; *Quarter Notes; Out of This, a Thread; Standardization; The Stirring Seed; World Design; Born of the Darkness,* by Helen C. Spear; *Wake,* by Mary Spicer; *In Spring,* by Rosemarian Staudacher; *Midwest U.F.O.,* by David Steingass; *In Very Country,* by James Stephens; *In a Field Before a Summer Storm,* by Scott Stromberg; *North Wind; Lament for Autumn,* by Anne Stubbe; *Mary Lincoln; Tom Lincoln,* by Lynn Surles; *We Thought We Knew,* by George Swoboda; *Treasures,* by Esther Tank; *Nostalgia; Wet Lilacs,* by Elizabeth Teicher; *West-Looking Window; Possessed,* by Nellie Burch Tennant; *Metaphysical Note; Two Songs from the Diaspora; Each Spring the Arbutus; Speak to Me, Sparrow,* by Sister M. Thérèse; *We Held On; This Is a Spring; Would You Mind?,* by Kathleen Thompson; *Night,* by Robert Thompson; *The Whistler; Loneliness; To an "Old Head",* by Don Thorne; *More than a Door; After Thirty Years; Remorse; Jimmy, 1923; The Last Spring; At Lawn's Edge; Lilac; Hour before Light; Miles; June Night,* by Rudy Topinka; *To the Full Ear of Corn,* by Maude L. Totten; *Night,* by John Tuschen; *Hope,* by Claude Venne; *The Fourth of July,* by Raymond Vils; *Identity; My Life,* by Edward J. von Steiner; *This Winter the Hawks; Abandoned Farm,* by George Vukelich; *The Lilacs of the Law of Love; Uneconomic Determinism; Consider the Locust Tree; A Gentleness,* by Chad Walsh; *Gull Wing Bone; The Stone of Truth,* by Michael Warlum; *Indian Song; Worst Poem,* by Robert Watt; *Explanation; Insular,* by Joyce W. Webb; *Torch Song,* by Jean L. Wester; *In High Fever; Tempest; White Dog Poetry; Duck Ground; Autobiography,* by Kathleen Wiegner; *Apple Tree,* by Grace Woodard; *December Fields; March Thaw; Timepiece; Storm over Woodstone; Night Landing,* by Warren Woessner; *On Lady Poets; I Come; Me and Clare and I,* by Suzanne Woods; *Cold Morning Sky; The Old House,* by Marya Zaturenska; *A Touch of the Earth; Old Man of Verse; Oh*

What a Terrible Grieving; First the Willows, by Josef Zderad; *RFD #3; Affirmation,* by Mary H. Zimmerman; *Afterword.*
A premium, voluminous anthology of regional poetry and a successor to *Poetry out of Wisconsin,* published in 1937. No reprints. $50/10

S16. Corn Village: A Selection, by Meridel Le Sueur. Short collection of four stories and a poem. (1970.) 74 pp. No print number given. Cover price $4.00. Jacket art by Gary Gore.
Contents: *Foreword,* by Ray Smith; *Preface; Corn Village; Persephone; Gone Home; Annunciation; Rites of Ancient Ripening (poem); Bibliography of Meridel Le Sueur,* by Mary K. Smith.
This title was printed by Villiers Publications Ltd. in London for Stanton & Lee. It was the last Stanton & Lee title to be published. No reprints. $40/10

7

The Thirty-five Most Valuable Arkham House Books

The books are listed in the order of current values. The number in parentheses is the book's entry number in the bibliography for Arkham House, Mycroft & Moran (designated with an M) or Stanton & Lee (designated with an S). The first value indicated is for books in "fine/fine" condition and in the original dust jacket. The second value listed is for books in "fine" condition without dust jacket or with facsimile dust jackets. A few titles were bound in boards and issued without a dust jacket; these are indicated as "bound" below. "Unbound" indicates a copy printed on loose sheets.

1. The Shunned House (bound) (1961)	(65)	$5,000
2. The Shunned House (unbound) (1961)	(65)	$3,000
3. The Outsider and Others (1939)	(1)	$3,000/400
4. Beyond the Wall of Sleep (1943)	(4)	$2,250/400
5. A Hornbook for Witches (1950)	(44)	$1,750/350
6. Someone in the Dark (1941)	(2)	$1,250/300
7. Dark Carnival	(25)	$1,250/300
8. Out of Space and Time (1942)	(3)	$1,000/250
9. The Dark Chateau (1951)	(46)	$1,000/250
10. AH: The First 20 years (bound) (1959)	(57)	$950
11. Skull-Face and Others (1946)	(17)	$800/125
12. Spells and Philtres (1958)	(54)	$750/125
13. The House on the Borderland (1946)	(16)	$600/120
14. Always Comes Evening (1957)	(53)	$550/100
15. A. Derleth: 20 Years of Writing (1946)	(19)	$500

16. A. Derleth: 25 Years of Writing (1951)	(45)	$500
17. A. Derleth: 30 Years of Writing (1956)	(51)	$500
18. 100 Books by A. Derleth (bound) (1962)	(69)	$500
19. Lost Worlds (1944)	(7)	$450/100
20. Demons and Dinosaurs (1970)	(112)	$450/100
21. Marginalia (1944)	(8)	$450/100
22. The Eye and the Finger (1944)	(5)	$400/100
23. The Opener of the Way (1945)	(10)	$400/100
24. Jumbee and Other Uncanny Tales (1944)	(6)	$375/100
25. Green Tea and Other Ghost... (1945)	(12)	$350/80
26. Slan (1946)	(22)	$350/80
27. Nightmare Need (1964)	(85)	$350/80
28. Something Breathing (1965)	(89)	$350/80
29. Three Problems for Solar Pons (1952)	(M4)	$350/80
30. Night's Black Agents (1947)	(27)	$300/60
31. Roads (1948)	(35)	$300/60
32. Who Fears the Devil? (1963)	(73)	$300/60
33. The Hounds of Tindalos (1946)	(14)	$250/60
34. Dark of the Moon (1947)	(24)	$250/60
35. Genius Loci and Other Tales (1948)	(36)	$250/60

8

Arkham House Books Ranked by Scarcity

These books are listed in order of scarcity (number 1 being the most scarce) in accordance with the numbers of first edition, first printing copies, not in accordance with current demand or availability. The number in parentheses is the book's entry number in the bibliography for Arkham House, Mycroft & Moran (designated with an M) or Stanton & Lee (designated with an S). Reprints are not included in the print numbers. The list does not include chapbooks, booklets, pamphlets and other limited, special publications whose print numbers are unknown. These are considered collectibles and in some cases are among the scarcest of Arkham House publications.

For further information on a book or clarification of print run figures, see the book's entry in Chapter 4, 5, or 6.

1. The Shunned House	(65)	100/50 copies
2. A Hornbook for Witches	(44)	253 for sale
3. Autobiography Notes on a Nonentity	(77)	500
4. Nightmare Need	(85)	500
5. Something Breathing	(89)	500
6. Demons and Dinosaurs	(112)	500
7. Spells and Philtres	(54)	519
8. The Dark Chateau	(46)	563
9. Always Comes Evening	(53)	636
10. The Arkham Collector, Vol. I	(126)	676
11. Poems by Midnight	(80)	742
12. AH: The First 20 Years	(57)	815
13. Wilbur, the Trusting Whippoorwill	(S10)	990
14. Three Problems for Solar Pons	(M4)	996

15. Poems in Prose	(87)	1016
16. Bright Journey	(S8)	1021
17. Restless is the River	(S11)	1021
18. Collected Poems (Tierney)	(160)	1030
19. Wind Over Wisconsin	(S9)	1032
20. Some Notes on Lovecraft	(58)	1044
21. Out of Space and Time	(3)	1054
22. Someone in the Dark	(2)	1115
23. Wisconsin Earth: A Sac Prairie...	(S5)	1186
24. The Arkham Sampler 1/1	(28)	1200
25. The Arkham Sampler 1/2	(29)	1200
26. The Arkham Sampler 1/3	(30)	1200
27. The Arkham Sampler 1/4	(31)	1200
28. The Arkham Sampler 2/2	(39)	1200
29. The Arkham Sampler 2/3	(40)	1200
30. The Arkham Sampler 2/4	(41)	1200
31. Beyond the Wall of Sleep	(4)	1217
32. The Curse of Yig	(49)	1217
33. 100 Books by August Derleth	(69)	1225
34. The Feasting Dead	(50)	1242
35. It's a Boy's World	(S7)	1244
36. The Outsider and Others	(1)	1268
37. Nine Horrors and a Dream	(56)	1336
38. 3 Tales of Horror	(99)	1522
39. Jumbee and Other...	(6)	1559
40. Invaders from the Dark	(62)	1559
41. The Eye and the Finger	(5)	1617
42. The Exploits of Chevalier Dupin	(M10)	1917
43. Black Medicine	(94)	1952
44. Wisconsin Murders	(M11)	1958
45. Portraits in Moonlight	(83)	1987
46. A Boy's Way	(S4)	1990
47. The Horror from the Hills	(76)	1997
48. The Arkham Sampler 2/1	(38)	2000
49. Strange Harvest	(91)	2000
50. Bill's Diary	(S1)	2002
51. The Abominations of Yondo	(60)	2005
52. Strange Gateways	(100)	2007
53. The Inhabitant of the Lake...	(79)	2009
54. Adv. of the Unique Dickensians	(M12)	2012

55. Collected Poems (Lovecraft)	(72)	2013
56. The Phanton-Fighter	(M8)	2022
57. Green Tea and Other Ghost...	(12)	2026
58. Fire and Sleet and Candlelight	(64)	2026
59. Number Seven, Queer Street	(M14)	2027
60. The Dark Man and Others	(75)	2029
61. Dreams and Fancies	(66)	2030
62. The Folsom Flint...	(109)	2031
63. Marginalia	(8)	2035
64. The Memoirs of Solar Pons	(M3)	2038
65. Nightmares and Daydreams	(104)	2040
66. Lost Worlds	(7)	2043
67. The Face in the Mirror	(118)	2045
68. Songs and Sonnets Atlantean	(123)	2045
69. The Travelling Grave	(32)	2047
70. The Quick and the Dead	(90)	2047
71. The Mask of Cthulhu	(55)	2051
72. The Reminiscence of Solar Pons	(M6)	2052
73. Something Near	(9)	2054
74. Who Fears the Devil?	(73)	2058
75. The Green Round	(102)	2058
76. Pleasant Dreams—Nightmares	(61)	2060
77. The Opener of the Way	(10)	2065
78. Not Long for this World	(37)	2067
79. Strayers from Sheol	(63)	2070
80. The Return of Solar Pons	(M5)	2079
81. The Survivor and Others	(52)	2096
82. Selected Poems (Smith)	(117)	2118
83. Sac Prairie People	(S6)	2131
84. Roads	(35)	2137
85. Thirty Years of Arkham House	(111)	2137
86. Lonesome Places	(67)	2201
87. Colonel Markesan ...	(93)	2405
88. The Trail of Cthulhu	(70)	2470
89. Tales of Science and Sorcery	(84)	2482
90. Selected Letters II	(103)	2482
91. Travellers by Night	(96)	2486
92. Dark Mind, Dark Heart	(68)	2493
93. The Arkham Collector 1	(97)	2500
94. The Arkham Collector 2	(101)	2500

95. The Arkham Collector 3	(105)	2500
96. The Arkham Collector 4	(106)	2500
97. The Arkham Collector 5	(107)	2500
98. The Arkham Collector 6	(110)	2500
99. The Arkham Collector 7	(114)	2500
100. The Arkham Collector 8	(116)	2500
101. The Arkham Collector 9	(119)	2500
102. The Arkham Collector 10	(122)	2500
103. In the Stone House	(200)	2500
104. The Far Side of Nowhere	(202)	2500
105. Selected Letters I	(86)	2504
106. Selected Letters III	(124)	2513
107. Over the Edge	(81)	2520
108. The Shuttered Room...	(59)	2527
109. Voyages by Starlight	(193)	2542
110. Mr. George and Other...	(74)	2546
111. New Poetry Out of Wisconsin	(S15)	2547
112. Deep Waters	(95)	2556
113. The House on the Mound	(S13)	2557
114. Flowers from the Moon...	(194)	2565
115. The Black Book of C.A.S.	(153)	2588
116. The Hounds of Tindalos	(14)	2602
117. This Mortal Coil	(23)	2609
118. Dark of the Moon	(24)	2634
119. A Praed Street Dossier	(M9)	2904
120. New Horizons	(196)	2917
121. In Mayan Splendor	(150)	2947
122. Witch House	(11)	2949
123. Evening in the Spring	(S2)	2990
124. Eight Tales	(120)	2992
125. Something About Cats	(42)	2995
126. Skull-Face and Others	(17)	3004
127. The House on the Borderlands	(16)	3014
128. The Casebook of Solar Pons	(M7)	3020
129. The Solar Pons Omnibus	(M17)	3031
130. West India Lights	(18)	3037
131. The Lurker at the Threshold	(13)	3041
132. The Mind Parasites	(98)	3045
133. The Wind from a Burning Woman	(163)	3046
134. Genius Loci and Other Tales	(36)	3047

135. Carnacki, the Ghost-Finder	(M2)	3050
136. Dark Things	(121)	3051
137. The Throne of Saturn	(43)	3062
138. The Web of Easter Island	(33)	3068
139. Revelations in Black	(26)	3082
140. Night's Black Agents	(27)	3084
141. Oliver, The Wayward Owl	(S3)	3089
142. Dark Carnival	(25)	3112
143. The Fourth Book of Jorkens	(34)	3118
144. The Darkling	(162)	3126
145. Disclosures in Scarlet	(127)	3127
146. The Dunwich Horror	(71)	3133
147. Other Dimensions	(113)	3144
148. Dreams from R'lyeh	(139)	3152
149. The Jaguar Hunter	(175)	3194
150. Watchers at the Strait Gate	(167)	3459
151. The Dark Brotherhood...	(92)	3460
152. From Evil's Pillow	(131)	3468
153. Dagon and Other Macabre Tales	(88)	3471
154. Demons by Daylight	(130)	3472
155. The Doll and One Other	(15)	3490
156. Mr. Fairlie's Final Journey	(M13)	3493
157. The Breath of Suspension	(189)	3496
158. Tales from Underwood	(47)	3500
159. Sixty Years of Arkham House	(198)	3500
160. Synthesis and Other...	(192)	3515
161. The Aliens of Earth	(187)	3520
162. The Zanzibar Cat	(165)	3526
163. Polyphemus	(176)	3528
164. A Wisconsin Harvest	(S12)	3532
165. Lovecraft's Book	(170)	3544
166. Meeting in Infinity	(186)	3547
167. At the Mountain of Madness	(82)	3552
168. The House of the Wolf	(164)	3578
169. Lovecraft Remembered	(195)	3579
170. Who Made Stevie Crye?	(168)	3591
171. One Winter in Eden	(166)	3596
172. "In Re: Sherlock Holmes"	(M1)	3604
173. The Caller of the Black	(125)	3606
174. New Tales of the Cthulhu...	(156)	3647

175. The Rim of the Unknown	(128)	3650
176. Tales of the Quintana Roo	(172)	3673
177. Alone with the Horrors	(188)	3834
178. Beneath the Moors	(132)	3842
179. Dwellers in the Darkness	(144)	3926
180. Dreams of Dark and Light	(173)	3957
181. At the Mountains of Madness (corr.)	(171)	3990
182. Dragonfly	(197)	4000
183. Arkham's Masters of Horror	(199)	4000
184. Book of the Dead	(201)	4000
185. Lord Kelvin's Machine	(185)	4015
186. Dagon and Other... (corrected)	(174)	4023
187. Tales of the Cthulhu Mythos	(108)	4024
188. Fearful Pleasures	(20)	4033
189. Prince Zaleski and Cummings...	(M16)	4036
190. The Clock Strikes Twelve	(21)	4040
191. Necropolis	(157)	4050
192. Slan	(22)	4051
193. In the Mist and Other...	(155)	4053
194. The Horror in the Museum...	(115)	4058
195. Blooded on Arachne	(161)	4081
196. Harrigan's File	(140)	4102
197. Her Smoke Rose Up Forever	(181)	4108
198. Gravity's Angels	(183)	4119
199. The Princess of All Lands	(154)	4120
200. Tales from the Nightside	(159)	4121
201. The Dunwich Horror... (corrected)	(169)	4124
202. Stories of Darkness and Dread	(129)	4138
203. The House of the Worm	(136)	4144
204. Born to Exile	(152)	4148
205. Collected Ghost Stories	(134)	4155
206. The Third Grave	(158)	4158
207. Nameless Places	(137)	4160
208. The Horror at Oakdeene...	(148)	4162
209. The Chronicles of Solar Pons	(M15)	4176
210. Crystal Express	(179)	4231
211. And Afterward, the Dark	(149)	4259
212. Xélucha and Others	(141)	4283
213. The Purcell Papers	(138)	4288
214. Half in Shadow	(151)	4288

215. The Height of the Scream	(143)	4348
216. Kecksies and Other...	(147)	4391
217. Night's Yawning Peal	(48)	4500
218. The Ends of the Earth	(184)	4655
219. Memories of the Space Age	(178)	4903
220. Cthulhu 2000	(190)	4927
221. Miscellaneous Writings	(191)	4959
222. Selected Letters IV	(145)	4978
223. Howard Phillips Lovecraft...	(135)	4991
224. A Rendezvous in Averoigne	(177)	5025
225. The Horror in the Museum... (corr.)	(180)	5062
226. The Watchers out of Time...	(133)	5070
227. Selected Letters V	(146)	5138
228. Literary Swordsmen...	(142)	5431
229. Tales of the Cthulhu Mythos	(182)	7015
230. The Final Adventures of Solar Pons	(M18)	No numbers
231. In Lovecraft's Shadow	(M19)	No numbers
232. Eyes of the Mole	(S14)	No numbers
233. Corn Village: A Selection	(S16)	No numbers

9

Arkham House Stock Lists and Catalogs

Stock lists and catalogs of new titles were issued periodically by Arkham House Publishers, Inc. Since it has not been possible to locate all issues, the list below is incomplete. All publications are bound in wrappers and center stapled. The values suggested are for copies in "fine" (unmarked) condition.

Books from Arkham House 1945	$75
Books from Arkham House,	
Mycroft & Moran and Stanton & Lee 1945	$75
Books from Arkham House 1946	$75
Books from Arkham House 1947–1948	$75
Books from Arkham House 1949 and later	$50
Stock List of Books from Arkham House,	
Mycroft & Moran and Stanton & Lee 1949 and later	$75
Stock List of Books from Arkham House 1950	$35
New Books Bulletin 1952	$20
New Books from Arkham House 1957	$25
Stock List of Books from Arkham House	
and Mycroft & Moran 1960	$65
Stock List of Books from Arkham House 1963	$35
Books from Arkham House 1964	$30
Stock List of Books from Arkham House	
and Mycroft & Moran 1965	$35
Stock List of Books from Arkham House	
and Mycroft & Moran 1969	$40
Stock List of Books from Arkham House 1970	$25

New and Forthcoming Books by August Derleth 1970	$30
Stock List of Books from Arkham House and Mycroft & Moran 1971	$35
Stock List of Books from Arkham House 1971	$25
Stock List of Books from Arkham House and Mycroft & Moran 1972	$25
Stock List of Books from Arkham House and Mycroft & Moran 1974	$25
Stock List of Books from Arkham House and Mycroft & Moran 1975	$25
Stock List of Books from Arkham House 1977	$15
Stock List of Books from Arkham House 1980	$20
Arkham House 50th Anniversary Stock List 1939-1989	$15
Arkham House 60th Anniversary Stock List 1939-1999	$10
Arkham House 2001	$ 5
Arkham House Publishers Catalog 2002	$ 5

10

A Representative Arkham House Book Collection

The following suggestions for an Arkham House book collection are personal choices and may not correspond with the opinion of other bibliographers or collectors. Which titles to include in any book collection, however, is a personal preference and therefore entirely subjective. Some Arkham House collectors focus on certain authors; type of fiction (genre); particular topics (such as the "Cthulhu Mythos"); poetry; or classic pulp magazine reprints. A few may have succeeded in acquiring a complete collection of Arkham House titles, but they are very few, for with the limited print numbers of some titles, such a collection is not easily obtained and the cost would be well beyond the reach of the ordinary collector.

The following is my personal recommendation for a smaller but representative selection of what I believe to be the best of the books published by Arkham House. The number in parentheses is the book's entry number in the bibliography for Arkham House or Mycroft & Moran (designated with an M).

Asquith, Cynthia	*This Mortal Coil*	(23)
Bear, Greg	*The Wind from a Burning Woman*	(163)
Bloch, Robert	*The Opener of the Way*	(10)
Bond, Nelson	*The Far Side of Nowhere*	(202)
Bradbury, Ray	*Dark Carnival*	(25)
Brennan, Joseph Payne	*Nine Horrors and a Dream*	(56)
Campbell, J. Ramsey	*Alone With the Horrors*	(188)
Coppard, A.E.	*Fearful Pleasures*	(20)
Copper, Basil	*Necropolis*	(157)

Derleth, August	*Someone in the Dark*	(2)
	Something Near	(9)
	Not Long for This World	(37)
Derleth, August		
(editor)	*Dark of the Moon*	(24)
	Fire and Sleet and Candlelight	(64)
	Dark Mind, Dark Heart	(68)
	Over the Edge	(81)
Dunsany, Lord	*The Fourth Book of Jorkens*	(34)
Hodgson, William		
Hope	*The House on the Borderland*	(16)
Howard, Robert E.	*SkullFace and Others*	(17)
	Always Comes Evening	(53)
Jacobi, Carl	*Revelations in Black*	(26)
Joshi, S.T.	*Sixty Years of Arkham House*	(198)
Lee, Tanith	*Dreams of Light and Darkness*	(173)
LeFanu, J. Sheridan	*Green Tea and Other Ghost Stories*	(12)
Leiber, Fritz	*Night's Black Agents*	(27)
Long, Frank Belknap	*The Hounds of Tindalos*	(14)
Lovecraft,		
Howard Phillips	*The Outsider and Others*	(1)
	Beyond the Wall of Sleep	(4)
	The Dunwich Horror and Others	(71)
	Collected Poems	(72)
	At the Mountains of Madness...	(82)
	Dagon and Other Macabre Tales	(88)
Machen, Arthur	*The Green Round*	(102)
Malzberg, Barry N.	*In the Stone House*	(200)
McNail, Stanley	*Something Breathing*	(89)
Quinn, Seabury	*The PhantomFighter*	(M8)
Shepard, Lucius	*The Jaguar Hunter*	(175)
Shiel, Matthew P.	*Xélucha and Others*	(141)
Smith, Clark Ashton	*Out of Time and Space*	(3)
	Lost Worlds	(7)
	Genius Loci and Other Tales	(36)
	Tales of Science and Sorcery	(84)
	Selected Poems	(117)
	A Rendezvous in Averoigne	(177)
Tiptree, James, Jr.	*Her Smoke Rose Up Forever*	(181)
Van Vogt, Albert E.	*Slan*	(22)

181

Reference Bibliography

The following sources were consulted during the research and preparation for this book. All are highly recommended for more in-depth information on book collecting and Arkham House titles and authors.

AB Bookman's Weekly Magazine. (1999). Clifton, New Jersey

Ahearn, Allen, and Patricia Ahearn (2000). *Book Collecting 2000—A Comprehensive Guide.* New York: G.P. Putnam's Sons. 536 pp.

_____. (2002). *Collected Books: The Guide to Values 2002 Edition.* New York: G.P. Putnam's Sons. 788 pp.

Behrends, Steve (1990). *Clark Ashton Smith.* Starmont Reader's Guide 49. Mercer Island, Washington: Starmont House. 112 pp.

Bell, Joseph, ed. (1987). *The Books of Clark Ashton Smith.* Ontario: Soft Books. 28 pp.

Derleth, August (1945). *H.P.L.: A Memoir.* New York: Ben Abrahamson. 123 pp.

_____. *Thirty Years of Arkham House: 1939–1969.* Sauk City, Wisconsin: Arkham House. 99 pp.

Greenfield, Jane (1992). *Books: Their Care and Repair.* 3rd ed. New York: H.W. Wilson Company.

Grobe Litersky, Dorothy M. (1997). *Derleth—Hawk and Dove.* Aurora, Colorado: National Writers Press. 238 pp.

Howlett-West, Stephanie, ed. (1999). *The Intergalactic Guide to Science Fiction, Fantasy and Horror 1999.* Peoria, Illinois: Spoon River. 253 pp.

Jaffery, Sheldon (1989). *The Arkham House Companion.* Mercer Island, Washington: Starmont House. 184 pp.

Joshi, S.T., ed. (1999). *Sixty Years of Arkham House.* Sauk City, Wisconsin: Arkham House. 281 pp.

Reference Bibliography

Long, Frank Belknap (1975). *Howard Phillips Lovecraft: Dreamer on the Night Side*. Sauk City, Wisconsin: Arkham House. 237 pp.

Price, E. Hoffmann (2001). *Book of the Dead—Friends of Yesteryear: Fictioners and Others*. Sauk City, Wisconsin: Arkham House. 423 pp.

Ruber, Peter, ed. (2000). *Arkham's Masters of Horror*. Sauk City, Wisconsin: Arkham House. 444 pp.

Wolfe, Charles K., ed. (1973). *Planets and Dimensions—Collected Essays of Clark Ashton Smith*. Baltimore: Mirage. 87 pp.

Zempel, Edward N., and Linda A. Verkler, eds. (1995). *First Editions: A Guide to Identification*. 3rd ed. Peoria, Illinois: Spoon River. 515 pp.

_____, and _____, eds. (1999). *Book Prices: Used and Rare, 1999*. Peoria, Illinois: Spoon River. 800 pp.

Author Index

185

Author Index (to bibliography serial numbers)

Dark Chateau (1951) 46; Spells and Philtres (1958) 54; The Abominations of Yondo (1960) 60; Tales of Science and Sorcery (1964) 84; Poems in Prose (1965) 87; Other Dimensions (1970) 113; Selected Poems (1971) 117; The Black Book of Clark Ashton Smith (1979) 153; A Rendezvous in Averoigne (1988) 177; A Rendezvous in Averoigne (reprint) (2003) 204
Starrett, Vincent (1886–1974): The Quick and the Dead (1965) 90
Sterling, Bruce (1954–): Crystal Express (1989) 179
Stuart, Jane: Eyes of the Mole (1967) S14
Swanwick, Michael (1950–): Gravity's Angels (1991) 183

Tierney, Richard L. (1936–): Collected Poems (1981) 160
Tiptree, James, Jr. (Alice Hastings Bradley Sheldon) (1915–1987): Tales of the Quintana Roo (1986) 172; Her Smoke Rose Up Forever (1990) 181
Turner, James (ed.): Cthulhu 2000 (1995) 190

Van Vogt, Albert Elton (1912–): Slan (1946) 22

Wakefield, H. Russell (1888–1965): The Clock Strikes Twelve (1946) 21; Strayers from Sheol (1961) 63
Walter, Elizabeth: In the Mist and Other... (1979) 155
Walton, Evangeline (1907–1996): Witch House (1945) 11
Wandrei, Donald (1908–1987): The Eye and the Finger (1944) 5; The Web of Easter Island (1948) 33; Poems for Midnight (1964) 80; Strange Harvest (1965) 91
Wellman, Manly Wade (1903–1986): Who Fears the Devil? (1963) 73
Whitehead, Henry S. (1882–1932): Jumbee and Other Uncanny Tales (1944) 6; West India Lights (1946) 18
Wilkins-Freeman, Mary E. (1852–1930): Collected Ghost Stories (1974) 134
Wilson, Colin (1932–): The Mind Parasites (1967) 98
Wright, Sydney F. (1874–1965): The Throne of Saturn 43

189

Title Index

Title Index (to bibliography serial numbers)

193

Title Index (to bibliography serial numbers)